THE MASONIC MYTH

THE MASONIC MYTH

Unlocking the Truth About the Symbols,
the Secret Rites, and the History of Freemasonry

Jay Kinney

HarperOne
An Imprint of HarperCollinsPublishers

Page 265 constitutes a continuation of this copyright page.

THE MASONIC MYTH: *Unlocking the Truth About the Symbols, the Secret Rites, and the History of Freemasonry.* Copyright © 2009 by Jay Kinney. All rights reserved. Printed in the United States of America. No part of this book may be used or reproduced in any manner whatsoever without written permission except in the case of brief quotations embodied in critical articles and reviews. For information, address HarperCollins Publishers, 195 Broadway, New York, NY 10007.

HarperCollins books may be purchased for educational, business, or sales promotional use. For information, please e-mail the Special Markets Department at SPsales@harper collins.com.

HarperCollins Web site: http://www.harpercollins.com

HarperCollins®, ▇®, and HarperOne™ are trademarks of HarperCollins Publishers

FIRST EDITION

Library of Congress Cataloging-in-Publication Data is available upon request.

ISBN 978-0-06-082256-9

16 17 18 19   RRD(H)   10 9 8 7 6 5

In memory of my father, Del Jay Kinney,
whose life was dedicated to universal brotherhood

Contents

Acknowledgments   *ix*

Author's Note   *xi*

Introduction   *xv*

1. **The Masonic Myth**   1
   Rumors, Accusations, and Hoaxes

2. **Square Roots**   17
   Where Did Freemasonry Come From?

3. **Continental Ops**   41
   The Craft Spreads to Europe

4. **Novus Ordo Seclorum**   59
   Freemasonry Comes to America

5. **The Powers That Be**   85
   Making Sense of the Masonic Power Structure

6. **Secret Rites and Rituals**   107
   What Do Masons Do?

7. **Out of the Blue**   125
   A Look at the "Higher" Degrees

8. **Veiled in Symbol and Allegory**   149
   Deciphering Masonic Symbolism

9. **The Illuminati Factor** 173
Does a Hidden Order Rule the World?

10. **Is Masonry Occult?** 195
And Is Occult Even a Useful Word?

11. **Back to the Future** 213
Is Freemasonry Doomed?

Appendix A: Further Light on Masonry
Recommended Resources for Research on Freemasonry 223

Appendix B: Masonic Lodge Officers
and Their Typical Duties 233

Notes 235
Credits 265

Acknowledgments

This book could not have happened without the assistance of numerous people and institutions. First and foremost are the Masonic libraries, whose resources are all too often underestimated and underutilized. (For the sake of brevity and so as not to emphasize an appearance of rank, I am dispensing with any degree honorifics after the names of any Masons that I name here.) I extend my appreciation to the House of the Temple Library and Museum of the Supreme Council, 33°, in Washington, D.C., whose assistant librarian, Larissa K. Watkins, has been unfailingly helpful in my research. Similarly, I've enjoyed the extensive use of the Harry G. Yetter Masonic Research Library at the Oakland Scottish Rite Temple, in Oakland, California, ably curated by Bro. Greg Rapp. A nod of appreciation as well to Bro. William Krueger, librarian at the Iowa Masonic Library of the Grand Lodge AF&AM of Iowa, and Helaine Davis, librarian for the Scottish Rite Masonic National Heritage Museum in Lexington, Massachusetts. Finally, and most significantly, I've had the good fortune to draw upon the resources of the H. Douglas Lemons Research Library of the San Francisco Scottish Rite, where I serve as librarian.

My thanks to friends Rich Coad, Spike Parsons, Jay Cornell, Richard Smoley, Bro. John Michael Greer, Bro. William Arney, Bro. Robert G. Davis, Bro. Jim Tresner, Bro. Thomas Worrel, Bro. Frits Cassée, Bro.

Al Miller, Bro. Edgar Fentum, and others unnamed, for reading my manuscript at various stages of completion and offering their comments. Thanks, too, to the brethren of Mill Valley Lodge no. 356 and Mission Lodge no. 169, Grand Lodge of California, F&AM, for the fellowship and insights they have offered over the course of my association with them.

A particular note of appreciation goes to my agent, Katherine Boyle, who has been an ongoing source of support and advice at every stage of the editorial process.

My thanks to Gideon Weil, my editor at HarperOne, without whose confidence and enthusiasm this book would not have happened. Thanks, as well, to Jan Baumer, Suzanne Stradley, Julie Burton, and the rest of the crew at HarperOne for their attention to detail and professionalism.

Finally, my love and gratitude go to my wife, Dixie, whose unwavering support saw me through the sometimes grueling process of writing my first full-length book.

Every writer is beholden to his sources, and I have tried to provide citations at every possible step in order to give credit where credit is due. Nevertheless, some may have been unintentionally omitted, in which case I express here my apologies in advance. It goes without saying that all opinions—as well as mistakes—are mine alone and should not reflect upon those cited or acknowledged here.

Author's Note

As a reader, you have the perfect right to wonder how I might presume
to uncover the truth about Freemasonry when so many before me have
wandered lost in a maze of hearsay and rumor. What qualifications do
I bring to this venture?

First and foremost, for the past thirty years I have studied the ever-
shifting sands of conspiracy theories and esoteric traditions—the two
overlapping milieus most often associated, whether rightly or wrongly,
with Freemasonry. As an observer, writer, and editor, I learned to distinguish between theories and facts, and between unwarranted assumptions and judicious conclusions. This sense of discrimination
served me well as publisher and editor in chief of *Gnosis: A Journal of
the Western Inner Traditions.* As the leading American journal dealing
with esoteric and spiritual traditions, *Gnosis* earned a reputation for
scholarly research that could be relied upon. In writing *The Masonic
Myth,* I have held myself to the same standards of accuracy and citation
of sources that *Gnosis* demanded of its authors.

Second, unlike many writers and researchers on Freemasonry,
I bring to my task the added perspective of having experienced the
Craft, as Freemasonry sometimes refers to itself, from within. For
many years I studied Masonry from the outside, but I didn't really "get
it" until I took a chance and joined a lodge in my area. This inside

experience has proved invaluable in assessing both Masonry's self-image and the image projected upon it by its critics.

In addition, membership in the Craft has placed me in close proximity to Masonic research circles and resources, such as little-known but substantial Masonic libraries. In investigating these resources, I quickly realized that they contain a wealth of information that can help a dedicated researcher develop a realistic picture of Freemasonry, past and present.

Now, I will admit that I had been reluctant to consider joining Masonry for a long time, out of fear that any vows of secrecy I might take would inevitably compromise my objectivity and my ability to discuss the Craft with the world at large. Such strictures could be damaging to my reputation and my work as a writer. I found, however, that Freemasonry—in the 21st century, at least—has far fewer prohibitions on what its members can discuss with others than I had feared. Accordingly, I have felt restrained only from revealing the modes of mutual identification between Masons (i.e., the passwords, grips, and signs) and the precise wording of ritual.

Regarding the intricacies of word usage, it would be helpful for me to clarify a few subtle differences between terms. References to "masonry" and "masons" (all lowercase) typically refer to working (or "operative") stonemasons. References to "Freemasonry," "Masonry," "Masons," and "the Craft" (all capitalized) usually refer to modern "speculative" (i.e., philosophical) Masons, who came to the fore after the gradual eclipse of operative masonry.

It is standard Masonic usage to capitalize the formal titles of lodge and grand lodge officers as well as the names of specific grand lodges. Thus, the presiding officer of a Masonic lodge who is formally addressed as Worshipful Master (an honorific dating back centuries, somewhat akin to calling a judge "your honor") invariably has that title capitalized or abbreviated to WM. To the modern eye this may seem like capitalization overkill, so I have trimmed back the capitals in some general references to officers and grand lodges. Other instances of capitalization in the book—such as references to the four cardinal directions within Masonic lodge rooms—generally follow Masonic usage.

I should point out that I did not join Masonry in order to write this book. However, after joining—and after familiarizing myself with the range of literature available—I discovered that there was a need for an accessible and reliable overview and guidebook to the Craft. In those few cases where there were decent books filling that need, there always seemed to be some crucial elements missing. Either the Masonry discussed was primarily British or the genuine mysteries about the Craft were given short shrift. *The Masonic Myth* is my effort to rectify the situation.

I invite the reader to accompany me as I hunt down the truth about Freemasonry. This book recapitulates my journey of discovery as I confront the many puzzles within puzzles that are strewn across the Masonic landscape.

Inevitably, in trying to make sense out of a host of competing claims and several libraries' worth of facts—not all of which support each other—I have constructed an account that reflects my own judgment calls. I make no claims to this book being exhaustive; instead, I have tried to produce an accessible narrative marked by common sense and a sense of proportion. Books on Masonry almost always succumb to a tyranny of minutiae, where a never-ending stream of names, dates, jargon, and organizational details numb the brains of all but the most dedicated readers. I have tried mightily to avoid this fate, and consequently, I have relegated many factual quibbles, asides, and relevant details to the endnotes. These may not interest the casual reader, but I hope they will provide additional insights for those who brave the fine print.

Masons are taught to seek "more light." With that in mind, I believe that it is time to open the doors of the lodge room, to let in some sunshine, and to allow the curious public to have access to the unvarnished truth about Freemasonry.

—Jay Kinney

Introduction

In 2001, just a month after I had received my first-degree initiation into Freemasonry, my wife and I took a trip to England. Our hotel in London, as it turned out, was within walking distance of Freemasons' Hall, the imposing stone headquarters of the United Grand Lodge of England, the administrative body overseeing English Masonry.

Normally, public tours of Freemasons' Hall are provided daily, but by happenstance the tours were not available on the day we first visited there. It was the day of the Grand Lodge's quarterly communication, when representatives from lodges and provincial bodies around England meet to take care of business. Do come again another day, we were told, and you'll be able to take a tour.

And then a most curious sight unfolded before our eyes as we turned to leave and stood at the top of the steps leading down to the street from the side entrance. A series of black taxicabs pulled up to the curb in front of Freemasons' Hall and proceeded to emit nearly identical passengers: the proverbial Men in Black—men dressed in black suits with black neckties, all carrying black briefcases. The men—all Masons—ran up the steps and through the doors of Freemasons' Hall as more taxis arrived, emitting more Men in Black.

Was this real life, or had we somehow stumbled into a scene from a Monty Python movie? To our American eyes, it was an almost comical sight, but I also felt a tiny shiver go up my spine. Masonry has been accused by some of being a cult, and the scene before us didn't exactly disprove the accusation. What *had* I gotten myself into, exactly?

It didn't take long for me to deconstruct the strangeness of the Men in Black episode. The quarterly meeting was about to begin. The arriving Masons had likely taken trains into London and caught cabs to take them to Freemasons' Hall. Most London taxis of that era were black, for reasons having nothing to do with Masonry. Unlike much of American Masonry, English Masonry has had a simple but narrow dress code for its meetings: white shirt, black suit and tie. (In a culture still given to subtle class distinctions such as old school ties, the requirement of a simple black tie for all can enhance the feeling of brotherhood.) And the black briefcases? Those were actually *apron* cases, in which brethren keep the ceremonial aprons that are worn during Masonic meetings. (The aprons commemorate the workmen's aprons used by the stonemasons, the supposed ancestors of modern Freemasonry.)

However, it would be a matter of years before I was able to answer the deeper question of what I had gotten myself into.

There are any number of legitimate questions that arise when one tries to grasp what Masonry is. Is it really a secret society—and if so, why all the secrecy? Where did it really come from? What's with all the ritual and regalia? Why the grandiose titles and honorifics? What's with the proliferation of degrees and orders and interrelated Masonic side organizations? And, when all is said and done, what's the point of all this rigmarole? Is there some secret payoff that justifies the enormous amount of time and effort that has been spent over centuries in maintaining this enigmatic institution?

Because the answers to these questions are not self-evident—even to some Masons, and especially to non-Masons—a barrage of pseudo-answers has too often rushed in to fill the void. Some of these, such as the imaginative speculations of "alternative historians," are harmless enough, at least if they aren't mistaken for historical facts. But other explanations, especially those of hostile anti-Masons, are dangerous, not merely to Masons but to society at large. The Nazis rose to power in Germany in part by scapegoating Jews and Masons, while in the present era Masonic lodges have been the target of Islamist terrorists. Dark accusations about Freemasonry as a satanic cult or a tool of a hidden power elite may be bestsellers for many publishers, but such pseudo-answers poison the well of public knowledge with delusional claims and paranoid misinterpretations.

Of course, everyone loves a good yarn, which is partly why Dan Brown's books have been so popular. Secretive brotherhoods can be excellent devices in suspense thrillers, but novels are, by their very nature, fiction. A novelist can make those links that raise the hair on one's neck, and a good writer can make you believe them. But once the novel is over, it is good to do a reality check. They say that truth is stranger than fiction. Let's see if that's true.

Fanciful book cover of the hoax-exposé The Mysteries of Freemasonry, by Léo Taxil, circa 1890s. Taxil's over-the-top accusations against Masonry are still taken as genuine by present-day anti-Masonic conspiracy theorists, who ignore his detailed public confession of his twelve-year-long scam.

1

The Masonic Myth

Rumors, Accusations, and Hoaxes

W hen most people think of Freemasonry—if they think of it at all—one or more contradictory images likely spring to mind. Freemasonry is (take your pick)

- a harmless bunch of aging men enacting strange rituals in odd costumes;
- a secretive cabal of elite power brokers at the highest levels of society;
- a group of conservative, patriotic, pious businessmen and civic do-gooders;
- a covert network of occultists, pagans, and New Agers intent on creating a "New World Order";
- a centuries-old tradition perpetuating ancient wisdom and esoteric teachings.

It is hard to think of any other social organization that has spawned such a wide-ranging and conflicting set of descriptions. People are fairly unanimous in their views of the Girl Scouts or the Mafia, but mention the Masons and confusion ensues.

When I first set out to discover the truth about Freemasonry, I found this strange brew of public perceptions to be curious indeed.

Was there something about the Craft, as Masonry sometimes calls itself, that fosters such a peculiar mix of reactions? I soon found that the deeper I dug, the more curious things became.

Freemasonry's self-description, according to its own literature, is innocuous enough. Masonry is "one of the world's oldest secular fraternal societies . . . a society of men concerned with moral and spiritual values. Its members are taught its precepts by a series of ritual dramas, which follow ancient forms and use stonemasons' customs and tools as allegorical guides."[1]

Could this be the same group that William Cooper, arch–conspiracy theorist, called "one of the most wicked and terrible organizations upon this earth"? "The Masons," according to Cooper, "are major players in the struggle for world domination."[2]

Another critic of Masonry, Martin L. Wagner, saw things a bit differently. He asserts: "[T]he proof is conclusive that Freemasonry is a sex-cult, in which the generative powers are adored and worshiped under disguised phallic rites and symbols. Phallicism is the essence of the religion of the mysteries, and phallicism is the essence of the religion of Freemasonry."[3]

Masonic leaders, of course, admit no such thing. They insist: "Freemasonry is not a religion, nor is it a substitute for religion. Its essential qualification [i.e., the belief in a Supreme Being] opens it to men of many religions and it expects them to continue to follow their own faith. It does not allow religion to be discussed at its meeting[s]."[4]

I found this same mix of competing claims and accusations displayed and toyed with in various fictional portrayals of the Craft. Numerous Masonic myths were deliciously satirized in a classic episode of the TV series *The Simpsons* devoted to a secret society dubbed the Stonecutters. In that episode, Homer Simpson craves membership in the exclusive club to which two of his co-workers and his boss belong. Once he gains admission he discovers, to his delight, that he now has access to all sorts of perks and privileges, including a secret, high-speed freeway just for Stonecutters. Gaining leadership of the group due to a significantly shaped birthmark that marks him as the prophesied "Chosen One," Homer revels in his near-godlike status until, satiated with always getting his way, he turns over a new leaf and redirects the Stonecutters from throwing beer bashes to doing community service. This breeds dissatisfaction in the ranks, and everyone quits to form a new club, the Ancient Mystic Society of No Homers.

A hundred years earlier, Rudyard Kipling had his own fun with Freemasonry in his short story "The Man Who Would Be King," later made into a memorable movie starring Sean Connery (a Mason in real life, as chance would have it) and Michael Caine. In that tale, two former British soldiers turned con artists make their way from northern India through the Hindu Kush to "Kafiristan," where they ascend to power over various warring tribes through the good fortune of being Masons. The local tribal priests, it turns out, maintain an ancient proto-Masonry marked by the same signs of recognition and symbol systems that latter-day Freemasonry uses. The two rogues enjoy godlike status among these mountainous Masons until, like Homer, one of them goes too far and angers the natives, and they have to run for their lives.

Kipling was himself a Mason of only a couple of years' standing when he wrote the story. Working in India as a young journalist, Kipling was initiated in 1886 in a lodge in Lahore, whose members included both British colonials and native Indians. It was a world as different from Homer Simpson's Springfield as one could imagine, yet the same themes of secrecy, power, and excess were ripe for the plucking, then as now.

The 2001 movie *From Hell*, starring Johnny Depp and Heather Graham, portrayed Jack the Ripper as a Masonic madman dispatched by Queen Victoria to take care of a royal scandal, which he does with bloody relish. He is finally reined in by his Masonic brothers, and his identity is covered up by Masons within the police.

The film was based on a mammoth graphic novel of the same name by Alan Moore and Eddie Campbell, itself loosely derived from a conspiracy theory elaborated

Action figure of Homer Simpson as a "Stonecutter"

by British author Stephen Knight in his 1976 book *Jack the Ripper: The Final Solution*. Knight went on to author *The Brotherhood: The Secret World of the Freemasons*, published in the United Kingdom in 1983. Knight's exposé alleged corruption and conspiracy within contemporary British police, judiciary, and business circles. The book's evidence was largely anonymous and anecdotal, and rather thin on particulars. Yet *The Brotherhood* was propelled to bestseller status by a public hungry for a glimpse inside the secretive order and for a confirmation of its worst fears.

Knight's book and the controversy surrounding it helped set off a wave of demands in the United Kingdom for official investigations, public disclosure of Masonic memberships, and the registration (and in some cases, banning) of Masons in public service. The pressure became so great that the Masonic leadership within the United Grand Lodge of England (UGLE) was finally forced to abandon its long-standing policy of turning a deaf ear to such accusations, and it embarked on a new era of "openness" and public-relations efforts designed to dispel the suspicious and insular image that had developed over the years.

Meanwhile, over the past decade or two a new genre of "alternative history" has enjoyed great popularity, with its predominantly British authors churning out books that purport, among other things, to reveal the real secrets of Freemasonry. These secrets turn out to consist, in most cases, not of mundane cronyism or far-reaching political control, but of allegedly ancient links between Masonry and the Knights Templar, Johannite Christians, Gnostics, Egyptian Mysteries, and the Divine Feminine. These "discoveries" are, in fact, a revival of romantic notions that were popular within Masonry in the 18th and 19th centuries and that live on today. We will see, shortly, how such ideas arose and whether there is any truth to these claims.

An Ocean Away

Freemasonry's reputation in North America has taken a different course from that of its British brethren, and with good reason. American Masons have long touted the Masonic membership of such key founding fathers as George Washington, Ben Franklin, and Paul

Revere, and fostered an image of patriotic benevolence. It has been a popular belief—among Masons and non-Masons alike—that Masons helped inspire the American Revolution.

The 2004 movie *National Treasure*, starring Nicholas Cage, took this premise and ran with it, spinning a plot around the notion that founding-father Masons hid clues to the location of a vast treasure on the back of the Declaration of Independence and in other historic spots. In a rare case of flattery, the Masons were portrayed as selflessly hiding the treasure away, as it was too vast for any one man, or even nation, to possess. Exactly why they would then have concocted a string of clues to the treasure's location and planted them up and down the eastern seaboard is never quite explained. Presumably, Masons are just that way: hoarders of secrets and droppers of clues.

While Masonry in the United Kingdom has often been associated with an upper middle class starchiness that draws the resentment of the working class, the Masons in the less class-conscious society of the United States have been typically seen as mainstream, white-bread Americans. At its peak of membership at the close of the 1950s, American Masonry could claim four million members, which amounted to eight out of every one hundred eligible adult males in the general population.[5]

Yet, Masonry's patriotic pedigree in the States hasn't entirely saved it from attack. Anti-Masonry runs deep in the American collective psyche, and once again questions of secrecy and power are responsible.

Scarcely thirty years after

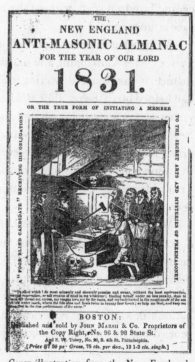

Cover illustration from the New England Anti-Masonic Almanac *for 1831, one of numerous anti-Masonic publications of that era. The picture presents a fanciful and hostile depiction of the initiation of an Entered Apprentice (first degree).*

George Washington was president, a scandalous incident involving Masons in upstate New York resulted in the founding of America's first third party, the Anti-Masonic Party. William Morgan, a disaffected Mason, was abducted in 1826 as he was about to publish a book supposedly revealing the "secrets" of the Craft, including its rituals. He was never seen again, and while some claimed that he was merely taken across the border to Canada and told to get lost, an accomplice to the kidnapping later confessed that Morgan was killed shortly after his disappearance.[6]

Were some of the rituals so shocking that their exposure could not be tolerated? That was many people's assumption. Yet the rituals had already been published numerous times in "exposures" over the preceding hundred years without the roof falling in. This fact made the case strange indeed.

Sadly, what followed next only made matters worse. Attempts to prosecute the kidnapping and murder were hampered by Masonic influence, it was rumored, leading to a general outrage. The Craft, which had helped birth the republic and had seemed the embodiment of civic virtue, was now viewed as corrupt and a threat to law and order. Indeed, New York Masonry at that time was split into rival "country" and "city" grand lodges, with charges of corruption against the grand master of the country faction. One historian has suggested that it was the fear of a possible exposure of this corruption that propelled the plot, not concerns for ritual secrecy.[7]

Whatever the case, before the affair was over, Masonry was in the doghouse and anti-Masonry had mushroomed into a political movement responsible for the election, in several states, of assemblymen, congressmen, and, in Vermont, the governor. By 1830, 124 anti-Masonic newspapers had sprung up, "an astonishing one-eighth of the young nation's newspapers."[8] American Masonry went into an eclipse for a generation, its members resigning ("demitting," in Masonic jargon) in hordes. Some 2,000 lodges turned in their charters to their grand lodges and dissolved.[9] It was only in the 1840s that Masonry began to revive and see its numbers grow once again.

By coincidence, the time and place of the Morgan Affair was 1826, smack-dab in the middle of the "Burned-Over District" of upstate New York, so-called for the fiery succession of evangelical Christian revivals and enthusiasms that swept through the area at that same time. Masonry was denounced from the pulpit and added to the list of pastimes earning damnation. The smell of fire and brimstone was in the air.[10]

Oddly enough, this same district was the birthplace of Mormonism, where Joseph Smith discovered the "golden tablets" of the Book of Mormon just a year later, in 1827, at Cumorah Hill, less than ten miles from Canandaigua, the site of Morgan's abduction. A good number of Smith's earliest converts were former or disenchanted Masons. Years later, in 1842, Joseph Smith and Brigham Young were to take up Freemasonry with fresh enthusiasm, interpreting its rituals as the remnants of ancient biblical initiations. When Smith introduced the doctrine of plural marriage among his followers, one of his earliest plural wives was none other than the widow of William Morgan![11]

Pulpit Bullies

The agitated nexus of anti-Masonic anxiety and evangelical fervor persists to this day. Christian preachers were prominent as leaders in the anti-Masonic movement in Morgan's day, and they still are. Within the thriving subculture of present-day born-again Christianity, anti-Masonic books are a mainstay in Christian bookstores, and several evangelical ministers have anti-Masonic ministries that peddle sensational allegations of Masonry as a satanic cult or a heretical honey trap.

Television evangelist Pat Robertson, in his 1991 book *The New World Order,* contends that Masonry is an integral part of a push toward an anti-Christian one-world government—a push that apparently began with the American Revolution. Robertson asks,

> Is it possible that a select few had a plan, revealed in the Great Seal adopted at the founding of the United States, to bring forth, not the nation that our founders and champions of liberty desired, but a totally different world order under a mystery religion designed to replace the old Christian world order of Europe and America?[12]

Robertson is here referring to the recurring notion that the United States' Great Seal, found on the back of the one-dollar bill, is a covert

Masonic symbol. This is a matter of much dispute, as we'll see in chapter 4, but Robertson's suspicions about its significance are indicative of a mind-set that has yet to reconcile itself to the modern era.

There's no question that contemporary Freemasonry is largely a product of the Age of Enlightenment in the British Isles. Eighteenth-century lodges commonly met in the upstairs rooms of pubs—accessible but private venues that enabled men from different classes to meet "on the level" for nonsectarian philosophical discussions supplemented by much food and ale. Whether by design or simply because they were in the air, various Masonic ideas of individualism, fraternity, and equality began to impact the political sphere.

Undoubtedly, this new era of science, reason, and universal values threatened the reins of power previously held by Church and Throne. One side effect of these new developments was a hostility toward Masonry on the part of conservative representatives of the old regime.

Commencing in 1738, the Vatican condemned Freemasonry on grounds that were often as political as they were religious.[13] Masonry represented a social milieu not under Church control, and its vows of secrecy constituted a challenge to the primacy of the confessional. Many among today's religious right, like Pat Robertson, have similar objections. (Ironically, so did Joseph Stalin, over the same issue of control.) Though current Freemasonry has traveled far from its revolutionary days, it still retains enough Enlightenment ideals—such as a universal brotherhood regardless of specific religious creeds—that those who wish to remake the world in the name of a single religion or ideology view it as a threat.

Mystery Babylon

Many of the suspicions about the Craft are traceable to the question of its nebulous origins. Conflicting claims about Freemasonry's history have been a problem ever since the first grand lodge was founded in London in 1717. As we'll examine in more detail shortly, individual lodges existed before 1717, and four of them formed what they called "the Grand Lodge" to regulate and systematize things. But it is still a matter of great debate whether modern Freemasonry, with its purely "speculative" (i.e., philosophical and ethical) focus, evolved directly out of "operative" (i.e., actual working stonemasons') lodges extending back centuries earlier, particularly in Scotland. We'll investigate this more fully in chapter 2.

With so much left to conjecture, numerous theories about Masonic origins have flourished. These theories invariably point far back, long before the Age of Enlightenment. One extreme of these romantic claims is illustrated by the following quote from Manly Palmer Hall, a prolific writer on mysticism and esoteric lore:

> Masonry is a university, teaching the liberal arts and sciences of the soul to all who will attend to its words. It is a shadow of the great Atlantean Mystery School, which stood with all its splendor in the ancient City of the Golden Gates, where now the turbulent Atlantic rolls in unbroken sweep.[14]

By Hall's reckoning, Freemasonry dates all the way back to the lost continent of Atlantis and its fabled advanced wisdom. When Atlantis sank, certain of its priests made their way to Egypt and were the source of the Egyptian Mysteries, according to Hall.[15] No matter that Atlantis itself has never been found, much less links to Egypt.

Yet, this is only slightly wilder than Freemasonry's traditional history of itself. The official history of Freemasonry, devised by the Rev. John Anderson in the 1723 and 1738 Constitutions of the premier Grand Lodge of England, traces Masonry back, by a long and pious lineage, to Adam as first possessor of Masonic knowledge!

In 1737, the Chevalier Michael Ramsay—a Scottish Mason living in France who supported the effort to restore the Stuarts to the British throne—composed a famous oration supposedly delivered to the Grand Lodge of France that linked Freemasonry's origins to the knightly Order of Saint John of Jerusalem, better known as the Knights of Malta—one of the orders of medieval crusaders. Nothing in the way of proof was offered, but this romantic suggestion was taken up by others and underwent various mutations, the most common being a claimed Masonic link to another crusading order, the Knights Templar.

Two of the most influential Masons of the 19th century, Albert Gallatin Mackey and Albert Pike, entertained the notion that Ma-

An imaginative depiction of the Chevalier Ramsay dressed in the garb of the Order of St. Lazarus

sonry was the inheritor, if not the direct descendant, of the Ancient Mysteries—an initiatory system of arcane wisdom that constituted an important part of mankind's spiritual heritage.

Such notions—more romantic than historical—were critically examined by Mackey in his *History of Freemasonry*, his *Encyclopedia of Freemasonry*, and other writings. Pike, for his part, discussed these ideas in his weighty compendium *Morals and Dogma,* and in various lectures and writings. Neither author could wholly buy into the theory of a direct link between the Ancient Mysteries and the Masonic mysteries, but they found certain parallels intriguing. In effect, Mackey and Pike were using Masonry as a context in which to speculate about and study what is now called the field of comparative religion. While their studies inspired some Masons to explore esoteric lore, classical philosophy, and ancient history, they also provided anti-Masonic critics with a treasure trove of pre- and non-Christian tidbits over which they could sputter and fret.

For example, the preoccupation with identifying ancient origins for Masonry takes a decidedly sinister turn in the elaborate conspiracy theories of David Icke. The charismatic Icke, whose past accomplishments include soccer announcer and U.K. Green Party spokesman, struck gold in New Age circles with a series of popular self-published books alleging that the human race is unknowingly under the sway of shape-shifting reptilian aliens from another dimension.

Icke identifies Freemasonry as a successor of an ancient Babylonian Brotherhood, wise men who originally sought to free human consciousness from the energy-sucking reptilians. The Brotherhood's necessary use of secrecy became, over the centuries, corrupted into a form of manipulation and power control, leading the membership to eventually sell out to the aliens. Material posted at Icke's Web site alleges that there are secret tunnels beneath every Masonic lodge to facilitate reptilian rendezvous.[16]

Luciferian Telephones

Such allegations are reminiscent of the extravagant and long-running anti-Masonic hoax perpetrated in France in the 1880s and 1890s by Gabriel Jogand-Pagès writing under the pen name Léo Taxil.

Taxil began his literary career as an anticlerical pamphleteer, evolved into a writer of anticlerical pornography, such as *The Secret Love Life of Pope Pius IX*, and founded the Anti-Clerical League in 1881. Circa 1885, he staged a dramatic conversion to the Catholic Church and hit upon a new racket: publishing anti-Masonic literature for Catholic consumption.[17]

Taxil, who seems to have taken great delight in putting one over on both the Masons and the Church, proceeded to invent increasingly wilder tales of Masonic scandal that took in even the pope. Women's lodges served as Masonic brothels, Masons secretly worshipped Lucifer, and so on. Taxil capped his creations with the invention of a secret

Léo Taxil,
„der große Schwindler".

Léo Taxil (born Gabriel Jogand-Pagès), anti-Masonic hoaxer extraordinaire

Masonic cabal, the New and Reformed Palladium, which supposedly directed world Masonry from Charleston, South Carolina.

In league with an accomplice who published under the name of Doctor Bataille, Taxil went so far into the realm of the unbelievable that his avid Catholic readers should have been tipped off to the existence of a hoax. In one memorable passage in *The Devil in the 19th Century* (1891), Bataille gives a description of a magical system of instantaneous intercontinental wireless communication among Palladium bigwigs that deserves quotation at length:

> In his house, Gallatin Mackey once showed me that Arcula Mystica (the Mystic Box), of which there are only seven examples in existence, at Charleston, Rome, Berlin, Washington, Monte Video [sic], Naples and Calcutta.
>
> The exterior of this small box resembles a liqueurs receptacle. A spring catch opens simultaneously its two doors and lid. Inside, in the middle, stands a telephone mouthpiece in silver, which, at first sight one would take for a very small trumpet or hunting horn. At the left is a little rope made of twisted silver threads, one end of which is attached to the machine while the other extremity ends in a kind of little bell which one holds to one's ear to hear the voice of the person with whom one is speaking, just like the telephone of today. At the right is a toad, in silver, with its mouth open. Placed around the opening of the mouth-piece, stand seven statuettes in gold, each on a small separate silver pedestal symbolically the seven cardinal virtues of the Palladian Ladder. . . .
>
> When the Supreme Dogmatical chief wishes to communicate, for example, with the head of political action, he presses his finger on the Statuette Ignis and on the Statuette Ratio: these sink into their sockets and at the same instant, a strong whistling is heard in Rome, in the office where Lemmi keeps his Arcula Mystica; Lemmi opens his box and sees the statuette of Ignis sunk, while tiny, harmless flames issue from the throat of the silver toad. Then he knows that the Sovereign Pontiff of Charleston wishes to speak to him. He presses down the statuette of Ratio in his box and from then on, the conversation between the two chiefs proceeds, each

speaking directly into the mouthpiece described above, while at the same time holding to his ear the small silver bell."[18]

Taxil's hoaxes, to which he confessed in a spectacular public event in 1897, have continued to hoodwink anti-Masons to this day.[19] There is hardly an anti-Masonic book in print that doesn't unwittingly incorporate one of Taxil's hoaxes as if it were real. Des Griffin's *Fourth Reich of the Rich*, a classic of far-right conspiracy theorizing, even attempts to swallow the Arcula Mystica tale by asserting: "Evidence gathered from a number of sources strongly indicates that scientists working with the Illuminati had discovered the secrets of wireless telephony decades before Marconi invented the radio."[20] Griffin fails to mention the silver flame-breathing toads.

A Tool of Zion

Perhaps the most infamous claim about Masonry—and one that is still found today in militant Islamist circles—is that Freemasonry is in league with, or a tool of, Judaism or Zionism. This mix of anti-Semitism and anti-Masonry was a mainstay of Nazi ideology and was present, early on, in Adolf Hitler's *Mein Kampf*, first published in 1925.[21] Nazi propaganda in the 1930s and 1940s railed against a Jewish-Masonic conspiracy, and Hitler matched actions to words by shutting down German Masonic lodges in 1935 and confiscating their archives. However, the claim didn't begin with Hitler.

It can be found, for instance, in the *Protocols of the Learned Elders of Zion*, the forged document from 1905 describing what are supposedly the world-conquering plans of Zionist elders. The Protocols—which seem to have originated in Russian czarist police circles and soon spread to Europe—were later promulgated by the Nazis. They take the form of a series of speeches or program items said to have been given at an international Zionist congress in 1897.

"Protocol No. 15" has the elders proclaiming:

[W]e shall create and multiply free masonic lodges in all the countries of the world, absorb into them all who may become or who are prominent in public activity, for in these lodges we shall find our principal intelligence office and means of influence. All these lodges we shall bring under one central administration, known to us alone and to all others absolutely unknown, which will be composed of our learned elders.[22]

A recent edition of the Protocols of the Learned Elders of Zion *published in Egypt.*

The notion of a manipulative link between Judaism and Freemasonry extends back at least through the whole 19th century. It is not too difficult to see how such a linkage could be made. British lodges had admitted Jewish members as early as 1732, and lodges in other countries followed suit over the following decades. The mixing of Christians and Jews in "secret" circumstances was sufficiently novel to provoke suspicions in societies long given to the segregation or exclusion of Jews. What's more, as we will see more fully later, Masonic ritual does draw upon biblical material and symbolism—sufficient proof, to some critics, of a Jewish-Masonic connection. Erich Ludendorff, a top German general in World War I and an early supporter of Hitler, wrote an anti-Masonic book accusing Jews of using Freemasonry to turn unsuspecting gentiles into "artificial Jews."

Such suspicions are echoed, with an Islamic twist, in the current Middle East, where Freemasonry is condemned as a Zionist and imperialist tool, despite its avowed nonsectarian stance. In March 2004, a Masonic lodge in Istanbul, Turkey, was bombed by Islamist militants, who rushed the front entrance with dynamite strapped to their bodies, shouting, "Down with the Israeli lodge." Meanwhile, the Protocols remain a popular "proof" of Jewish-Masonic goals in a number of Islamic countries.

Lifestyles of the Rich and Famous

Part of the Masonic allure—and a source of some bewilderment—is the long list of prominent men who have been Masons over the last several centuries. What is one to make of a fraternity that has attracted both the composer Wolfgang Amadeus Mozart and Gene Autry, the singing cowboy? Both the philosopher Voltaire and *Seinfeld*'s Kramer, Michael Richards? Both liberal icon Franklin D. Roosevelt and ultraconservative Strom Thurmond?

The list of famous Masons goes on and on. Authors? Arthur Conan Doyle, Jonathan Swift, Anthony Trollope, Oscar Wilde, and P. G. Wodehouse. Composers? Bach, Haydn, Liszt, and Mozart. World leaders? Napoleon, King Kamehameha, Winston Churchill, Aga Khan III, and Salvador Allende. American frontiersmen? Davy Crockett, Kit Carson, and Lewis and Clark. Performers? Harry Houdini, Clark Gable, Ernest Borgnine, and Peter Sellers.[23]

Clearly there is something about Freemasonry that has attracted and inspired men from all walks of life. While some, such as Lyndon Baines Johnson, took the first degree and were insufficiently interested to proceed any further, others have proudly displayed their enthusiasm. Apollo astronaut "Buzz" Aldrin went so far as to transport a Masonic flag to the moon in 1969—a Scottish Rite flag sporting its double-headed eagle.[24] Two centuries earlier, in 1791, Mozart composed his opera *The Magic Flute* as a combination of fairy tale and Masonic allegory that was intended to propagandize in Masonry's favor, according to Mozart's librettist.[25]

The Masonic Myth is a rich tapestry of contradictory images and accusations, of half-truths and romantic dreams, of paranoia and hubris. Reality, however, is richer still, and therein hangs a tale.

Drawing of the Goose and Gridiron tavern in St. Paul's Churchyard, London, site of the founding of the premier Grand Lodge of England on June 24, 1717, convened by four local Masonic lodges. This is the official date of the beginning of modern "speculative" Freemasonry.

2

Square Roots

Where Did Freemasonry Come From?

The central story around which Freemasonry has built itself is its claim of descent from medieval guilds of stonemasons. As the celebrated builders of the great gothic cathedrals of Europe, these craftsmen are said to have protected their trade craft with oaths of secrecy and maintained quality control by channeling members through a progressive advancement in skills from apprentice to fellow craft to master.[1] These masons, who were "free" by dint of their ability to move from one job site to another (as opposed to serfs, who were tied to the land), formed temporary "lodges" to maintain order and oversee the work at those job sites.[2]

This, at least, is the venerable tale that generations of Freemasons have told themselves for some three hundred years. It is to this medieval model, with its secrets, its oaths, its advancement by degrees, and its local lodges, that modern Masonry has looked for its inspiration, structure, and symbolic vocabulary. However, similar features are not the same thing as historical evidence of direct connections. If we want to discover where Freemasonry really came from, we have to dig a little deeper.

In trying to trace the origins of Freemasonry, historians are faced with a knotty question: how do you uncover the history of an entity that is supposedly a secret society? If, as many claim, Masonry has had something to hide, wouldn't its lack of clear-cut origins and certain holes in its historical record be circumstantial evidence of some sort of cover-up? Many "alternative" historians and anti-Masonic critics seem to think so.

However, as any family genealogist will be happy to testify, having difficulty in finding records of one's great-great-great-grandfather doesn't necessarily mean that he had something to hide or that there is a family conspiracy at work. Sometimes the records are simply lost. But often the records are out there—and the big challenge is to find them and interpret them correctly.

As it so happens, for a supposed secret society, Freemasonry has a staggering amount of records preserved: lodge meeting minutes, membership rolls, charters, certificates, correspondence, and commemorative objects. These are scattered all over the place: in local lodges, Masonic libraries, private collections, and grand lodge archives. Due to considerations of privacy, these records are not always available to everyone, and certainly not to someone just walking in off the street. But legitimate historians and researchers, both Masonic and non-Masonic, have combed through many of these sources over the years as part of an effort to construct an objective history of the Craft.

Admittedly, most of this research has been tucked away in the transactions of Masonic research lodges such as the celebrated English Lodge of Research, Quatuor Coronati No. 2076, or within scholarly books published by university presses, such as David Stevenson's *Origins of Freemasonry* and Steven C. Bullock's *Revolutionary Brotherhood.* These writings are not always easy to locate, and even when one does, the sheer quantity of minute details can be difficult to digest. But any serious researcher seeking the truth about Freemasonry should at least make an attempt to familiarize himself with their high points.

Alas, the twin sources of Masonic fabulation—the alternative historians and the anti-Masonic conspiracy theorists—apparently do not bother. Christopher Knight and Robert Lomas, themselves Masons and authors of such alternative tomes as *The Hiram Key, The Second Messiah,* and *The Book of Hiram,* grumble bitterly about a "Masonic Mafia" of scholars who refuse to take Knight and Lomas's "new ideas" seriously.[3] Indeed, reviewers in *Ars Quatuor Coronatorum,* the transactions of the previously mentioned research lodge, have made short work of Knight and Lomas by calling them on numerous errors of fact, unwarranted assumptions, and research gaffes.[4] Perhaps the sticklers of *Ars Quatuor Coronatorum* would be less dismissive if Knight and Lomas had shown any evidence of bringing themselves up to speed on the current state of Masonic research. The pair's bibliographies and citations—when they have them at all—display a conspicuous absence of such sources.[5]

Instead, early on in their first book, *The Hiram Key,* Knight and Lomas take all of two pages to dismiss what they call "the stonemason theory," which, they admit, "has found acceptance in virtually every quarter, Masonic and non-Masonic."[6] By rejecting it, they clear the path for *their* theory, which attributes Freemasonry's origins to the Knights Templar and the Sinclair family of Rosslyn Chapel fame. We'll take a further look at that theory shortly, but first let's look at Freemasonry's own account of its origins.

The Official Records

Present-day Masonry as an organized order marks its official beginning as June 24, 1717 (St. John the Baptist's Day), when four London lodges, which were already in existence, met to found an administrative grand lodge and to elect a Grand Master. These lodges were originally identified by the names of the taverns in which they met: the Goose and Gridiron, the Crown, the Apple Tree, and the Rummer and Grapes. From that day on to the present, Freemasonry has maintained itself in uninterrupted fashion, eventually spreading around the world.

But how exactly did those four lodges come to be, and how did men come to call themselves Freemasons in the first place? This is where the fog begins to roll in and the mysteries multiply.

Masonic records indicate that one of the four lodges was founded in 1691 and the others were apparently of more recent vintage.[7] But even this is uncertain. According to Masonic tradition, the four lodges were considered "time immemorial" lodges, which means that they were presumed to have existed prior to such records.[8]

Masonic records and historical accounts also show that there were other lodges peppered around England and Scotland, some dating back to at least the 16th century. However, this is where we have to tread very carefully. For the oldest of those lodges, which were in Scotland, were still "operative" lodges—that is, actual craft lodges of working stonemasons. The London lodges that came together in 1717 to found a grand lodge were not.

One of them, the Rummer and Grapes, Westminster, was largely composed of aristocrats and gentlemen. The other three had less rarefied members, including a few actual stonemasons, interspersed with various "nonoperatives."[9] In short, the London lodges of 1717 were already well on their way to being purely "speculative"—that is, philosophical and social in nature, which is how present-day Freemasonry describes itself.

This brings us to one of the most disputed questions in Masonic history: did speculative Freemasonry actually descend from operative masonry? And if it did, are its secrets and rituals a continuation of traditions handed down from the cathedral builders or even earlier?

Anderson's Constitutions

Everyone loves a mystery, and the Masons themselves have been among the biggest consumers (and producers) of fanciful theories about their own historical roots and impact upon history. The "traditional" history that Dr. James Anderson published in 1723, soon after the founding of the premier Grand Lodge of London in 1717, is as good a place to start our search as any, since it makes up a major portion of the official Masonic Constitutions endorsed by the fledgling grand lodge.

The history identifies the origin of geometry (and hence Masonry) with Adam, who had that knowledge "implanted in his heart" by God, the Great Architect of the Universe. Adam passes on this knowledge to Cain, who builds the first city, and to another son, Seth. Masonry is preserved through the Flood by Noah and his sons, and is passed on to the builders of the Tower of Babel, whence it is dispersed around the world.

Anderson threads his history through each of the seven wonders of the ancient world, the greatest being the Temple of Solomon.[10] The Egyptians, Greeks, and Romans all get their due, and eventually the history comes up to the present (1723) reign of King George I. Along the way, Moses, King Solomon, and Caesar Augustus, not to mention the kings of Scotland, are all dubbed grand masters of Masonry.

This is, of course, a charming tale, but it is of little help as far as verifiable history goes. The situation is no better if we go further back, to the so-called Old Charges that Anderson drew upon in writing his traditional history of the Craft.

The Old Charges

The Old Charges are the earliest surviving manuscripts that preserve what the British operative masons (i.e., the actual working stonemasons) taught their new members about their craft's history and the ethical behavior that was expected of them. The earliest of these charges, the Regius Manuscript (or Regius Poem), dates from 1390 or so, while the next oldest, the Cooke Manuscript, from 1425, is said to be a copy of an earlier charge dating back to the mid–14th century.[11] More than one hundred of these Old Charges have been preserved and identified, and most of them share the same general content, although with numerous variations in details.

One might think (or hope) that such early documents would provide the most authentic information about the Masonic tradition. However, their accounts of Masonic ancestry are no more reliable than Anderson's, as the following brief passage in Middle English from the Regius Poem demonstrates:

> On thys maner, thro[g] good wytte of gemetry,
> Bygan furst the craft of masonry:
> The clerk Euclyde on thys wyse hyt fonde,
> Thys craft of gemetry yn Egypte londe.
> Yn Egypte he taw[g]hte hyt ful wyde,
> Yn dyvers londe on every syde;
> Mony erys afterwarde, y understonde,
> [G]er that the craft com ynto thys londe,
> Thys craft com ynto Englond, as y [g]low say,
> Yn tyme of good kynge Adelstonus day;[12]

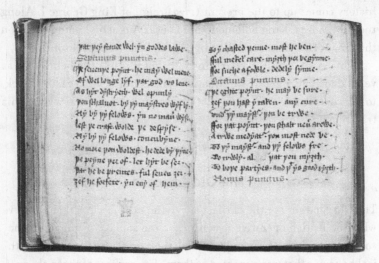

The Regius Manuscript, the oldest of the Old Charges, circa 1390

This roughly translates as:

> In this manner, through good knowledge of geometry,
> Began first the craft of masonry.
> The clerk Euclid in this wise founded,
> This craft of geometry in Egyptian land.
> In Egypt he taught it full wide,
> In divers lands on every side;
> Many years afterward, I understand,
> Before the craft came into this land.
> This craft came into England, as I now say,
> In the time of the good king Athelstan's day.[13]

This amounts to saying that Masonry grew out of geometry, was taught in Egypt by Euclid, and was brought to England at the time of King Athelstane (circa the early 900s). As historian David Stevenson notes, "If studied in search of the historical truth about the origins of the mason craft, the Old Charges may be dismissed as rubbish, impressive exercises in the dubious skills of name-dropping and creative chronology. But in so far as they reflect the craft's image of itself they should not be dismissed with ridicule."[14]

Concocting impressive traditional histories was a common practice among medieval craft guilds; in this the Masons were hardly unique. The fact that Anderson drew upon the Old Charges in devising his traditional history for modern Freemasonry is, at best, ambiguous evidence of a direct lineage from the operative masons to the speculative Masons who founded the premier Grand Lodge in London in 1717. Anderson might simply have been using the legends and customs of earlier stonemasons in order to create an appearance of continuity between them and speculative Masonry.

The Scottish Factor

In fact, if one focuses solely on England, there *is* a problem with a direct operative-speculative Masonic link. This is because the historic record in England is both spotty and ambiguous—when there is a record at all. There *was* a masons' craft guild, the London Masons' Company, which regulated the trade in London. But guilds were urban organizations, and as Masonic historian Harry Carr has pointed out, the majority of masons' work was "at castles, abbeys, monasteries and churches, away from the large towns, usually under circumstances which were not conducive to any kind of municipal or gild controls."[15] Masons working at those locations are believed to have formed lodges—perhaps in shacks adjoining the job sites—but these lodges do not seem to have been permanent, ongoing entities.

There were masons' guilds in France and Germany, but they didn't evolve into speculative groups. Yet it was in England, where stonemasons were largely organized in a more ad hoc fashion, that speculative lodges seem to have first appeared. The four London lodges of 1717 fame, and others in England in the 1600s, all appear to have been entirely or largely speculative.[16]

The records of the London Masons' Company seem to indicate that there was an inner club within that guild called "the Acception," into which nonoperatives were initiated, thus becoming "accepted masons." But there is no clear-cut evidence linking this club within the Masons' Company to separate outside lodges, either operative or speculative.[17]

Where we *do* find records of ongoing operative masons' lodges in the British Isles is in Scotland. It is a matter of historic record that a number of these lodges (some of which still exist) did make the transition over time from operative to speculative, largely in the early 18th century. Their lodge minutes, some dating back to 1599, indicate that operative lodges in Scotland began to accept members who were not working stonemasons in the early to mid–1600s.[18]

For instance, nonoperatives joining the Lodge of Edinburgh included two generals (1641), a physician to the king (1647), an Edinburgh merchant (1649), three lawyers (1670), and a mathematics teacher (1679).[19]

So one prominent theory is that an incremental shift happened over the years until a point was reached where nonoperative members began to outnumber operative members. This eventually led to purely speculative lodges where the old stonemasons' working tools, garb, and symbolism were retooled for philosophical and allegorical purposes.

There are numerous variations on this theory, which we needn't go into in detail here. Some historians have posited a stage of "transitional" lodges between the operative and speculative ones. This might account for, if not explain, the pre–1717 lodges peppered around England.

Others have suggested that there were speculative/philosophical strains (those elusive secrets!) within operative masonry from the beginning and that it was an interest in learning these that induced some nonoperative gentlemen and others to seek to join. An alternate theory is that it was the nonoperative intellectuals who brought their philosophical concerns with them into the Craft and redirected the focus of the lodges away from the practical concerns of working masons.

Historian David Stevenson has suggested that after William Schaw was appointed Master of the Works by King James VI of Scotland in 1583, Schaw reorganized the Scottish lodge system in a more orderly fashion—including the taking of minutes—and introduced some elements of Renaissance esotericism into Masonic practice. The formal rules for this reorganized Masonry, known as the first and second Schaw Statutes, include an order that entered apprentices and fellow crafts be tested in "the art of memory and science thairof." Stevenson suggests that this may well refer to "the Art of Memory"—a practice championed by such Renaissance esotericists as Giordano Bruno, which entailed constructing elaborate mental images of "memory palaces," which could then serve as aids for prodigious feats of memory. Stevenson thus credits Schaw with hatching a deeper, more speculative Freemasonry within Scottish Masonry itself.[20]

It is at this point that what little historical consensus there is among Masonic historians begins to break down and the question of Masonic origins becomes a free-for-all. On the one hand, the earliest evidence of flat-out speculative lodges resides on the English side of the border. On the other hand, the records kept by Scottish lodges demonstrate, in Scotland at least, an evolution from operative stonemasons to the speculative Masons of today.

Given that the first recorded Masonic initiation on English soil was the Scotsman Robert Moray's 1641 initiation by members of the Lodge of Edinburgh serving in the Scottish army then occupying northern England, and that James Anderson, the author of the Constitutions for the Grand Lodge of London, was himself a Scot, it doesn't seem too far-fetched to suggest that the Scots and the English may have traded Masonic influences back and forth, especially once James VI, king of Scotland, became James I, king of England, in 1603 after the death of Queen Elizabeth I; and further still after the 1707 union between Scotland and England.

But exactly how this Masonic influence trading may have taken place remains obscure. The Scottish lodges were still predominantly operative stonemasons' lodges at the time that the English Grand Lodge was organized in London in 1717, so it is difficult to credit the Scottish lodges with founding speculative Masonry as such.

Shadows of Knight

The alternative historians, though largely English, have been partisans of the claim for Scottish roots, but with a twist: they view the late-medieval operative masons as merely a link back to an earlier source of wonder and mystery: the Knights Templar. According to them, the Freemasons are, in one way or another, a survival or creation of the Templars.

The Templars, as you may recall, were an order of warrior-monks that was ostensibly founded to protect pilgrims on their way to the Holy Land

Jacques de Molay, final grand master of the Knights Templar

at the time of the Crusades, circa 1118. It appears that the Christian king of Jerusalem granted them headquarters on what is now known as Temple Mount, the legendary site of the original Jewish Temple, better known as the Temple of Solomon, and the present location of the famous Islamic shrine the Dome of the Rock. That fateful gesture placed the Templars at the epicenter of one of the most celebrated and myth-laden spots in Jewish, Christian, and Islamic history. Even if the Templars were using the mount only as a barracks, their proximity to a locale of such projected significance virtually guaranteed that some of it would rub off on them.

And indeed it has. Among the alternative historians, the Templars enjoy a commanding position as the most lionized (and mythologized) group of knights this side of the Knights of the Round Table. Supposedly, they

- excavated beneath the site of the old Temple and found a fabulous treasure of some sort—either the Ark of the Covenant, the Holy Grail, explosive early Christian teachings, or great wealth;
- absorbed heretical and esoteric wisdom and secrets from Shiite Ismailis and/or Johannite Gnostics in the Jerusalem vicinity;
- brought both their treasure and the secret teachings back with them to Europe once the Crusades were crushed;
- underwrote and oversaw the building of the great Gothic cathedrals;

• survived the 1307–12 attempt by the French monarch Philip IV and his Avignon pope, Clement V, to wipe them out, escaping variously to Scotland, Portugal, North Africa, and even North America.

Unsurprisingly, real-world, noncircumstantial evidence is lacking for all of these allegations, with the exception of the fact that some Templars did manage to survive the order's abolishment and were absorbed into other chivalric orders, such as the Knights Hospitallers. But the lack of solid evidence hasn't fazed the ever-growing cottage industry of Templar mythologists, who happily take each other's suppositions as given facts and build further suppositions upon them.

The most commonly cited "link" between Templars and Freemasons is the myth that the persecuted knights found refuge in Scotland, helped win the key battle of Bannockburn for Robert the Bruce in 1314, clandestinely survived within Masonry (or within Masonic-linked orders such as the Royal Order of Scotland), and hid their celebrated treasure in a vault beneath the Sinclair family's Rosslyn Chapel near Edinburgh.[21]

Unfortunately, none of these assertions is backed up by solid evidence, either, though Rosslyn Chapel keeps turning up like a bad penny in the speculations of the alternative historians.

Chapel Perilous

Rosslyn Chapel should be familiar to readers of *The Da Vinci Code* as the climactic destination of the grand chase that fuels that novel's plot. The chapel is real enough, a 15th-century architectural oddity that still survives as a historical tourist attraction. Originally intended as the choir of a larger "collegiate" church whose construction was halted in 1484 upon the death of Sir William St. Clair (Sinclair), the chapel features extensive stone carvings on both its exterior and interior.[22]

The interpretation of those carvings has played a central role in the efforts of alternative historians to identify a connection between Freemasonry and the Knights Templar. Unfortunately, "evidence" of this

Rosslyn Chapel near Edinburgh, Scotland

sort is akin to reading tea leaves: everyone sees what they want to see, and no single interpretation can be considered indisputably correct.

One typical piece of "evidence" connecting Rosslyn to the Knights Templar is a weather-worn ornamental carving of two rather bloblike figures—one supposedly a Templar and the other identified as a blind-folded and kneeling man with a noose around his neck and a Bible in his hand. Knight and Lomas see this as a depiction of a Templar conducting a Masonic first-degree ritual.[23] This neatly links the Templars, Rosslyn, and Masonry into a tidy package.

The only problem is that there is no record of the Templars having had such an initiation ritual; the Templar figure is not clearly a Templar; the head of the supposedly kneeling man is at the same height as the head of the standing "Templar"; it isn't clear that he is in fact holding a Bible or anything at all; and the appearance of a blindfold may just be due to the erosion of the carving. This leaves us with the noose, which appears more like a leash than a rope.

Similarly, decorative carvings within the chapel are identified by Knight and Lomas as depicting maize (corn) and aloe plants, both "New World" flora—this in a building built before Columbus ever set sail. This constitutes proof that the missing Templar fleet, which sup-posedly took off just as Philip IV launched his attack on the Templars, actually made it to America before Columbus. Again, photos of the

carvings show vegetative motifs that could be any number of plants—
or simply made up.[24]

Suffice it to say that any links between Rosslyn and the Templars
are highly dubious, not least because there is a 134-year gap between the
Templars' abolition in 1312 and the start of construction on the chapel in
1446. Moreover, members of the Sinclair family are on record as having
testified *against* the Templars during a hearing and trial in Scotland held
by Bishop Lamberton in 1309.[25]

The most solid link between Rosslyn and Freemasonry—if link
it is—is the Sinclair (sometimes St. Clair) family's claim to being the
hereditary patrons of the Masons in Scotland since at least the 15th
century. This claim has been a matter of controversy ever since it first
arose in the 17th century, and serious historians within both Masonry
and academia view it with skepticism.

Much has been made of the so-called St. Clair Charters of 1600 and
1627–28, which were not so much charters as letters of commission
signed on behalf of various Scottish lodges seeking the king's recognition of William Sinclair as their traditional patron. Such a confirmation was not forthcoming, and
indications that the Sinclairs acted
as actual patrons are spotty.[26]

Other than employing skill-
ful masons to build and decorate
Rosslyn Chapel in the 1400s, and
the aborted attempts to gain recognition with the two charters, the
main Sinclair interaction with the
Craft on record seems to have been
the appointment of a Sinclair descendant, William Sinclair, as first
Grand Master of the Grand Lodge
of Scotland in 1737, when that
grand lodge was founded, twenty
years after the founding of the premier Grand Lodge in London. Sinclair received this largely honorary
position with the understanding

*Interpreting weatherworn bloblike carvings
is a game anyone can play. These appear
on the exterior southwest corner of Rosslyn
Chapel. Is it a Templar "masonic" ritual or
wishful thinking?*

that in accepting the post he was relinquishing any further hereditary claims to Masonic leadership. The wording of the document that Sinclair was forced to sign before induction suggests that the Masons were eager to be done with Sinclair pretensions to hereditary leadership. Sinclair's statement reads, in part:

> I, William St. Clair of Rossline, Esquire . . . for me and my heirs renounce, quit, claim, overgive, and discharge, all right, claim, or pretence that I, or my heirs, had, have, or any ways may have, pretend to, or claim, to be patron, protector, judge or master of the Massons [sic] in Scotland, in virtue of any deed or deeds made and granted by the said Massons, or of any grant or charter made by any of the Kings of Scotland, to and in favours [sic] of the said William and Sir William St. Clairs of Rossline, or any others of my predecessors.[27]

William was replaced as grand master by a non-Sinclair the following year.[28]

Be that as it may, it seems to have been a long-running Sinclair family tradition to promote their claims about Rosslyn and about Masonic patronage. Claims of a specific Rosslyn–Knights Templar connection are of a more recent vintage—they date back only twenty-five to thirty years—and there are no signs of Templar claims in Sinclair family histories prior to that. Thus we have the privilege of witnessing a myth still in the making.

Born in Blood

The other most prominent recent attempt to make a case for a direct line between the Knights Templar and Freemasonry has been the work of John J. Robinson, whose 1989 book *Born in Blood: The Lost Secrets of Freemasonry* became quite popular in Masonic circles. Robinson doesn't attempt to draw Rosslyn Chapel or the Sinclairs into his speculations, though he does recount the legend of fugitive Knights Templar coming to the rescue of Robert the Bruce at the Battle of Bannockburn.[29]

Instead, he draws intriguing correlations between components and phrasing supposedly found in Masonic rituals and motifs associated with the Templar myth. Thus, he claims that in "the lecture that sums up the initiation of a new Master Mason, the newly admitted candidate is told that this degree 'will make you a brother to pirates and corsairs.'"[30] Robinson surmises that this most makes sense as a reference to the eighteen Templar ships said to have escaped King Philip's attack, some of which supposedly then took up piracy to survive. Similarly, there is the parallel between the famous pirate flag and the skull and crossbones sometimes found as one of the symbols associated with the Master Mason degree in Masonry.

But as is so often the case in such speculations, Robinson—who was not a Mason at the time he wrote the book—was relying on exposés and thirdhand sources for his information about Masonic ritual. In eight years of research, I have never found any version of the Master Mason's lecture or ritual (or that of any other degree) that refers to "pirates and corsairs." According to a Mason who spoke with Robinson about this detail, Robinson confessed that he'd found the phrase in the novel *The Count of Monte Cristo*—hardly a reliable Masonic source.[31]

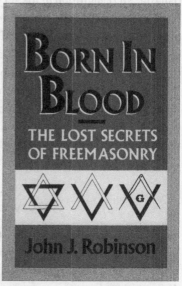

Worse still, there seems to be no historical evidence of the escape of eighteen Templar ships (which Robinson readily admits, although he seems to find this lack of evidence to be a confirmation of the Templars' successful stealth).

The motif of skull and crossbones has a much wider usage than just pirates and Masonry, symbolizing as it does mortality or danger. It can be found on numerous (non-Masonic and non-Templar) tombstones, and its employment as a symbol associated with the Masonic third degree simply refers to that degree's legend of the slain Grand

Born in Blood, *John J. Robinson's popular 1989 book linking the Knights Templar to Freemasonry*

Master Hiram Abiff.[32] While it is true that the black aprons of the Masonic version of the Knights Templar used to feature a skull and crossbones, this was a reference to Hiram (and possibly a commemoration of the martyrdom of the original Templars' leader, Jacques de Molay). However, the Masonic Knights Templar weren't organized until the late 1700s, while the original Knights Templar did not, to the best of my knowledge, employ the skull and crossbones as a symbol.

Robinson, to his credit, recognized that his musings were highly speculative and never claimed them as "discoveries." Nevertheless, Robinson's very readable book seized the imagination of many romantic Masons, and it became a bestseller in Masonic circles.

The sum total of Robinson's research and his subsequent contacts with Masons gave him a positive impression of Masonry (references to pirates aside), and within a few years of the publication of *Born in Blood*, Robinson decided to become a Mason. He continued to write and lecture in defense of the Craft, and on his deathbed in 1993, while succumbing to cancer, he received an honorary 33rd degree in the Scottish Rite, in recognition of his service to Masonry.[33]

As for any concrete connection between Masonry and the Templars, this remains unproven. Masons in the latter half of the 18th century were sufficiently taken with the notion of a linkage, however, that they devised so-called Templar degrees and organized Masonic Knights Templar orders. By the middle of the 19th century, "traditional" (i.e., mythological) histories had been invented that claimed actual lineal descent from the famous Templars. These have continued to muddy the historical waters right up to the present.[34]

History vs. Tradition

So far we have seen that the "traditional histories" of Masonry—whether Anderson's Constitutions or the Old Charges or Ramsay's Oration—are of little help in determining the Craft's real history. Traditional histories serve many purposes, including providing romantic rallying points and working templates for group cohesion, but they are unreliable as actual history.

The alternative historians are not much better. Their complex theories may touch on many intriguing ideas and offer a smorgasbord of "discoveries," but the end results more resemble the Old Charges than they do reliable history.

By all indications, modern Freemasonry can rightfully claim to have inherited certain of its components (some terms, some traditions, some ritual elements) from the operative stonemasons of the late Middle Ages and Renaissance, but any attempts to identify earlier roots than that are purely conjectural. Why is this so difficult for so many to accept, many Masons included? I would argue that it is because the way in which Freemasonry evolved from 1600 on created a kind of "optical illusion" that suggested ancient origins, teachings, and secrets. Let's look at how this could have come about.

The Optical Illusion

We are accustomed in the modern era to having new products or social innovations sold to us on the basis of the wonderful future that they will bring us. The modern gaze is largely forward looking—more concerned with what might be and what is to come than with what came before.

By contrast, the 16th through 18th centuries—the time span in which speculative Freemasonry slowly emerged—were home to more traditional societies in which new inventions and developments were defended and justified by associating them with a fabled past.

The Renaissance, for instance (c. the 15th through 17th centuries), arose through the rediscovery and translation of ancient texts believed to embody the universal wisdom of the pre-Christian Greeks and Egyptians, who were championed as the source of Western culture.[35] This repaganizing of high culture resulted in an efflorescence of new art, music, and drama, such as Shakespeare's plays and da Vinci's creations, and it helped loosen the grip of the Church on the culture at large.

Similarly, Martin Luther and the Protestant Reformation (c. the 16th century) justified their innovations and upheavals with an appeal to the past—to a primitive and purer Christianity, shorn of corrupt papal accretions. Even the era of the Enlightenment, with its scientific skepticism and the first moves toward democracy (c. the 17th through 18th centuries), was ushered in with a return to classical architecture and references to Greek and Roman predecessors.

The genesis of Freemasonry can be found in the midst of these overlapping eras of ferment and change, when the medieval guilds were on their way out and a new breed of gentlemen scholars, eluding church control, were making their presence known.

The Renaissance quest for ancient wisdom and knowledge was undertaken by some participants through the pursuit of such arcane practices as alchemy, magic, and Cabala (a Christianized form of the Jewish mystical tradition of Kabbalah). These were commonly carried out in secret, in order to avoid persecution by the Inquisition and other unsympathetic authorities. Their status in England was unpredictable, depending on the whim of Church and Crown. A ban on alchemy was enacted by Henry IV in 1403 out of fear of counterfeit money, but later monarchs, such as Henry VI and Charles II, were more favorably disposed.[36] Within such an uncertain terrain, these studies were risky, but they still held an interest for some of the finest minds of the kingdom. Two of the fathers of modern science, Isaac Newton and Robert Boyle, undertook alchemical studies as part of their investigations of nature, as did Elias Ashmole.

If we place ourselves in the shoes of a 17th-century inquisitive gentleman with such preoccupations, including a fascination with architecture—a very fashionable interest of the time—it isn't hard to imagine that the Masonic lodges, with their fabled histories, their oaths of secrecy and mutual aid, and their practical knowledge of the building arts, might have exerted a profound interest. The need for the lodges as trade institutions was on the wane, but their potential as confidential gathering places for seekers of a certain bent was on the rise.

The Old Charges, with their suggestive history of the Craft, were read aloud in lodge whenever a new Mason was initiated—a tradition that began in the operative era and was upheld in the speculative era.[37] These provided a romantic myth of the handing down of ancient knowledge, and it seems apparent that as the Masonic degree rituals evolved in the speculative era, this myth was interwoven into the rituals themselves.

And to complicate matters further, it appears that the unknown authors of the evolving rituals introduced new elements and symbols—or highlighted old ones—in ways that invited alchemical, astrological, or philosophical interpretations.[38] Because we do not know who authored the rituals or, with absolute certainty, which parts date back to operative days and which do not, the rituals as a whole have acquired a "time immemorial" quality.

And here is one source of the "optical illusion": the initiatory rituals that all Freemasons have undergone give the impression of ancient origins, and the lectures that accompany those rituals add to that impression. But the ritual components that create this impression may be later additions that earlier stonemasons wouldn't recognize at all.

Yet there is another significant cause of the illusion as well—this one coming from outside Masonry.

The Optical Illusion II

One important side effect of the loosening of Church control over the pursuit of knowledge during the 17th and 18th centuries was a new interest in the critical scrutiny of religion. New concepts, such as Deism and a natural religion supposedly inherent in mankind, began to gain currency in educated circles, and Christianity began to lose its privileged status as the only true religion among educated Europeans. It became, instead, just one among many religions—a view driven home by the expansion of the British and European colonizers into the Far East.

A favorite assumption among many gentleman scholars of the day—including Isaac Newton—was that there had once been a primordial religion or religious impulse originally shared by all mankind. As the Frenchman "Baron" d'Hancarville put it in 1785, there was originally "one cult, one theology, one religion, and very likely one language."[39] This primordial religion was often attributed to Noah, from whom post-Flood humanity was said to descend. Newton in his private papers surmised that Jesus merely confirmed this original religion when he taught that one should "love God above all things, and

ANTIQUARIANS.
A LA GREQUE.

Eighteenth-century satirical print by Thomas Rowlandson mocking the obsessions and enthusiasms of antiquarians. While such amateur researchers did expand the boundaries of acceptable thinking about religions and cultures of the past, they also entertained many exotic notions not supported by historians and anthropologists. Many of their ideas were echoed in the writings of romantic Masons.

our Neighbour as our self."[40] Indeed, Anderson's revised and expanded Constitutions of 1738 defined a Mason as "a true Noachida" who was charged "to adhere to that Religion in which all Men agree (leaving each Brother to his own particular Opinions) that is, to be Good Men and True, Men of Honour and Honesty, by whatever Names, Religions or Persuasions they may be distinguish'd."[41]

Since the oldest surviving evidence of the religious past consisted of temples and monuments presumably built by masons, certain of these proto-anthropological scholars of the day assumed that the rituals and symbols of Masonry must offer clues to that primordial religion. For instance, the antiquarian William Stukeley joined the Craft in 1721 with the preformed idea that he would find evidence linking the Masons to the ancient Druids, supposedly one manifestation of this early proto-religion.[42]

Two of the more popular theories about this hypothetical root religion were that it involved the worship of the sun and of the phallus, respectively. These were, in turn, projected onto Freemasonry by proponents of these theories, including, oddly enough, the colonial freethinker Thomas Paine. (Paine, who had no special regard for Christianity, either, contended: "The christian religion and Masonry have one and the same common origin: both are derived from the worship of the Sun.")[43]

The activities of these antiquarian "mythographers," as scholar Joscelyn Godwin calls them, continued well into the 19th century and were influential enough that some Masons came to share the view that Masonry originally derived from the Ancient Mysteries. It was much more exciting and impressive, after all, to trace oneself back to the pyramid builders of Egypt or the temple builders of Greece than to a cluster of Scottish stonemasons. Masonic ritual and writings abounded with references to "our ancient brethren," helping to bolster the illusion.

And thus the second source of the optical illusion was set in place: non-Masonic mythographers in search of humanity's religious roots linked their version of a mythic past to Masonry's own mythic past, resulting in grand theories that bore little resemblance to actual history. Ritual components and symbols that weren't added until the 18th or 19th century were interpreted as if they had been present in Masonic tradition for millennia. It is ironic that some anti-Masonic critics—especially fundamentalist Christians who view Masonry as a rival religion—often use the assertions of the mythographers to bolster their arguments, even though the mythographers often had reductionist attitudes toward Christianity as well.

Rivals Arise

If the history of Freemasonry before its "official" 1717 founding is confounding and elusive, its post–1717 history is no less puzzling, despite the presence of much better kept records and more thorough historical research.

As we have seen, the initiative for founding the first grand lodge was undertaken by four London lodges, and London and its immediate surroundings were the extent of its claim of jurisdiction. However, there were a good number of lodges, both in London and around England, that had their own traditions and resisted the premier Grand Lodge's efforts to organize the Craft. Exactly where these lodges came from to begin with is part of the mystery.

Before long, at least two rival grand lodges sprang up, both claiming roots more ancient than those of the premier Grand Lodge in London. The first of these, a local lodge in York, renamed itself the Grand Lodge of All England, although its few associated lodges were mostly in Yorkshire, Lancashire, and Cheshire. It derived its claim to preeminence from references in various of the Old Charges to an annual assembly of Masons held in York in previous centuries. It never amounted to much, chartering only fourteen other lodges in its sixty-seven years of existence (1725–92).[44]

The other rival, the Grand Lodge of the Antients, was formed in 1751 and gave the premier Grand Lodge—which they disparagingly dubbed "the Moderns"—a more serious run for its money.[45]

The Antients claimed, with some justification, that the Moderns had tinkered with the degree rituals, neglected certain traditions, and inserted other new "innovations," although it was unclear as to how far back these cherished traditions actually dated. The lodges that came together to form the Grand Lodge of the Antients had kept their independence from the London Grand Lodge, and so the formation of this newer, yet supposedly more authentically "antient," grand lodge wasn't really a schismatic move, although the Moderns liked to think so.[46]

There is little point in delving into the minutiae of the Antients/Moderns dispute. For our purposes, the salient detail is that many of the lodges composing the Antients' Grand Lodge had members who were Irish and Scottish Masons living in England, and in some instances they may have been privy to customs and traditions that predated or at least differed from those of the premier Grand Lodge in London.[47]

The other significant difference is the Antients' defense of an additional degree ritual, the Holy Royal Arch, which they considered to be a "completion" of the third-degree Master Mason's ritual. Together the two rituals tell an intriguing tale, which we will consider in more depth in chapter 7.

For the next sixty years, the Antients and Moderns continued on parallel tracks, sometimes persuading lodges to switch allegiance to one camp or the other. However, after more than a decade of negotiations, the rival lodges finally made peace and merged in 1813, forming the United Grand Lodge of England (abbreviated as UGLE, which many Masons delight in pronouncing "ugly"). It is this body that has continued on down to the present as the sole governing body of "free and accepted" Masonry in England.

An Entered Apprentice candidate's "hoodwink" is removed in this depiction of a French-style first-degree ritual, from an "exposure" published in Amsterdam in 1745, The Secrets of the Order of Free Masons. *Swords are not a part of degrees performed in English-speaking Freemasonry.*

3

Continental Ops

The Craft Spreads to Europe

egend has it that at the public execution by guillotine of Louis XVI in 1793, a stranger (often described as a Freemason) jumped onto the platform, dipped his hand in the dead king's blood, and called out, "Jacques de Molay, thou art avenged!"

Despite the lack of evidence for this anecdote, it has become a favorite of those who like to think that the Masons were behind the French Revolution and that behind the Masons were the Knights Templar.[1] Or, in other words, that the regicide of the French Revolution was the revenge of the Templars enacted via the Masons.

To better understand how this idea could gain any currency, we need to grasp the subtle—and not so subtle—changes that Freemasonry underwent as it spread abroad shortly after 1717.

Masonry in Britain and its colonies was and remains all of a piece, with closely shared rituals, experiences, and values. European Masonry, as it developed, was something else again. The differences between English-speaking Masonry and the Masonry of other tongues and cultures account for much of the confusion people have in trying to understand the Craft as a whole—especially when all flavors of Masonry are lumped together indiscriminately.

Europe is home to some of the finest specimens of the stone-masons' craft, from the sky-touching spires of Cologne to the rose-window-infused interior space of Chartres. During the course of the Middle Ages, Europe's operative masons were organized into guilds and lodges—institutions with, in many cases, more stability and durability than their counterparts in the British Isles.

Nevertheless, there seems to have been some vital spark missing, or perhaps an absence of fortuitous circumstances, that would have led to a self-generated evolution from operative to speculative Masonry on the Continent.

According to most historical accounts, it was only after the establishment of the premier Grand Lodge in London in 1717 that the idea of a philosophical and fraternal speculative Masonry appeared on the Continent, and when it did, it was initially derived from the British phenomenon.

The earliest record of Masonry's spread to Europe seems to be the founding of a lodge in Rotterdam in 1721, among Englishmen and Scots living there.[2] However, this was apparently a short-lived phenomenon and did not, it seems, directly spawn other lodges. A Bohemian "Lodge of the Three Stars" was founded in June 1726 in Prague, under a charter from the premier Grand Lodge in London.[3] Some sources speak of native French lodges as early as 1725–26, or even preceding 1717, but this is disputed by others.

A Jacobite Ploy?

The introduction of Masonry into France is sometimes attributed to the arrival in that country of English and Scottish exiles (commonly called Jacobites) who were supporters of the Stuart royal line. This was the line that had ascended to the English throne in 1603 when James VI of Scotland was crowned James I of England, following the death of Elizabeth I. Alternative historians are fond of portraying James I as a key supporter of Masonry. Knight and Lomas go so far as to state that James VI "brought Freemasonry with him" when he "went to London to become James I of England."[4] Often cited in favor of James's supposed Masonic stature is the apocryphal claim that he was made a mason in 1601 at the Lodge of Scone in Scotland while still James VI.[5] Unfortunately, this is one of those legends for which there is no proof.[6]

While king of Scotland in 1583, James did appoint William Schaw as Master of the (Royal) Works, with the charge to reorganize the masons—a task that led eventually to the Schaw Statutes, which detailed that reorganization. And Schaw did lend his signature in 1601 to the first of the two ill-fated Sinclair (St. Clair) "charters" addressed to the king and requesting his confirmation of the Sinclairs as hereditary patrons of Masonry in Scotland. But as previously mentioned, this came to naught, and whether James's relation to Masonry was any more special than that of most sovereigns remains unsettled.[7] King James I is perhaps most famous for commissioning the 1610 translation of what became known as the King James Bible.

The course of Stuart rule in England and Scotland throughout the 17th century was not smooth, to say the least, and James I and his successors Charles I and Charles II were often at odds with Parliament and the rest of the kingdom, suffering two civil wars and the temporary eclipse of the monarchy (1650–60). The conversion of Charles II to Catholicism, following a stroke in 1685, and the staunch Catholicism of his brother James II only made matters worse, as Britain had been firmly Protestant since Henry VIII's reign the century before.[8]

Much of this drama came to a close in 1688 with the so-called Glorious Revolution, which settled fears of a Catholic restoration and stabilized conflicts among the Protestants by solidifying the Church of England's position in England and that of the separate (Presbyterian) Church of Scotland. James II was forced to abdicate and took refuge in France, along with his six-month-old son, James Edward (who was to become the pretender, James III). After an interim with William III (of Orange) and Mary (Stuart) as monarchs (1689–1702), the last of the Stuart rulers, Queen Anne, ruled fitfully until her death in 1714.

At this point, George I of Hanover was installed as king of England, and the Hanoverian succession began. Shortly thereafter, the Stuart pretender, James Edward (James III), exiled in France, made an aborted attempt to claim the throne in a Jacobite rebellion that was rather easily quashed.

This did not, however, bring an end to Jacobite hopes, and a Stuart court in exile continued in France (and later, Rome) with the indulgence of the French kings. The Stuart cause finally culminated in a second aborted attempt to regain the throne in 1745–46, this time by James Edward's son, "Bonnie Prince Charlie."

I have made this slight digression in order to provide a better understanding of the context of the Jacobite camp in France.

A French Mason, Paul Naudon, contends in his book *The Secret History of Freemasonry* that Scottish nobility decamped to France following the beheading of Charles I in 1649 and, during the Cromwell years, "acted under the cover of the Masonic lodges, of which they were honorary members. Under the protection of so-called trade secrecy and without too much risk of committing an indiscretion, they could thereby communicate with their brothers who had remained in Great Britain to plot the overthrow of the 'dictator.'"[9] Precisely which lodges and which nobles were supposedly involved in this plot is never specified.

He further notes that the earliest chartered lodge on French soil is claimed to be a lodge associated with a military regiment, the Royal Irish (which soon became the Irish Guard), formed by Charles II in 1661. This unit left Britain for France in 1689 following the Stuart defeat and was garrisoned at St. Germain, at least until 1698, when it was absorbed into the French army.[10]

Naudon argues that the Masonry that came to France along with the Stuart court and its supporters was Scottish and Irish, not English, and, perhaps most significantly, that it was Catholic. Alternative historians Michael Baigent and Richard Leigh make a similar argument for a distinctive Jacobite Masonry associated with the Stuarts, in contrast to the Enlightenment-influenced Masonry of the premier Grand Lodge in England. This idea of a Jacobite Masonry stationed in France was a mainstay of 19th-century Masonic historians such as George Oliver and J. G. Findel, but more recent historians have drawn their claims into question.[11]

However, it is difficult to discern exactly what this theory contributes to an understanding of French Masonry's development. True, craft guilds in Scotland, prior to the 1560 Reformation, were integrated within a Catholic social order, celebrated their patron saints' days, marched in religious processions, and espoused pious sentiments. The pre–1560 Scottish operative masons, like the other guilds, were Catholic in this sense. But the Reformation and ascendance of the Calvinist Church of Scotland would have made ties between Scottish Masonry and Catholicism rather difficult to maintain.

Moreover, the Stuart kings James I and Charles I were not themselves Catholic, nor was Charles II until the final year of his reign, and then only secretly so. Any covert "Catholic Masonry" between the 1560 Reformation and the conversion of Charles II to Catholicism in 1685 would have been at odds not only with Scottish society at large, but with its Stuart rulers. Thus it seems likely that if Masons within the Stuart court in exile portrayed themselves as the exponents of an original Catholic tradition within Scottish Masonry, this was probably more an ideological stance than a historical fact.

This would seem to be borne out by a letter written by the Chevalier Ramsay, a Scottish convert to Catholicism who overlapped with the Stuart entourage in exile in France, and whose famous 1737 Oration intended for the Grand Lodge of France helped set the stage for the spread of "higher grade" Masonry in France. In this letter, also composed in 1737, Ramsay engaged in some historical spin:

> The unfortunate religious discords which set afire and tore Europe in the sixteenth century caused our order to degenerate from the greatness and nobility of its origin. In order to satisfy the parricidal usurper Elizabeth who looked upon our lodges as so many nests of Catholicism which had to be suppressed, the Protestants altered, disguised and degraded many of our hieroglyphs, stamped our brotherly meals as Bacchanals, and polluted our sacred assemblies. Mylord Earl of Derwentwater [at that time Grand Master of the Grand Lodge of France], martyr of Royalty and of Catholicism, attempted to bring everything here [i.e., in France] back to its origin and to restore everything upon its ancient footing.[12]

This would seem to be a creative case of ideological mythmaking and self-justification in the midst of what was a very volatile situation. As recent Masonic historians have traced it, on March 20, 1737, Ramsay submitted a draft of his Oration to Cardinal Fleury, Cardinal Minister to King Louis XV, for his approval, prior to Ramsay's scheduled delivery of the Oration to the Grand Lodge of France. The Oration was, in part, an effort to create a sympathetic resonance between Masonry and Catholicism. Cardinal Fleury, however, was having none of it and, unbeknownst to Ramsay, had already instructed the Lieutenant General of the Police, three days before, to allow no more meetings of Freemasons. As soon as he was apprised of the cardinal's disapproval, Ramsay, loyal Catholic that he was, withdrew from Freemasonry and apparently never delivered the Oration to the grand lodge, although it was later published in several different print editions.[13]

Ramsay's letter quoted here was written three weeks later, on April 16, 1737, and seems to be pleading the case that Stuart-sympathizing Freemasonry, then temporarily banned, was a good Catholic restoration of ancient Masonry. This was an attractive marketing angle, and it was soon to meet with some success as "Éccosais" (Scottish) Masonry became synonymous with degrees and rites that purported to be the oldest or the highest. Whether such degrees actually originated in Scotland is something else again, as we'll shortly see.

In any event, one stream of Masonry promulgated in France does seem to have been de facto Catholic, a not too surprising development in a country where Catholicism was the only legal religion. The 1738 bull of Pope Clement XII against Masonry, which came on the heels of Cardinal Fleury's ban, was never ratified in France, and hence although Masonry did experience a temporary abolition, it soon bounced back. Numerous lodges had Catholic clergy as members and officers—a situation that continued right up to the time of the French Revolution.

Meanwhile, there were other streams within French Masonry reflecting the philosophical ferment present in intellectual circles. A veritable smorgasbord of Masonic bodies assured that there were lodges suited for every persuasion. Despite the efforts of some, no single grand lodge was ever able to successfully claim jurisdiction over all Masons in France—a situation that has continued on down to the present, when there are no less than four grand lodges (including the largest, the Grand Orient) coexisting and enjoying various degrees of mutual "recognition."[14] Only one of them, the GLNF (Grande Loge Nationale Française), is recognized as legitimate by the United Grand Lodge of England. Most French Masons, one assumes, lose little sleep over this.

In summation, most historians agree that by the 1730s Freemasonry had jumped the Channel and was spreading in elite French and German circles, including both the clergy and the aristocracy. Its popularity in such circles shaped it in ways that would create puzzling contradictions between its theory and practice.

Espousing universal brotherhood is one thing, but practicing it is something else again, and it is difficult to imagine the bewigged brethren of the French aristocracy and intelligentsia sitting in lodge with anyone too far beneath them in social standing. Indeed, Masonry on the Continent rapidly expanded from merely honoring the symbolic meaning of stonecutters' tools and customs into a whole new universe of armchair chivalry, "higher" degrees soaked in mystical and esoteric symbolism, and grandiose titles accompanied by ornate regalia and jewelry.

Continental Masonry also became a playing field for philosophical and religious skirmishes between the Catholic Church, which was determined to maintain its political and cultural power and influence, and proponents of Enlightenment values and republicanism, who were intent on opening up a cultural space outside of the Church's control.

A Proliferation of Rites

Masonry's spread to Europe and beyond was not an orderly process. Prior to the founding of the Grand Lodge in London in 1717, individual lodges were often ad hoc, "occasional" affairs with few formal procedures. A handful of Masons in close geographical proximity might call a meeting, form a "lodge" for that occasion, initiate some new candidates, enjoy a meal together, and dissolve back into the woodwork. The Warrington lodge into which Elias Ashmole was initiated in 1646 seems to have been one of this sort.

Other lodges, however, assumed a more stable and continuous existence, and the impulse for founding the English Grand Lodge came from lodges of this latter kind. The 1717 grand lodge sought to enforce a consistency among its member lodges in matters of ritual, record keeping, regulations, and the creation and recognition of new lodges. Ad hoc groups of Masons were no longer supposed to initiate new Masons without receiving a charter (or warrant) from the grand lodge to do so, and individual lodges were forbidden from spawning further lodges without grand lodge approval.

The premier Grand Lodge had nominal success in enforcing such rules in England among its constituent lodges and its regimental lodges stationed overseas. But as much as it would have liked to enjoy a monopoly over the spread of the Craft, that was not to be. The founding of the Grand Lodges of Ireland (1725) and Scotland (1738), not to mention the English rival York Grand Lodge (1725) and the Antients' Grand Lodge (1751), created a panoply of competing chartering entities. And there was really nothing to stop individual Masons from traveling abroad and creating new "irregular" and "unrecognized" lodges of their own inspiration.

Thus there was already a proliferation of lodges in France before a lodge or grand lodge formally recognized by England was ever formed there. Masonic carpetbaggers and native French impresarios founded a variety of Masonic orders and rites, many of them claiming to have earlier roots than England's premier Grand Lodge, and some offering additional degrees on top of the three traditional degrees of Entered Apprentice, Fellow Craft, and Master Mason.

According to recently rediscovered records, a "Scottish Union Lodge" was founded in Berlin in 1742 by a handful of French, Italian, and German Masons. It initially conferred one "higher" degree, that of Scottish Master, which was supplemented in 1743 by a chivalric degree, Knight of the Scottish Order (also called the Order of St. Andrew). Exactly where these degrees came from remains a mystery, although it appears that they did not come directly from Scotland.[15]

Masonic Scholar Alain Bernheim points out that there are references to a "Scotch" or "Scott's" Mason Lodge in London as early as 1733, and records of a lodge in Bath where "Scots Mastr Masons" [sic] were initiated in 1735. These conferrals of Scots or Scottish Master degrees appear to be supplemental to the three basic degrees, and thus the earliest instances of so-called higher degrees. What is most curious, however, is that these "Scottish" lodges are in England, while in Scotland there was no record of any such higher degrees at that time.[16]

Whatever its origins may have been, the Scottish Union Lodge in Berlin soon spun off further "Scottish" lodges in Leipzig, Frankfurt, Copenhagen, Transylvania, and several other locales.[17] According to the respected Masonic historian Robert F. Gould, similar "Scottish" lodges were meanwhile multiplying throughout France.[18]

It may be beyond the ability of any single author to accurately trace the subsequent proliferation of "higher" degrees and Masonic-related chivalric orders in Europe over the course of the latter half of the 18th century. Masonic historians offer different dates for the start of the same organizations, quibble over who may or may not be claimed as members, and engage in intricate arguments over matters of minor importance that it would be pointless to recount here. Instead, I will briefly look at a few of the better-known rites and personalities of so-called higher Masonry in order to give the reader a taste of the baroque efflorescence of Continental Freemasonry.

Hierarchies du Jour

As you'll recall, in the last chapter we touched on the cottage industry of alternative historians who have labored to draw connections between the crusader order of the Knights Templar and Freemasonry. Although this explosion of books is a recent publishing phenomenon, we can trace its roots back to the French and German "higher" degrees and rites that emerged around 1740–50. Many of these groups conferred Templar degrees or claimed a lineage from the Templars.

One such order was the Chapter of Clermont in France, whose genesis is variously dated to 1743 or 1754. It is said to have had a system of seven degrees, including the first three craft degrees, the Scots Master degree, the Knight of the Eagle or Select Master degree, the Illustrious Knight or Templar degree, and, finally, the Sublime Illustrious Knight degree.[19]

Gould suggests that the Chapter of Clermont was "probably composed only of high nobility, courtiers, military officers, and the *élite* of the professions."[20] It would appear that the Chapter was succeeded (or superseded) by a yet grander order named the Council of the Emperors of the East and West, Sovereign Prince Masons, Substitutes General of the Royal Art, Grand Surveillants and Officers of the Grand Sovereign Lodge of St. John of Jerusalem—also known by the shorter appellation Heredom of Perfection. As we pause to catch our breath, two points are worth noting: first, the Council of the Emperors continued to confer Templar degrees; and second, their system of degrees blossomed into no less than twenty-five degrees, which were later to form the ritual core of the thirty-three degrees of the Ancient and Accepted Scottish Rite, one of the two main bodies of "higher" degrees to flourish in North America in the 19th century.[21]

Despite the presence of Templar degrees in both the Chapter of Clermont and the Council of the Emperors, I have found no indication that those orders claimed actual descent from the Knights Templar. Instead, that claim was first floated by a Prussian Masonic order, the Rite of Strict Observance. Its early leader Baron Karl Gottlieb von Hund claimed to have been initiated into higher degrees and to have been dubbed a Knight Templar in Paris in 1743 at the hands of a masked "Unknown Superior," known only as the "Knight of the Red Feather," who von Hund apparently assumed was none other than Charles Edward Stuart, "Bonnie Prince Charlie."

Recent research has discovered that another of the leaders of the Rite of Strict Observance, the deliciously named Baron Friedrich von Vegesack, likely contributed a second Templar-Masonic link from an obscure French Masonic group, the Sublime Order of Elected Knights, into which he was initiated in 1749. A recently discovered manuscript that appears to be the degree lecture for the order traces a traditional lineage from the Essenes and the later Christian desert fathers to the Knights Templar and thence to Scotland, where they supposedly changed their name to Elected Knights, and whence they ultimately brought the lineage back to France. Such a claim was no more provable than von Hund's, but it clearly had a romantic appeal to some.[22]

The Rite of Strict Observance is noteworthy for achieving a dominant presence in German Masonry during the latter half of the 1700s and for introducing the legend of the order being led by "unknown superiors"—that is, a secret leadership unknown to all but the top officers.[23]

The meme of unknown masters behind the scenes was not entirely new; it was first seen as part of the myth of the Rosicrucian Brotherhood in the early 1600s. But this was its first appearance in Masonic circles. As we'll presently see, this meme was to take on a life of its own, fueling anti-Masonic suspicions for centuries to come, and culminating in Theosophical and esoteric motifs of "secret masters" and hidden adepts.

The Templar Temptation

At this point, we might do well to pause and ponder why the Knights Templar theme reemerged at this juncture as a motif within Freemasonry. The alternative historians would likely say that the Templars' reappearance makes perfect sense: they were there all along, carried within Masonry like the hidden contents of a diplomatic pouch. However, I have found this impossible to swallow, not least because most of the circumstantial evidence evaporates under critical scrutiny.

If the Templars were destroyed by a French king and the pope, and their remnants supposedly found refuge in Scotland because the Scottish king, Robert the Bruce, was under excommunication, why would they later, in the guise of Masons, align themselves with the Jacobite cause, which had the blessing of both the Vatican and the French court? The usual alternative-history explanation is that the Stuarts were the hereditary grand masters of Scottish Masonry, a claim for which there is no credible evidence. Thus, the Templar-Mason-Jacobite daisy chain seems extremely far-fetched.

The Templar–Strict Observance connection seems little better. According to Gould, for the Rite of Strict Observance:

> The sequence of Grand Masters was presumed never to have been broken, and a list of these rulers in regular succession was known to the initiates; but the identity of the actual Grand Master was always kept—during his life-time—a secret from every one except his immediate confidants, hence the term, "Unknown Superiors." In order to ensure their perfect security these Knights are said to have joined the Guilds of Masons in Scotland, and thus to have given rise to the Fraternity of Freemasons. At the time of the origin of the Strict Observance system, the period was assumed to have arrived when it would be advantageous to boldly proclaim the continued existence of the Ancient Order of the Temple, and to endeavor to reinstate it in its former possessions, organization, and privileges.[24]

This tale seems equally far-fetched. If the Templars had consolidated themselves within Scottish Masonry (for which there was no

Sigil of the Knights Templar. It depicts two knights riding a single horse.

evidence), why not make their comeback there rather than in Prussian Berlin? The whole story had all the hallmarks of a classic con job, and one that was ultimately undercut by the fact that the Rite of Strict Observance made no effort to actually take back Templar possessions and privileges.

What struck me as a far more likely explanation for the rise of the Templar motif in French and German Masonry at the time was the romantic appeal of the Templars as elite outsiders. If one assumed that the Templars had been wrongly accused of heresy and unjustly disbanded—which was certainly the assumption of the Masons who lionized them—then they might represent different things to different Masons. For Protestants, they could symbolize a heroic martyrdom to religious persecution by the Catholic Church. For aristocratic and military circles jockeying for more power under the Bourbon regime, their martyrdom could symbolize a telling illustration of the injustice of royal tyranny.

The devisers of additional degrees, in casting around for motifs on which to build appealing dramas, ransacked the treasure house of history and myth and created innumerable stories with accompanying "honors" and lessons. The Knights Templar motif was one that stuck.

The Temple Trope

But there's another aspect of the choice of Templars as an initiatory theme. And that is the edifice to which their name alludes: the ancient Temple of Solomon. The Templars were forever linked to that trope by virtue of their having occupied Temple Mount in Jerusalem during the Crusades.

And—coincidentally or intentionally—the Temple of Solomon and its construction provide the central myth and symbols of Freemasonry. As we'll presently see, the Masonic lodge room is roughly patterned after the layout of the Temple, while the rituals of the second and third degrees each convey their teachings through having the initiate portray a mason at work on this ancient Temple to the Most High.

The alternative historians' explanation for the Temple as the theme shared by Templars and Masons is that the latter derived from the former—that the Masons were the offspring (or protégés or concealers) of the banished Templars.

According to this theory, the true secrets of Freemasonry boil down to the Templars' purported secrets: either their hidden and heretical teachings or their much-vaunted treasure, supposedly found while excavating beneath the former site of King Solomon's Temple. Indeed, certain of the "higher" degrees have to do with finding a treasure beneath the Temple.

But one can play this game in both directions, and it seems equally plausible that the Temple of Solomon motif derived from the intellectual currents feeding into the rise of speculative Masonry.

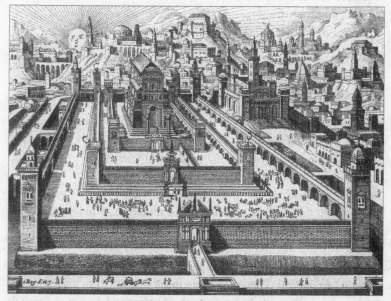

Artist's depiction of the Temple of Solomon in
Jerusalem (from Matthaeus Merian's Icones Bibliae*)*

Both Francis Bacon (1561–1626) and Isaac Newton (1642–1727), though a century apart, were fascinated with "the House of Solomon." Bacon employed it as a model for his vision of a "New Atlantis," a new civilization of learning and enlightenment.[25] Newton, for his part, hypothesized that a close study of the Temple, whose dimensions are described in great detail in the Bible, and which he thought served as a microcosmic symbol of the greater universe, might reward him with additional insights into the laws of nature.[26]

Of course, neither Bacon nor Newton is on record as having been a Mason—though there are theories afloat of Bacon having been instrumental in the rise of speculative Masonry, while the new grand lodge (c. 1717) was rife with associates of Newton's from the Royal Society, most notably John Theophilus Desaguliers, grand master in 1719, who worked closely with Newton in devising demonstrations of Newton's theories.[27]

By this logic, speculative Masons who were already disposed to use Solomon's Temple as a mythic symbol latched onto the Knights Templar as a further symbol of interaction with the Temple.

Until specific new evidence is unearthed, it would be most truthful to simply note that the Knights Templar motif struck a resonant chord with Masons and, from the mid-1700s on, provided a theme for additional degrees and orders.

Esoteric Influences

The Templar motif was not the only one to be found in Continental Masonry's multidegree rites. A cluster of interrelated themes—derived from Rosicrucian, alchemical, and magical traditions—provided the underpinnings for several Masonic orders.

A Benedictine monk, Dom Antoine-Joseph Pernety, became intrigued with the study of alchemy in the mid-1700s and left the Benedictines in 1765 to found his own order, the Rite Hermétique. This rite's system was thoroughly grounded in alchemical symbolism and consisted of six degrees eventually capped by a seventh, Chevalier du Soleil (Knight of the Sun). Though the rite never amounted to much, its 7th degree eventually made its way into the Ancient and Accepted Scottish Rite, where it provided material for two degrees, the 27th and 28th.[28]

Dom Pernety went on to found another order, the Illuminés d'Avignon, in 1783. This group enjoyed greater popularity and prominence, enough to earn Pernety's arrest in 1793 in the wake of the French Revolution. Luckily, Pernety was later released. He died in Avignon in 1796.[29]

More influential still was Martines de Pasqually, like Pernety the founder of two Masonic groups, in this case the Scottish Judges (1754) and the Order of the Elus Cohen (Elect Priests) (1760). Pasqually drew upon magical traditions and his own mediumship in devising the Elus Cohen's rituals. He sailed to the West Indies in 1772, leaving the order in others' hands.

One of the Elus Cohen was Jean-Baptiste Willermoz, who has been credited with authoring the Rose-Croix degree, one of the longest lasting and most celebrated of the higher degrees.[30] Willermoz is also said to have imported the doctrine of the Elus Cohen into two higher grades of the Rite of Strict Observance in Germany after he subsequently joined that order.[31] Finally, Willermoz is notable for founding the Rectified Scottish Rite, which preserved a reformed version of the Strict Observance.

However, the most significant of Pasqually's followers was Louis Claude de Saint-Martin, who had joined the Elus Cohen in 1768. Saint-Martin went on to develop his own system of Christian mystical teachings, heavily influenced by the great German mystic Jacob Böhme.[32] After Saint-Martin's death in 1803, this system became known as Martinism, and it has continued up to the present via various Martinist orders, most of which have little or no connection with recognized Freemasonry.

It is into this European landscape of a hundred and one rites and orders that the self-styled Count di Cagliostro strode in the 1770s. Cagliostro, who fancied himself the Grand Copt of the Egyptian Rite of Freemasonry, is widely considered to have really been one Giuseppe Balsamo, a Sicilian bunco artist. Manly Palmer Hall, who has an unfailing instinct for propagating a good yarn, calls Cagliostro "a man of insight and supernatural power" and "the mysterious agent of the Knights Templars, the Rosicrucian initiate whose magnificent store of learning is attested by the profundity of the Egyptian Rite of Freemasonry."[33]

Whatever the true facts of his origin, Cagliostro does seem to have been initiated into a Strict Observance lodge in London in 1777 and into higher-degree bodies on the Continent thereafter. As historian Christopher McIntosh succinctly summarizes:

> He claimed to have received, at the pyramids of Egypt, a full initiation into the "mysteries of the veritable Grand Orient" and to be able to make gold and silver, renew youth, give physical beauty and evoke the spirits of the dead. He also proclaimed that he had lived for 2000 years. Cagliostro found France an ideal environment for his posturings and enjoyed enormous success in the salons.[34]

Cagliostro and his wife ingratiated themselves in aristocratic circles by initiating ladies into a "lodge of adoption" at his Temple of Isis in Paris.

However, he ran afoul of the law in an intrigue involving a necklace of Marie Antoinette and relocated to Rome, where he tried to organize an Egyptian Rite lodge. This attracted the attention of the Inquisition, which tried him for heresy and sentenced him to life imprisonment. He subsequently died in prison, although the ever-hopeful Manly Hall relates that "there are rumors that he escaped, and according to one very significant story Cagliostro fled to India, where his talents received the appreciation denied them in politics-ridden Europe."[35]

Ultimately, the Egyptian Rite's actual relationship with Egypt was slim, but it was to serve as a prototype for subsequent Masonic groups trading on the Egyptian myth, such as the Rite of Memphis and the Rite of Misraim.

Vive la Différence

We will pass over the much-argued question of a possible Masonic influence on the French Revolution. If there was one, it did not succeed in influencing events in its own favor, as Masonry was soon banned as the revolution unfolded. Its status in France and in other European countries was subsequently at the mercy of the whims of whatever regime was in power at a given moment. Amid these shifting tides, the

Grand Orient emerged as the dominant grand lodge in France, and it was able to bring some order to the gaggle of competing rites by providing an organizational umbrella under which they could maintain their records and their systems of degrees.

By way of contrast, Swedish Freemasonry consolidated by the late 1700s into a single Christians-only system under the patronage of the king of Sweden, which it remains up to the present day.

Freemasonry in Austria, as elsewhere on the Continent, was an elite affair, with lodges such as True Harmony in Vienna, which served as a powerful intellectual forum for Enlightenment ideas. While Mozart was initiated in 1784 in another Viennese lodge, Charity Lodge, he also frequented True Harmony. He soon composed several Masonic pieces, including music for a Masonic funeral, and, in 1791, the score for his opera *The Magic Flute*.

The Magic Flute is Mozart's most famous "Masonic" composition, although its relationship to Masonry resides mostly in the libretto, which was written by a theater producer named Emanuel Schikaneder, who was apparently a Mason for six months in 1789 before being expelled. Schikaneder later claimed that the opera was written to propagandize on behalf of Freemasonry, but it is equally possible that the libretto touched on Masonic themes and virtues in order to attract a popular audience intrigued with Masonry's alleged mysteries.[36]

Mozart died barely more than two months after the opera was first performed at the end of September 1791. While conspiracy theorists have suggested that Mozart's untimely death (he was only thirty-five) was instigated by Masons who were unhappy with Mozart revealing their secrets in the opera, this notion falls apart on several grounds. First, the opera reveals no such secrets; in fact, any Masonic content is highly allegorical and indirect. Second, paranoid rumors aside, Masons have never stooped to murder for the punishment of revealing their supposed "secrets."[37] And third, the opera's libretto was by Schikaneder, not Mozart, and Schikaneder lived until 1812, continuing to produce plays and operas "often with either Masonic content or scenery."[38]

There's more to be said about Masonry as it evolved on the Continent and beyond, but first let us turn our attention to the controversial role of Freemasonry in the founding of the United States and its spread in the New World.

One of numerous prints and engravings showing George Washington in the regalia of the Master of a Masonic lodge. While Washington certainly was a Mason, and was elected Master of a Virginia lodge after the War of Independence, that position was largely honorary. Compared with some other founding fathers who were Masons, such as Benjamin Franklin and Paul Revere, Washington was not especially active in the fraternity.

4

Novus Ordo Seclorum

Freemasonry Comes to America

One of the most common beliefs among Americans is that the Masons somehow managed to leave their mark on the back of the most widely circulated slips of paper in the land—the dollar bill. Each time we pull a dollar from our wallet or purse, we catch a glimpse of the Great Seal of the United States, one face of which depicts a pyramid composed of thirteen stacked layers of stone, capped by a shining all-seeing eye in a triangle.

Surely this must be indisputable evidence of a deep connection between the Founding Fathers and Freemasonry, mustn't it?

Or what about the many paintings, etchings, and woodcuts dating back to the early 1800s showing George Washington attired in his Masonic apron and wearing the jewel of a Worshipful Master (master of a lodge)? These imply, none too subtly, that Masonry was there at the birth of the United States and represented by none other than our first president.

And perhaps most suggestive, the Bible with which George Washington was sworn in as president belonged to a New York lodge that is still in existence and that has continued to lend the same Bible for the swearing in of nearly every subsequent president.

To be sure, it *is* part of the historical record that Washington did participate, while president, in a public Masonic ceremony for the laying of the cornerstone for the new Capitol in 1793. Washington had been first initiated in a lodge in Fredericksburg, Virginia, in 1753, and remained a Mason for the rest of his life.[1]

Second only to Washington in the Masonic pantheon of Founding Fathers is Benjamin Franklin. Franklin became a Mason as early as 1731, served as Grand Master of the fledgling Provincial Grand Lodge of Pennsylvania, and was a member, and eventually Master, of the prestigious Lodge of the Nine Muses in Paris, while serving as an envoy to France during the Revolutionary War.

A number of other Founding Fathers, such as Paul Revere and John Hancock, were Masons as well, as we will see.

All these things would seem to indicate that *something* is (or was) going on—that Freemasonry's immigration to America had a significant impact on the course of history, and that Masonry was somehow intertwined with the American Revolution and the establishment of the new republic. Yet when one begins to venture beneath the surface, the mysteries once again multiply and it becomes difficult to distinguish between myth and fact. Let us begin with a few indisputable facts.

Masonry Comes to the New World

With the founding of the premier Grand Lodge in London in 1717, it didn't take long for Masonry to make its way to the British colonies in North America. While there are a few scattered references to individual Masons in the colonies—one as early as 1705[2]—the first official record of a Mason being appointed by the English Grand Lodge to represent Masonry in the colonies dates to 1730, when Daniel Coxe was designated Provincial Grand Master of New York, New Jersey, and Pennsylvania. Unfortunately, Coxe seems not to have actually done anything in this role, and it wasn't until three years later, in 1733, that a group of Masons in Boston requested a charter from a new Provincial Grand Master, Henry Price, in order to start their own lodge.[3] Upon receiving the charter, they were assisted by members of a military lodge of British soldiers in formally constituting their lodge, now known as St. John's Lodge, and installing lodge officers.

Military lodges were a growing phenomenon, and they were to play a significant role in helping the spread of Masonry in British colonies.

Not long after the lodge was established in Boston, other requests for charters began to come from Pennsylvania, Virginia, and other colonies. Not all of these requests were solely directed to the premier Grand Lodge in London. Perhaps reflecting the diverse makeup of the immigrants to America, charters for lodges were also requested from the recently established Grand Lodge of Ireland (formed in 1725) and Grand Lodge of Scotland (formed in 1736). And once the Antients' Grand Lodge was formed in England in 1751, it, too, granted charters for lodges in the New World.

Please take note of this diversity of sources and loyalties, as it will help explain the differing responses that arose among Masons as the desire for American independence gathered steam.

A Political Puzzle

When I first began to investigate what role Masonry might have played in the War of Independence, I was struck by a crucial, but often over-looked, fact: a key passage in Anderson's Constitutions—which Masons were sworn to uphold—seemed to command loyalty to the Crown. The passage reads, in part:

A Mason is a peaceable Subject, never to be concern'd in Plots against the State, nor disrespectful to Inferior Magistrates. . . . But tho' a Brother is not to be countenanced in his Rebellion against the State; yet if convicted of no other Crime, his Relation to the Lodge remains indefeasible.[4]

This raises the obvious question of how a conscientious Mason could have taken part in the Revolutionary War without violating his own oath "never to be concern'd in Plots against the State." True, there is that small loophole in the final sentence—that should he rebel, a Mason should still be accepted as a brother—but the overall thrust was distinctly against political rebellion. This suggests that although some of the Founding Fathers and rebellious colonials were Masons, they were not acting *as*

Masons in engaging in what could be seen as "Plots against the State."

One Masonic historian has suggested a solution to this puzzle. Upon the formation of the Continental Congress and its Declaration of Independence in 1776, the Continental Congress became "the lawful supreme civil authority," and patriotic Masons would be keeping their vows by supporting it, not the Crown.[5] If this was the logic of some, it failed to convince others. Many Masons, especially those linked to the premier Grand Lodge (the "Moderns"), remained loyal to England, and some fled to Canada. Lodges with ties to other grand lodges, especially that of the "Antients," were more likely to side with the cause of independence.[6]

But there are no easy generalizations here. Ben Franklin's Provincial Grand Lodge of Pennsylvania had originally been chartered by the "Moderns," yet he supported independence. A rival grand lodge, chartered by the "Antients," became the dominant force in Pennsylvania Masonry in the mid-1700s, and although it sided with the patriots, it failed to grant Franklin any honors upon his death in 1790.[7]

The only thing that can be said for sure is that there was not a uniform Masonic stance toward the American Revolution. Masons came down on both sides of the conflict and could point to Masonic ethics and ideals in doing so. Nevertheless, a case can be made for Masonry laying the philosophical groundwork for principles embodied in the new American experiment.

A Model for a New Order

Consider some of the social practices that Masons had implemented within their lodges. First, there was the principle of a brotherhood of equals. Masons "meet on the level, act by the plumb, and part upon the square," as one Masonic ritual puts it. Although the premier Grand Lodge in London sought respectability and status soon after its 1717 founding by persuading members of the nobility (or better yet, royalty) to take on the largely honorary post of Grand Master, the basic idea of Masonic equality remained a potent ideal. In theory, at least, within the lodge a gentleman might rub elbows with a peer or a merchant as equals, whatever their differences of status outside the lodge.

Further, the election of officers and the formal conduct of Masonic business meetings followed a democratic pattern of self-governance that was bound to leave its mark on those who experienced it.

While no direct evidence of an organized Masonic influence on the direction of American political ideas has been found, it seems a safe bet that the Masons among the Founding Fathers were able to draw upon their lodge experiences when envisioning "a new order for the ages."

Historian Steven Bullock has suggested that many colonialists sought to improve their social standing and status by joining Masonic lodges and that up until the William Morgan scandal in the late 1820s, Masonry played a prominent part in establishing a civic culture in the new country.[8]

He also argues that military lodges, within both the Crown's forces and the Continental Army, served to create cohesion among officers. We do know that out of approximately 14,000 American officers, 2,018 (just over one-seventh) were Masons.[9] Whether General George Washington was part of any military lodge is unclear, but he did visit a West Point lodge at least three times during the war years and even marched in a Masonic procession in Philadelphia in December 1778.[10]

Some Masons have claimed that the Boston Tea Party may have had a Masonic inspiration, as the men who undertook that famous action set off from the Green Dragon Inn in Boston, which was home to a Masonic lodge, St. Andrew's, suggesting that the men may have gathered as Masons and left as "Indians." In fact, the action took place on December 16, 1773, a night on which the lodge was scheduled to meet; however, the Sons of Liberty were also meeting at the inn that same night. Lodge records indicate that a brief and sparsely attended meeting was attempted—perhaps more as an alibi than to transact Masonic business, it has been suggested.[11] The most intriguing circumstantial evidence of Masonic involvement in the Tea Party comes from the hand of the lodge secretary. He made a brief record of the aborted meeting and then covered the rest of the page with "flourishes, each one of which is a well defined T."[12]

In any event, there is little or no direct evidence of who actually participated in the "party," which at least indicates an effective practice of secrecy, whether Masonic or not.[13] According to a source cited by Michael Baigent and Richard Leigh, a partial list of 110 men who took part was compiled in 1837 with the help of seven participants who were still alive. This list, modified by Baigent and Leigh, identifies twelve members of St. Andrew's Lodge as participating, including Paul Revere, John Hancock, and Joseph Warren.[14]

General Joseph Warren was an early Grand Master of Antients Masonry in Massachusetts, and his death at the Battle of Bunker Hill in 1775 might well have galvanized revolutionary support among Masons. Similarly, Paul Revere was Master of St. Andrew's Lodge in Boston for 1771 (and again for 1778–82), and his famous Midnight Ride has played a key role in the romantic myth of the American Revolution. Once the Revolutionary War was won and normal life resumed, Paul Revere continued his association with Masonry, eventually serving as Grand Master of the Grand Lodge of Massachusetts from 1795 to 1797. But despite the fact that such prominent participants in the Revolution were Masons, I could find little direct evidence of a specifically Masonic angle to their rebellious actions.

Retrospective Grandeur

What does seem to have happened is that Masons in the post-Revolutionary era rallied to the notion of George Washington as the great hero of the war and the preeminent statesman. By celebrating Washington's Masonic membership, Freemasonry was able to hitch a ride on his coattails and boost its own prestige—a penchant that the Antients' and Moderns' Grand Lodges in England satisfied by persuading peers of the realm to serve as grand masters.

In fact, there had been a call circa 1780 for a grand master over all American lodges, with Washington as the top choice. But Washington declined the honor, and leadership of American Masonry remained apportioned among state grand lodges.[15]

Nevertheless, the reminder of Washington as Mason remained a useful tool in Freemasonry's self-defense. While the William Morgan episode and the subsequent anti-Masonic movement in the late 1820s scuttled Masonry's reputation for a generation, Masonry was eventually able to regain lost ground, in part through reminders that its members included some of the most famous Founding Fathers.

For instance, Masons were the driving force behind the original effort to erect the Washington Memorial, starting in 1846, just twenty years after Morgan's disappearance.[16] The design of a Mason, Robert Mills, was chosen, its most prominent feature being an obelisk.

The raising of funds for the monument and its construction proceeded nicely for some years—this was largely a pay-as-it-goes operation—until the project was derailed, the monument only half built, in 1856 by another wave of political hysteria, not anti-Masonic this time, but anti-Catholic.

The same fear of conspiracies that had fueled the now-spent Anti-Masonic Party arose again in Protestant anxieties over the threats represented by Catholic immigration and papal influence.

The original design for the Washington Monument by Robert Mills. The obelisk was originally designed to be six hundred feet high, but the height was later shortened to five hundred feet. The pantheon at the monument's base was never constructed.

This resulted in the rise of a nativist secret society, the Order of the Star Spangled Banner, which mutated into the American Party, aptly nicknamed the "Know Nothings."

It also resulted in a group of Know Nothing supporters raiding the construction site of the Washington Monument on the night of March 6, 1855, when they seized a block of marble that had been donated to the monument's construction by Pope Pius IX and transported it to the Potomac River, into which they unceremoniously dumped it.

This incident and the subsequent takeover of the Washington National Monument Society by the Know Nothings, followed shortly thereafter by the Civil War, effectively stopped the construction of the monument in its tracks. It wasn't until December 6, 1884, that the monument was finally completed—a day marked by a Masonic ceremony at the site, as was the monument's dedication on February 21, 1885, Washington's birthday.

The Eye and the Needle

Some alternative-history tomes, such as David Ovason's *Secret Architecture of Our Nation's Capital* and Graham Hancock and Robert Bauval's *Talisman,* suggest that the location of the Washington Monument fits into a sacred geometric grid originally mapped out for Washington, D.C., by the French engineer Pierre-Charles L'Enfant. Hancock and Bauval hint that the transporting of obelisks from Egypt to Rome, Paris, London, and New York—underwritten or engineered in most cases by Masons during the 19th century—is part of a grand quasi-Gnostic scheme to encode ancient Egyptian Isis worship into Western urban centers.[17] Throw in the Statue of Liberty for good measure (sculpted by a French Mason), and it is possible to have an *aha!* moment when one sees the big picture: a psychic power grid of phalli and goddess statues crisscrossing the globe.

Of course, what the alternative historians thread together in order to tell an enchanting tale the anti-Masons seize upon as evidence of Masons covertly worshipping Egyptian gods and goddesses. To anyone with a whit of common sense this would seem exceedingly far-fetched, but the deeper I delved into old Masonic writings, the more I could see where notions like this might have come from.

For instance, the 1737 Oration of the Chevalier Ramsay—prepared for the Grand Lodge of France and subsequently published, but apparently never actually delivered—was full of grand assertions as imaginative as the "historical" claims of the Old Charges and Anderson's Constitutions. Ramsay orates:

> Yes, sirs, the famous festivals of Ceres at Eleusis, of Isis in Egypt, of Minerva at Athens, of Urania amongst the Phoenicians, of Diana in Scythia were connected with ours. In those places, mysteries were celebrated which concealed many vestiges of the ancient religion of Noah and the Patriarchs.[18]

To the conspiratorial mind, this would seem to constitute "evidence" that Masonry admits that it derives from ancient pagan goddess worship. However, this is the same speech in which Ramsay associates Masonry with the Knights of St. John of Jerusalem, among other extravagant claims. Ramsay, like Anderson in London, was constructing a grand mythic history going back to Noah and to that supposedly single primordial religion bequeathed to mankind. By linking Masonry with ancient civilizations like those of Egypt and Greece, Ramsay and other romantic Masons were arrogating to themselves the glory of the mighty builders of old.

Ramsay goes on to expound:

> The secret science was handed down by oral tradition from [Noah] to Abraham and the Patriarchs, the last one of which carried our sublime Art into Egypt. It was Joseph who gave the Egyptians the first idea of labyrinths, of pyramids and of obelisks, which have become the admiration of all centuries.[19]

This fascination with things Egyptian was not restricted to Masonic ranks. By the late 18th century, Egypt had become a fashionable motif within French high society. Cagliostro exploited this interest with his Egyptian Rite, but he was just one manifestation of the trend. In America, the Egyptian Revival style, in the first five decades of the 19th century, produced a remarkable array of public buildings and monuments—not to mention cemetery mausoleums—aping Egyptian edifices and markers.[20]

In choosing to memorialize Washington with an obelisk, the Masons involved were participating in a broad social trend of the day, albeit one that had an added frisson of meaning in subtly linking Egypt to Masonry to Washington.

The pleasures of a romantic Egyptomania and a romantic Masonry were certainly present in the transport of the obelisk of Thothmes III ("Cleopatra's Needle") from Alexandria, Egypt, to Central Park in Manhattan in 1880. As related in published reports at the time, the Masonic sponsors of the project were convinced that they had discovered Masonic symbols on the base of the obelisk when it was first excavated in Egypt to ready it for removal. They considered these symbols to be an exciting confirmation of the antiquity of Freemasonry.[21]

Of course, on closer examination this "discovery," like so many others, mainly confirmed the power of the human imagination. Three parallel lines carved in one base stone were interpreted to symbolize

Plate from John Weisse's The Obelisk and Freemasonry, *supposedly depicting "Pharaoh Osiris, King of Egypt, in Masonic communication with one of that Order, whose head is covered by a mask which represents the head of an Ibis," according to the fantastic theory of Madame Belzoni*

the three degrees. Similarly, another stone, which had rough, smooth, and carved components, was considered as offering "at a glance the labours of the three symbolical degrees—the apprentices being represented by the rough parts, the craftsman by the worked portions and the masters by the finished and ornamented parts of the stone."[22]

An oxidized trowel of unknown age, found at the base, was linked to the symbolism of the trowel found in the present Masonic ritual of the third degree. A "perfectly white stone found . . . in the centre of the eighteen stones forming the first step" was interpreted to "represent the purity that should distinguish the applicant for initiation."[23]

Not all Masons bought into these claims—which were quietly abandoned after the initial excitement dissipated—but they achieved enough vogue to inspire a curious volume, *The Obelisk and Freemasonry,* by John Weisse, a homeopathic doctor, who was also a Mason, an early officer of the Theosophical Society, and a Spiritualist.[24]

Weisse not only passed along the claims about the "Masonic symbols" found in the base of the obelisk; he upped the ante by relaying startling revelations derived from unpublished papers entrusted to him by Madame Belzoni, the widow of the celebrated Italian explorer of Egypt Giovanni Battista Belzoni. These amounted to a claim that certain depictions in the tomb of Seti I, discovered by Belzoni in 1817, illustrated Masonic initiation ceremonies, thus decisively linking modern speculative Freemasonry to ancient Egypt.[25]

Belzoni's résumé included working in his father's barbershop and a stint as a strongman, "the Patagonian Samson," in a London theatre. He had originally traveled to Egypt in 1816 with his English wife, Sarah, in hopes of selling the Pasha on a hydraulic machine to be used for crop irrigation. Failing in that endeavor, he obtained a contract from the British consul general to recover a seven-ton bust from the Temple of Ramses II at Thebes and any other antiquities he could find.[26]

While Belzoni's excavations and recoveries earned him a rightful place in the annals of Egyptology, he was untrained as an archaeologist, and his efforts at interpreting tomb reliefs and hieroglyphs were fanciful at best, as exemplified by his description of the tomb of Seti I as a "Masonic Temple." Upon his return to England, he became a Mason in 1820 and a Masonic Knight Templar in 1821.[27] It is safe to say that, like so many others, he retroactively projected the forms and rituals of modern speculative Masonry onto the culture of ancient Egypt.

Sadly, it is half-baked speculations such as these that were to plant the seeds of the current crop of alternative historians and anti-Masons who have shaped the present popular perception of Masonry.

Similarly, the common notion that the Great Seal of the United States serves as evidence of a Masonic hand in early American government disintegrates upon close examination. Masonic researcher S. Brent Morris has explained:

> The Great Seal . . . grew out of three separate Congressional committees. The first of 1776 was composed of Benjamin Franklin, Thomas Jefferson, and John Adams, with Pierre Du Simitière as artist and consultant. Each of the three committee members proposed an allegorical design: that of Franklin, the only known Freemason involved at any stage of the design process, was Moses at the Red Sea with Pharaoh being overwhelmed. . . .
>
> Du Simitière, the committee's consultant and a non-Mason, contributed several major design features that made their way into the final design of the Great Seal: the shield, "E Pluribus Unum," and the eye of providence in a radiant triangle.[28]

Francis Hopkinson, a consultant to a second committee, of 1780, contributed the image of an unfinished pyramid. A third committee, in 1782, amalgamated elements from the preceding two committees and finally produced a design that won Congressional approval.[29]

Thus it would seem that any Masonic input was minimal, though American Masonry was only too happy to have the Great Seal taken for some kind of Masonic emblem. Through mistaken impressions such as this, Freemasonry developed a mystique that would attract potential members and enhance its own image of benign power and influence.

A Fraternal Boom

Despite Masonry's temporary eclipse from 1826 to the early 1840s—or perhaps because of it—fraternalism really began to flourish in the young country. When Masonry made its comeback, it was a part of a general upsurge in fraternal orders, including the Independent Order of Odd Fellows, the Knights of Pythias, and the Improved Order of Red Men, followed a couple of decades later by the widespread rural organization the Order of the Patrons of Husbandry, better known as the Grange (which admitted both men and women). Many of these groups were actually founded by Masons, and most of them featured elaborate initiation rituals of their own. The Grange, for example, had seven degrees, the last three of which were named for Roman goddesses: Pomona, the goddess of fruit and gardens; Flora, the goddess of flowers; and Ceres, the goddess of food plants.[30]

Historian Mark Carnes has posed the pertinent question of why so many men of the Victorian era felt the need to undergo and perform these rituals, with their secrecy and initiatory ordeals. He suggests that the fraternal orders served a need that many men had for both a spiritual experience and a masculine social sphere unfettered by feminine influence. As Carnes points out, as the 19th century unfolded, churches increasingly catered to a feminine sensibility. And as industrialization took hold, men's former authority in the home was supplanted by an ethic of the home as the realm of the homemaker.[31]

What's more, the predominance of a ritual-poor Protestantism failed to satisfy the need that some men felt for a meaningful ritual in their lives. The fraternal orders spoke to that need and provided a male-only refuge from the expansion of women into a greater social presence. Within that refuge, men were encouraged to remain in touch with values that might otherwise be identified by the culture at large as feminine: a sense of fairness and ethical virtue, cooperation, charity, and spiritual inquiry. In addition, as settlers moved ever westward, founding new towns and societies, fraternal orders served as support groups for men who had left behind old family ties and social networks.

It is likely that much of the hostility directed at Masonry by churchmen, who reviled it as a rival "religion," was due to their shrewd perception that Masonry and other fraternal orders were, in some fashion, satisfying needs that their churches failed to address.

There may also have been a conflict between the organizational values and styles of Church and Lodge. Masonry encouraged a measured, orderly demeanor in the lodge, and its members were instructed to "circumscribe their desires" and "keep their passions within due bounds"—that is, not fall prey to excesses of emotion and desire. This was in direct contrast to the evangelical "revivals" that were popular during the time of the anti-Masonic uproar and thereafter. The revivalist technique was to intentionally raise participants' emotions to a fever pitch, the better to trigger repentance and conversion experiences.[32]

In addition to ritual and masculine companionship, Masonry also provided a social safety net through its members' vows to look after each other's widows and children, and through its custom of providing "relief" for brothers in need. While many fraternal orders were little more than insurance providers whose relief funds helped cover members' expenses while unemployed, Masonry (and the Odd Fellows) institutionalized their relief efforts into homes for widows and orphans. Many of these have continued to operate right up to the present, evolving along the way into more general retirement homes.

The Civil War

Freemasonry's resurgence after the anti-Masonic nadir was actually boosted by the War Between the States. As Masonic historian Allen E. Roberts summarizes:

Many lodges had lost their officers and well-informed members to the armed services, both North and South. The faithful few at home were exerting every effort to keep their lodges alive, and their success was amazing. More new lodges were formed during the war years than gave up their charters. The membership in Freemasonry increased to a greater extent during the four years of war than during any similar period in its history.[33]

This is perhaps not surprising when one considers that the bonds of Masonic brotherhood served as an additional support for men undergoing the stress of war. While the phenomenon of military lodges among the troops during the Revolutionary War had dissipated once the Continental Army was disbanded, the idea reasserted itself with the Civil War. No less than 244 military lodges (94 among the North's military and 150 among the South's) were formed under dispensations from various state grand lodges.[34]

Not surprisingly, the war disrupted formal relations between grand lodges, throwing them into a conceptual dilemma. Were the bonds between Masonic brethren stronger than the divisions between the North and South? On at least an organizational level, they were not. However, there is anecdotal evidence that at the individual level those bonds helped mitigate some of the war's cruelty.

One typical story tells of a captured Confederate soldier who fell severely ill in a prisoner camp in Illinois. "He was able to let a Union officer know he was a Mason, and that officer, himself a Mason, took him to his home, nursed him back to health, and when the war was over, gave him money, and a gun, and saw him off for Texas."[35]

The Color Line

If Lincoln's Emancipation Proclamation marked the end of legal slavery in the United States, it certainly didn't mark the end of racial segregation or discrimination of whites against blacks. As advocates of the Brotherhood of Man, one might have thought that Freemasons would have been in the forefront of efforts to integrate and reconcile sectors of society alienated from each other. Unfortunately, this was hardly the case.

As early as 1775, a free black man by the name of Prince Hall had been initiated into Masonry, along with fourteen other free black men, by a British military lodge attached to a British regiment in Boston. Though details are in dispute, it would seem that these men were given a limited charter to form their own lodge (although not to "raise" new Masons). One should perhaps note that the military lodge in which Prince Hall and his fellow blacks were initiated was a military lodge chartered by the Grand Lodge of Ireland, not one under the jurisdiction of the Provincial Grand Lodge of Massachusetts. Nevertheless, according to the customs of Masonry at that time, their status as Masons and that of their lodge were not irregular. Once the Revolutionary War was over, they petitioned the Grand Lodge of England for a full charter, which they received in 1784.[36]

At this point, Prince Hall's lodge found itself in an awkward position. Either it could seek inclusion in one of the newly sovereign grand lodges in the states, or it could strike out on its own. It chose the latter course, later declaring itself a de facto grand lodge and chartering further lodges among free black men. Thus was set in motion a parallel Masonry among American black men, which Masonic historians now concede was as "regular" in its rituals and other philosophical components as the more "mainstream" (i.e., largely white) grand lodges.[37]

(The concept of "regularity" looms large in the affairs of grand lodges, it being one of the main standards that grand lodges use in deciding whether to officially "recognize" each other. *Regularity* is usually defined as adherence to the traditional defining rules, or "landmarks," of the Craft—a set

Prince Hall, founder of the first African-American Masonic lodge in the United States, depicted in a traditional painting

of principles that include belief in Deity, belief in an afterlife, the presence of a Volume of Sacred Law [usually the Bible] in the lodge, a policy of making Masons only of men, certain organizational standards, and so on. To complicate matters further, there is no single set of landmarks agreed upon by all grand lodges.)

Leading up to and following the Civil War, American society was divided along racial lines, and, with parallel institutions now in place, Masonry maintained those racial lines as well. Prince Hall lodges went on to play a significant role within black communities, serving as a crucial means of self-help among the black middle class. (Whenever black men, such as Booker T. Washington, Duke Ellington, and Count Basie, are included in lists of famous Masons, it is a safe bet that they were members of Prince Hall lodges.)

Unfortunately, the mainstream grand lodges' doctrine of jurisdictional exclusivity (according to which there could be only one "recognized" grand lodge per state) assured that Prince Hall grand lodges and their component local lodges were consigned to the outsider categories of "clandestine" and "unrecognized." This legalism within Masonic jurisprudence granted mainstream grand lodges the excuse that they were not being racially biased in prohibiting contact between their members and "clandestine" black Prince Hall brethren—they were merely holding to Masonic principles.

Eventually, this rationale began to crumble and mainstream Masonry began to rethink its hypocritical racial stance. But first there was to be considerable water under the bridge.

The Eastern Star

From the very beginning, one of Masonry's defining rules was that only men could become Freemasons. This was perhaps unremarkable in an age when most civic groups, political parties, and social clubs were men-only affairs, and it reflected the divide between the sexes within British and American society.

As mentioned earlier, this Masonic rule was rapidly waived on the Continent, and "adoptive" lodges for women were soon created. While these enjoyed a great popularity in Europe, they were typically frowned upon by English-speaking Masonry.

Nevertheless, some degree rituals for women made their way to America in the early 19th century, where they gained a few adherents. Among those were a very active Kentucky Mason, Rob Morris, and his wife, Charlotte, who received the degree of "Heroine of Jericho" in 1847, and another degree, "Martha's Daughter," shortly thereafter.[38]

Not satisfied with these degrees, which Morris described as "poorly conceived, weakly wrought out, unimpressive," Rob Morris set out to devise his own adoptive rite in 1850. This became the Order of the Eastern Star (OES), its name referring to the star in the east that guided the three magi to the infant Jesus.

As was the case with adoptive Masonry in Europe, the Eastern Star's degrees and rituals shared some Masonic characteristics but were largely new creations, drawing inspiration from biblical heroines of the Old and New Testaments.

The OES was not an immediate hit, in part because many American grand lodges were initially opposed to "Freemasonry for Women." After a series of organizational false starts and the intervening Civil War, Morris turned over the order's reins to Robert Macoy, a Masonic publisher, in 1867, when Morris decided to set off for the Holy Land in search of Masonic historical sites.

Macoy proved a more able leader, and the OES began to spread in the latter decades of the 1800s. In order to qualify, women had to be wives, daughters, or other relatives of Masons, and following the paternalistic pattern set by adoptive lodges, at least one male Mason who was also an OES member had to be present at all Eastern Star meetings, which were typically held in Masonic lodges.

Whatever Rob Morris's original intentions may have been in terms of group autonomy, the OES largely succumbed to the fate of a "women's auxiliary," often providing cooking and cleanup for Masonic lodge dinners and supervision for Masonic youth groups such as Job's Daughters and Rainbow for Girls. Still, its ritual and ceremonial work was to prove satisfying and inspirational to millions of women over the years, giving them entrée into the Masonic world.

Journey to the East

Buffeted by criticisms from anti-Masons that it was elitist, anti-Christian, and morally suspect, Masonry in the 19th century responded by underscoring its patriotic fervor and pious rectitude. While the Masons of the 1700s had commonly met in private rooms at pubs and taverns, with lodge meetings attended by much food, drink, and conviviality, American Masons in the 1800s increasingly built their own lodge halls, distanced themselves from a free-drinking reputation, and fashioned an image of themselves as solid pillars of their communities.

However, this regimen of bourgeois respectability did not sit well with all Masons. Every action engenders a reaction, and one response to the suffocating atmosphere within Masonry arose within the cosmopolitan environs of Manhattan in the 1870s. This was the Ancient Arabic Order Nobles of the Mystic Shrine (AAONMS), better known as the Shriners or simply the Shrine. (For what it's worth, the initials AAONMS are an anagram of "A MASON.")

The precise genesis of the Shrine is a matter of some dispute, but

Fantastic illustration from a Shrine Annual Proceedings report of 1886. Titled "Commemorative Ceremonies of a Grand Shareef," it depicts the Shrine's romantic image of Middle Eastern culture. Note the pharaohlike headdress of the officiating mourner. The wizardly men on the left are presumably alchemists, always good to have around during a funeral.

the most common account attributes its origin to the mutual inspiration of two New York Masons, a stage comedian and actor, William "Billy" Florence, and a physician, Dr. Walter M. Fleming. According to the Shrine's potted histories, Florence and Fleming felt that the Masonry of their day provided insufficient opportunities for fun and fellowship, and they brainstormed a new organization for Masons that would help redress this imbalance.[39]

Florence, according to his own account, was traveling in Marseille, France, in 1870, when he was invited to a ceremony hosted by a possibly mythical figure, "the celebrated Yusef Churi Bey," apparently an attaché of the Persian consulate. In the course of the evening, Yusef Bey presided over the lavishly staged proceedings of what was dubbed the "Bokhara Shrine," the attendees including the cream of Marseille society.[40]

Florence prevailed upon his host to supply him with copies of the rituals, and these provided the inspiration and ceremonial seed for the Orientalist motif of the Shrine. Or so the story goes.[41] As John Patrick Deveney has noted in his examination of the Shrine's complicated roots, the Shrine's cofounder, Walter Fleming, later attributed the lion's share of both inspiration and ritual creation to himself, while a third collaborator, Albert Leighton Rawson, a fascinating character in his own right and something of a fringe Masonic confidence man, claimed to have translated the original rituals from the Arabic and to have provided the new organization with actual contacts with Eastern brotherhoods, most notably the Bektashi order of Sufis. Indeed, correspondence and reports published in the early annual proceedings of the Shrine's Imperial Council made reference to supposed branches of the Shrine in the Middle East and North Africa as "Bektashy" or "Bektashee." It is highly dubious that these branches ever actually existed, and it is equally unlikely that there was any organizational link between the Shrine and the Bektashis. Such references appear to be part of an elaborate mythos concocted by Rawson and a few others intent on fleshing out the Orientalist motif.[42]

Whatever the truth may be, there is little question that the Shrine soon flourished as "the playground of Masons," a purely social respite from the solemn proceedings of Masonic ritual and rhetoric. The Shrine's founders introduced a touch of gentlemen's-club elitism into the Shrine's requirements by opening membership only to Masons

Murat Temple in Indianapolis (originally built in 1909). Many Shrine temple buildings imitated the architectural motifs of Islamic cultures. Though sometimes called "mosques," they had no religious function, but served as meeting halls and private clubs.

who held the 32nd degree in the Scottish Rite or were Knights Templar in the York Rite, these being the respective summits of the two primary rites of "higher" degrees in the United States.

In line with the Masonic fascination of the era with Freemasonry's mythic history back to Egypt and beyond, the Shrine cultivated quasi-Egyptian, quasi-Islamic trappings, many of which—such as the red fezzes and Janissary marching-band costumes—boiled down to Western cliché versions of Ottoman Turkish customs. Islam and the Middle East were sufficiently distant and exotic at that time that there was little risk in employing their motifs in a playful fashion.

Viewed today from a post–9/11 perspective, the Shrine's lightheartedness seems a telling example of an earlier era's cultural insensitivity, but to give the Shrine its due, it is just as likely that it represented an early accommodation of Middle America to a wholly foreign Other.

Charity and Americanism

If the 19th century was the heyday of fraternal orders as refuges from a changing world, the 20th century saw Masonry take a more active public stance in the culture at large. This had both good and bad aspects.

The Shrine, whose love of "fun" had begun to earn it a hedonistic reputation at odds with Masonry's idealistic self-image, devoted considerable resources to founding free hospitals for crippled children—an admirable endeavor that garnered much praise. Other Masonic bodies, such as the Scottish Rite and the Knights Templar, founded free clinics for children with language disorders, dyslexia, eye injuries, and a host of other maladies. The old criticism that Masons' charity was mainly extended to themselves and their kin was rendered increasingly obsolete.

Further, in a new, prosperous era of civic boosterism, with increased competition from clubs like Rotary and the Lions, Masons were drawn out of their lodge rooms and into local community activities and service. As chronicled by scholar Lynn Dumenil, this marked a shift from the more inward-looking lodges of the 19th century to the outward-directed Masonry of the 20th century.[43]

Unfortunately, with greater engagement came a greater temptation to break with long-standing Masonic traditions of studied neutrality on matters of sectarian religion and politics. Masonic rules had long enforced a ban on the discussion of religion and politics in the lodge room on the grounds that such discussions would likely create disharmony between members. However, as a largely white, middle-class, Protestant, and conservative institution, Masonry could be said to have a de facto religious and political stance that deferred to what a majority of its members saw as their own interests.

Just as earlier waves of Irish Catholic immigrants in the previous century had triggered fears of papist plots and Romanism, further immigration from Eastern Europe and other non-Anglo-Saxon countries, and the success of the Russian Revolution, now fed fears of "alien" subversives and political upheaval. Some Masons had already shown a propensity for anti-Catholicism and for support of nativist/antiradical groups such as the American Protective League, which had received the endorsement of the attorney general.[44] In the tense years of World War I, followed by the 1919 Palmer Raids and the attendant Red Scare, Masonry as a whole underscored its patriotism and came out in favor of "100% Americanism."[45]

This amounted to advocating the capping of further immigration (at least by non–Northern Europeans) and assimilating immigrants already here to "American" values—that is, white, middle-class, Protestant, and conservative. One means to this end was the rallying of support for compulsory public education—a goal that would have resulted in the elimination of parochial schools.

The revival of the Ku Klux Klan from 1915 on was precisely under this rubric of "100% Americanism," and in some locales there was a significant overlap between the local Masonic lodge and the local Klan. The KKK particularly targeted Masons for recruiting, and it claimed in 1923 that as many as 500,000 Masons were members of the Klan.[46]

In Texas, starting in 1922, a succession of eight Grand Dragons, the top Klan leader for the state, were all Masons. One of them, a San Antonio lawyer, even became Grand Dragon while serving as Grand Senior Warden of the Grand Lodge of Texas in 1924. Only a few months after resigning as Grand Dragon, he became Grand Master of Texas Masonry in 1926—an especially egregious case of political corruption.[47]

This blurring of boundaries between the KKK and Masonry was also facilitated on a national scale by George Flemming Moore, the Sovereign Grand Commander of the Scottish Rite (Southern Jurisdiction), who was forced to resign that post in 1921 after he began publishing a weekly newspaper, the *Fellowship Forum*. Though the paper described itself as "a national weekly newspaper devoted to the fraternal interpretation of the world's current events," it "continually stressed the relationship between the Klan and Masonry—a policy that brought criticism from Masonic officials and authors."[48]

Indeed, the cozy relationship between some Masons and the Klan during the 1920s, while prevalent in some areas, was hardly universal, and many grand lodges denounced the Klan and forbade their members from joining the clandestine organization.[49] Nevertheless, the damage was done, not least in contributing further confusion to the public's perception of Masonry.

Boom, Bust, and Boom

Between 1910 and 1929, American Masonry lifted its membership figures by nearly two million, an extraordinary boom for an organization that had numbered only 854,000 in 1900 and an estimated 70,000 in

1850.[50] As the economy peaked in 1928–29, Masonry peaked with it, with more than 3,295,000 men. According to one estimate, this came in at 12 percent of the native white adult male population in the United States.[51]

This upsurge in numbers and dues helped Masonry undertake its greatest period of building imposing edifices for its grand lodges, Scottish Rite cathedrals, and Shrine temples. In 1923 alone, Masons spent over thirty million dollars in erecting Masonic temples, according to one estimate.[52]

The Detroit Masonic Temple, the largest Masonic structure in the world, was dedicated in 1926—a fourteen-story behemoth with some 1,037 rooms. It included eight lodge rooms, decorated respectively in Egyptian, Doric, Ionic, Corinthian, Italian Renaissance, Byzantine, Gothic, and Romanesque motifs. The third-floor mezzanine housed a drill hall of 17,500 square feet of open floor space in which Knights Templar drill teams and Shrine patrol units could practice for parades.[53]

The building mania wasn't limited to large cities. The Scottish Rite Valley of Guthrie, Oklahoma, benefiting from a surge of oil money among its membership, erected a stunning temple in classic Greek style, featuring two auditoriums, a magnificent pipe organ, and its own series of lavishly decorated theme rooms, including a Pompeian room, an Assyrian room, an Italian lounge, an Egyptian room, and a library in Gothic vaulted style. The temple, begun in 1921, was dedicated in 1929, just in time for the stock-market crash.[54]

Not surprisingly, such a boom could not last. The lean times of the Great Depression caused lodge membership to shrink, year by year, wiping out the growth of the 1920s. Only with World War II did membership start turning around as many enlisted men petitioned to join before shipping overseas. Still, membership didn't recover to its 1929 level until 1948, as Masonry benefited from a new postwar boom.

Many explanations have been given for Masonry's renewed cycle of popularity. Returning veterans, coming back from the war with a shared sense of danger and comradeship, found in Masonry a way to translate those emotions into a satisfying ritual and new fraternal bonds. Just as Masonry had demonstrated its value as a support group for men and a supportive social institution during the westward expansion of the 19th century, it now played a similar role in the explosion of suburbs populated with new families taking advantage of the G.I. Bill.

Masonry was intertwined with the temper of the times, whether it was the bourgeois pursuit of the American Dream or the heightened anti-Communism of the Cold War years.

Masonry's success in the 1950s was celebrated with a famous pictorial cover story in *Life* magazine in 1956, which featured a cover photo of the forty-eight states' grand masters, bedecked in ceremonial aprons and jewels, standing in a triangular formation on the steps leading up to the Scottish Rite's imposing House of the Temple in Washington, D.C.[55]

By 1959 the Craft's American numbers had grown to their greatest ever at 4,103,161. And then came the '60s.

Shaken, Not Stirred

As the '60s began, the great bulk of Freemasonry's members were the fathers and grandfathers of the baby boom generation, and they fared no better in comprehending the cultural changes that were afoot than their non-Masonic neighbors. Conditioned by their service in World War II and Korea, many Masons shared a reflexive patriotism that assumed that God, flag, and country were all of a piece and that one naturally supported the government in times of war. Their children's opposition to the Vietnam War was nearly inconceivable to them.

At the same time, the complacency of many Masons was shaken by a civil rights movement that employed civil disobedience to challenge racial injustice. Masons' obligations included vows to be law-abiding citizens, and the thought that some laws might be simply wrong—or might be challenged by breaking them—was not easily digested.

And then there was the little matter of sex, drugs, and rock 'n' roll. The Masons with their crew cuts left over from their time in the service, and their suits and ties with flag pins next to their square-and-compass lapel pins, largely lined up on one side of the cultural chasm, their long-haired children in jeans on the other.

Beginning in 1960, Masonry's numbers began to shrink incrementally. Masons weren't leaving, exactly, but not enough new members were coming in to make up for attrition due to older Masons' deaths. The decline wasn't drastic at first: in the course of the '60s, the shrinkage was roughly 30,000 per year for the whole country.[56] But by 1971, Masonic membership was back down to that of 1951 (roughly 3,600,000), and the numbers kept going south. By 2007 they would be down to 1,483,449 in the United States.

Families with long-running traditions of Masonic involvement found that their sons had little interest in putting on a suit and tie and heading on down to the lodge. And they had even less interest in hanging out with guys whose idea of casual attire was a polyester leisure suit. The beatniks' characterization of the unhip as "square" fit Freemasonry all too aptly, and most Masons were not about to change—even if they could have.

Time marches on, however, and as Masonry continued to shrink, its leaders became more sensitive to the need to rethink some of its customs. Many lodges made efforts to include their members' wives and families in dinners and activities that previously would have been for members only. And belatedly, state "mainstream" grand lodges began to grant "recognition" to their Prince Hall equivalents (starting with the Grand Lodge of Connecticut in 1989), allowing members to visit each other's lodges and acknowledge each other as brothers.

Grand lodges also began to experiment with new ways to attract potential members, including much-advertised "one-day classes" in some states, where groups of new candidates could receive all three degrees in one day. The Grand Lodge of Ohio, for instance, initiated some 7,700 new members in one day in 2002.

Whether such efforts will prove sufficient to make the fraternity more attractive to younger men remains to be seen.

It is tempting to suppose that Masonry's uncomfortable position as an aging social institution dooms it to irrelevance and consigns its traditions and rituals to the dustbin of history, but that would fail to take into account the enduring nature of its core values and its initiatory function.

As we'll see shortly, Masonic ritual, and the symbolism that it draws upon, can still provide an emotionally potent transformative experience for men, free of sectarian dogmas.

Nighttime electrical display on the front of the Masonic Temple in Boston, during the Triennial Conclave of the Masonic Knights Templar Grand Encampment in 1895. Through parades and public displays such as this, the Knights Templar made their presence felt in American culture at large.

5

The Powers That Be

Making Sense of the Masonic Power Structure

Tucked away in the dusty stacks of Masonic libraries around the country is a mind-boggling oversize leather-bound volume of over five hundred gold-trimmed pages. This rare 1895 book, the *Photo Souvenir of the 26th Triennial Conclave* of the Masonic Knights Templar, offers stunning photographic evidence of an earlier era of public display, when Masonic Knights Templar—the summit of the York Rite series of "higher degrees"—gathered every three years to parade in military formation through the streets of America's urban centers. This particular volume commemorates the gathering of August 26–31, 1895, in Boston.[1]

One Masonic historian described the conclave's impressive extent:

> Elaborate preparations had been made for the reception and the meeting of the Grand Encampment. The streets and main build-ings were dressed in holiday attire. The parade consisting of 20,000 Knights Templar in line and accompanied by 140 bands, required more than five hours to pass the reviewing stand. It was the greatest pageant so far presented by the Grand Encampment, surpassing all previous efforts. It is estimated that five hundred thousand people viewed the parade.[2]

The souvenir book provides photo documentation of the hundreds of Knights Templar commanderies from around the continent, each dressed in plumed black hats and banner-bedecked black uniforms with swords at their side, ranged in drill formation, with some entire units mounted on black horses. Most knights wore the distinctive black triangular Templar apron, with a skull and crossbones embroidered in silver thread displayed front and center. Dozens of buildings that served as headquarters for the visiting commanderies were draped in Templar bunting and banners, and the entire front of the multistory temple of the Grand Masonic Lodge of Massachusetts was lit up with an enormous Knights Templar cross fashioned out of electrical lights—this at a time when electrical displays were still quite novel.[3]

The average citizen watching this spectacle might reasonably have assumed that Freemasons were a powerful force to be reckoned with, and more than a little scary.[4] This image was driven home by the Knights Templar every three years in a different major city. Histories of other Knights Templar triennials, such as that in New Orleans in 1922 and in Seattle in 1925, invariably include photos of major urban thoroughfares surmounted by giant temporary arches and electrical

Masonic Knights Templar parading in Boston in 1895, during their 26th Triennial Conclave. The parade of some 20,000 knights and 140 bands took more than five hours and was watched by a half million spectators. Such public displays affirmed an image of power and prestige.

displays, all sporting Templar crosses and other Masonic symbols, American flags, and bunting.[5] Even as late as 1934, in the midst of the economic depression, the Knights Templar triennial in San Francisco featured Templar flags and banners spanning the length of Market Street from the Ferry Building to the Civic Center, as well as a large electrical display at Newspaper Square and, most amazingly, a specially constructed "massive Gothic Cathedral tower, built around the Dewey Monument in Union Square Park."[6]

Granted, these lavish displays of presence and posture took place in earlier times, when Americans were much more given to parading around at the drop of a hat. Parades and related public spectacles provided free entertainment, both for the participants and for the spectators. Cities were more inclined to allow civic organizations and visiting conventions to decorate public space with their insignias for special occasions. The Knights Templar were not, by any means, the only group throwing impressive pageants.

Still, none of that diminishes the fact that these Knights Templar parades and displays were clearly intended as assertions of public presence and power, and undoubtedly carried the whispered subtext that the Knights Templar were the elite of Freemasonry. Many "Sir Knights" (as members called each other) probably considered themselves just that: a Masonic elite.

But was it really so? Was there then—and is there now—a Masonic elite whose power and status dwarf that of ordinary Masons? If so, who are they? Knights Templar? Thirty-third-degree Masons? Shapeshifting reptilians?

As this is a subject that is riddled with urban legends and confusion, let us take a good hard look into the controversial question of Masonic authority and organization. Official titles such as Worshipful Master, Grand Master, and Sovereign Grand Commander may sound powerful and awe-inspiring if not dictatorial, but is this really the case, or is it simply an illusion fostered by fancy titles? Who is really calling the shots within the Craft?

There is no question that from the very beginning of the premier Grand Lodge of England in 1717, the issue of Masonic authority and hierarchy has been a bundle of contradictions. On the one hand there was the strong egalitarian impulse in the Craft exemplified by the slogan that all Masons meet "on the level," a pun invoking the builder's tool as a metaphor for across-the-board equality. On the other hand, the very act of founding an administrative grand lodge created an überhierarchy of grand officers, and it subordinated individual local lodges to a central body. This tension between equality and hierarchy was further complicated by the development of "higher" degrees and Masonic chivalric orders, such as the Knights Templar, which introduced further opportunities for elitism within Masonry.

Modern speculative Masonry may have officially begun in 1717 with clear-cut ideals of universal brotherhood, but the human fondness for rank, prestige, honor, and power asserted itself almost immediately, complicating matters greatly. Yet there is a method to the madness that is important to understand, and once one grasps a few basics, much that is confusing at first glance falls into place.

Brethren of the Lodge

The basic building block of Masonry remains the individual local lodge, often called a "blue lodge" after Masonry's signature color, which is also the color of the trim on Masonic officers' aprons. In Masonic parlance, a "lodge" refers to a group of Master Masons (known to each other as "brothers" or "brethren") assembled together under the leadership of a "line" of officers in order to confer degrees, transact lodge business, enjoy communal dinners, perform community service, and so on. Such lodges can vary in size from several dozen men up to several hundred or more.

Although many lodges meet in their own buildings, this is not always the case, and technically a lodge consists of the men composing it, not the building in which they meet, although the terms are often used interchangeably. Some Masonic temples or centers are shared by several local lodges, each meeting on a different night of the week or month. In some major cities, such as New York and Detroit, large Masonic temples are furnished with several lodge rooms, enabling more than one lodge to meet at the same time.

A candidate typically petitions to join a blue lodge in his general locale—whether neighborhood, town, or city—and it is this lodge that performs his degree rituals. A Mason's blue lodge remains his most basic link to the Craft, although if he moves elsewhere he might shift his membership to another blue lodge. A Mason who doesn't maintain his membership in his blue lodge (and through it, his grand lodge), and who doesn't pay its annual dues, is no longer considered a current Mason, no matter how famous or powerful he may be.

In the United States, the blue lodges within each state operate under the umbrella of a state grand lodge. Technically, a grand lodge is composed of its blue lodges, each of which has certain voting rights in Masonic matters. However, on a day-to-day level, a grand lodge amounts to a line of grand officers (some elected, some appointed) and a paid staff at central offices where membership records are kept, contacts with other Masonic bodies are maintained, state Masonic charities are supervised, and statewide Masonic activities and guidelines are coordinated.

In most countries around the world, with some notable exceptions, there is generally just one primary grand lodge per country. However, in the United States, each state has its own grand lodge, which is a sovereign power unto itself. There is no national grand lodge supervising things or setting policy on a national scale.[7]

This is the first fact that undercuts conspiracy theories of top-down Masonic hierarchy and control. Instead of one giant coordinated combine, American Masonry is akin to fifty-one little duchies, each jealously guarding its own independence and prerogatives.[8] A further obstacle to coordination is the custom of having the grand officers (like their counterparts at the blue-lodge level) serve one-year terms, after which other officers take their chairs.[9] Thus the Masonic leadership is annually shuffled like a deck of cards.

Within this miniature bureaucratic universe, the main forces of continuity are the Grand Secretaries of each grand lodge, who may commonly serve for many years but whose powers are limited to acting within the legal guidelines and limits set by the votes of the blue lodges that make up each grand lodge.

These guidelines and limits are codified, much like state or federal law, into an ordered Masonic code of law that defines the proper conduct and responsibilities of officers, lodges, and individual Masons. Again, this body of Masonic jurisprudence differs subtly (and sometimes dramatically) from state to state.

Thus, the grand lodge in one state may forbid alcohol at lodge dinners, while a grand lodge in another state may allow it. Some grand lodges keep a tight rein on their lodges' public activities, while others are looser, and so on. The Grand Lodge of Georgia, for instance, has a strict set of rules about what its local blue lodges can and cannot have on their lodge Web sites.[10] The Grand Lodge of California doesn't allow its lodges to "accept any of the proceeds or profits of any raffle, lottery or other gambling enterprise."[11]

Typically, changes to Masonic code must be proposed as resolutions to be voted on by representatives from the local lodges at grand lodge annual meetings, the results of which are published in grand lodge proceedings and, these days, often posted on grand lodge Web sites.

While there are two associations—the Conference of Grand Masters of North America, and the Conference of Grand Secretaries of North America—that meet every year for two or three days to discuss issues and problems that grand lodges may have in common, these associations are purely advisory and consultative. They hold no formal power or control over individual grand lodges.

If Freemasonry really were a top-down conspiracy, it would be hard to come up with a more cumbersome way of organizing things.

Further Confusion

Even if we set aside for the moment questions of conspiracy, we are still left with the confusion surrounding the "higher" degrees and their relationship to blue-lodge Masonry. Many people assume that the possessors of higher degrees must hold power over those with lower degrees.

More than once, acquaintances have proudly told me, "My grandfather was a 32nd- (or 33rd-) degree Mason," with the obvious assumption that Gramps must have been pretty high up in the Masonic pecking order.

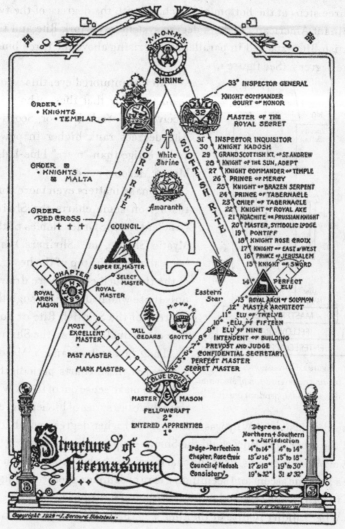

An example of a well-meaning but misleading chart showing the degrees of the York Rite and
Scottish Rite rising above those of the blue lodge and implying a culmination in the Shrine.
Also shown are other social, charitable, and women's groups for Masons or their relatives.

Widely disseminated charts of Masonic degrees have unintentionally deepened such confusion by showing the three blue-lodge degrees as three steps at the bottom of the chart, with the degrees of the two dominant American "higher" degree systems—the York Rite and the Scottish Rite—stacked in parallel pillars rising above the three blue-lodge degrees. (See figure 1.)

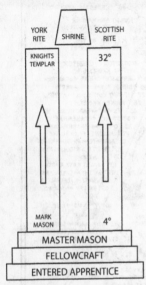

Figure 1. *Conventional and misleading representation of Masonic degrees and appendant orders*

To the untutored eye, this would seem to imply that those who have received the York Rite or Scottish Rite degrees rank higher in power and prestige than "mere" blue-lodge Master Masons.

To make matters even more confusing, on some charts the Shrine (Ancient Arabic Order Nobles of the Mystic Shrine, or "Shriners") has been shown at the top of the heap, as at the time such charts were drawn, only those who had gone through the degrees of the Scottish Rite or York Rite could qualify to join the Shrine.

Long before I became a Mason, I stared at these charts periodically, trying to make sense out of them. Why were there *two* series of higher degrees instead of just one? Why was one series of higher degrees numbered and the other not? How could the Shrine—apparently the most exclusive of Masonic groups, or so the chart implied—be both the pinnacle of one's Masonic ascent and seemingly a club of drunken good-time Charlies in fezzes, loud ties, and minicars? None of it seemed to add up.

What I didn't realize at the time was that such charts are subtly misleading. In stacking the degrees of the two concordant rites vertically above those of the blue lodge, the charts lead the casual reader to assume that a 32nd degree has more power and prestige than a third degree because that degree is both higher on the chart and has a greater number. However, in terms of Masonic organizational standing this is akin to comparing apples and oranges. If one were to put these additional degrees on the same chart as the three blue-lodge degrees, it would be more accurate to have them branch out horizontally from the core of the three degrees. (See figure 2.)

Figure 2. More accurate representation
of Masonic degrees and appendant orders

This is because the two "rites" of additional degrees, the York Rite and the Scottish Rite, exist outside of the core Masonic system of local lodges and state grand lodges.[12] The degrees they confer, no matter what their numerical designation or elevation, are not recognized by grand lodges as raising any Mason above the status of Master Mason (third degree).

Within Masonry, these groups are referred to as "concordant" bodies (i.e., Masonic groups in "concord" with grand lodges, but organizationally independent) or "appendant" orders (i.e., Masonic groups appended to or supplemental to other bodies). While these rites perform additional degrees that impart their own moral and philosophical lessons, Masons who choose to take these additional degrees gain no further official status within blue-lodge Masonry. And even more to the point, the York and Scottish Rites and their leadership have no authority over grand lodges.

The possession of additional degrees merely indicates that a Mason has undergone the rituals associated with those degrees and ideally has gained some further insights into Masonic symbols and philosophy, but this doesn't automatically translate into greater power or prestige. A Mason might receive every additional degree offered by both the York and Scottish Rites and gain little status thereby among his blue-lodge brothers, particularly if he merely "takes" the degrees and ceases to be active in any meaningful way.

Indeed, it could be said that no status is more highly regarded in Masonry as a whole than that of Past Master, a title that indicates that its holder has served at least one term as Worshipful Master of his blue lodge—a task of considerable responsibility and leadership.

We saw earlier how numerous rites and orders with higher degrees sprang up in Europe in the latter half of the 18th century. Many of them included the three "blue" degrees within their systems, adding additional degrees above them in a linear hierarchical order. In many of those groups, more power and prestige *did* accrue the higher one went up the ladder.

For instance, the Grand Constitutions of 1762 of the Rite of Perfection, the twenty-five-degree predecessor to the Scottish Rite, gave the rite's Inspectors General "governing authority" over the three blue-lodge degrees, at least as performed within its own lodges.[13]

It would be only natural to assume, therefore, that the same patterns of power and rank would hold true with "higher" degrees elsewhere, yet this was not to be the case, especially in the British Empire and North America. By the early years of the 1800s, the United Grand Lodge of England, as well as the North American grand lodges, required that any additional degrees beyond the core three degrees were to be given by separate organizations whose right to have Master Masons join them was dependent on the permission of the grand lodges. This effectively eliminated the possibility of any higher-degree bodies presuming to pull rank on blue-lodge Masonry. The Scottish Rite, for instance, was able to gain a foothold in America only once it deferred any jurisdiction over the blue degrees to the state grand lodges and agreed to confer degrees only from the 4th degree on.

Nevertheless, the York Rite and the Scottish Rite are sufficiently intertwined with the evolution of Freemasonry in America that it is important to grasp what they have provided if we want to gain an understanding of the Craft as a whole, especially how it is organized.

The York Rite: Swimming Upstream

As with so many things in Masonry, to really understand the development of higher degrees in America, we must first go back to speculative Masonry's early days in Britain.

While Masons on the Continent became enthusiastic propagators of additional degrees, their Masonic brethren in the British Isles were much more conservative in their attitude toward such "innovations." The creative energy that in Europe went into creating new degrees was funneled in Britain into deepening the three blue degrees, with Masonic notables such as William Preston and William Hutchinson composing extended degree lectures and fleshing out the array of Masonic symbolism for the three blue degrees.

Nevertheless, a modest number of additional degrees (less than a dozen) did turn up in British lodges during the 1700s. A few were probably native British creations, while some may have been imported from France. Masonic lodge minutes record that such degrees were usually conferred within normal blue lodges, although their conferrals were sporadic and not officially sanctioned.

These relatively few higher degrees, which included the Royal Arch, the Mark Master, and a Knights Templar degree, were promptly imported into American blue lodges, presumably by individual Masons bringing their memorized knowledge of the degrees with them to the colonies. Ironically, the first recorded instance of a Knights Templar degree conferral in any English-speaking lodge was in August 1769 in Boston, not in England.[14] Paul Revere, for instance, is on record as having received both the Royal Arch and the Templar degrees later that same year, on December 11, 1769.[15]

What was notable about these select additional degrees is that, with the exception of the Templar degrees, they all expanded upon and offered further details regarding the building of Solomon's Temple or its later rebuilding. In short, the tales they told and the lessons they imparted fit into and further detailed the self-contained mythos of the blue-lodge universe: the story of the slain Grand Master Hiram Abiff, and the craft of biblical-era stonemasons.

These degrees—especially the Royal Arch degree—were most often worked within lodges associated with the Antients' Grand Lodge, the rival to the premier Grand Lodge of 1717. It was the Antients' traditional claim "that they were York masons [i.e., that they upheld the Masonic traditions of York, England, the legendary fount of English Masonry and the supposed site of annual Masons' assemblies in olden

Jewel of a Past Eminent Commander of a Masonic Knights Templar Commandery

days according to some Old Charges] and were handing down to posterity a rite that had been worked at York for hundreds of years."[16] This claim was historically unfounded but romantically attractive—so much so that when these degrees were gathered together into a more orderly system in America, they were collectively referred to as the York Rite, even though they are not collected under that designation in England.

This systematization eventually resulted in the degrees being overseen and conferred by three York Rite subgroupings: Chapters of Royal Arch Masons (conferring the Mark Master, Past Master, Most Excellent Master, and Royal Arch degrees); Councils of Royal and Select Masters (aka Cryptic Masons, conferring the Royal Master, Select Master, and Super Excellent Master degrees); and Knights Templar Commanderies (conferring the Order of Red Cross, Order of Malta, and Order of the Temple [Knights Templar] degrees). As with blue-lodge Masonry with its local lodges and grand lodges, the local York Rite bodies are governed by their own state grand bodies.[17]

It is customary for a Mason who chooses to pursue the York Rite to receive the degrees and join the respective bodies in the above order, culminating in a Commandery, but this is not always the case. While any Master Mason can petition to join a Royal Arch Chapter (and, following that, a Cryptic Council if he so chooses), the Knights Templar Commandery specifically reserves itself for Christian Masons, commemorating as it does what were, after all, Christian military orders.

One must first have joined a Royal Arch chapter in order to petition to join a commandery, but only those Royal Arch Masons who are Christians need apply. Because the Knights Templar present themselves as the capstone of the York Rite, the York Rite as a whole has often been characterized as a Christian rite, even though the mythic content of the chapter and council degrees is largely drawn from the Hebrew scriptures and other Jewish sources such as Josephus, and mostly expands upon the Temple-building mythos.

This perception of the York Rite as Christian has fostered some resentment over the years from Masons who consider it a central principle of Freemasonry that a Masonic group should not discriminate based on religion and that *all* believers in Deity should be welcome in any Masonic group, regardless of specific religion. To those with such views, the Masonic Knights Templar are not truly Masonic, nor are the several other invitational and honorary side orders within the Masonic milieu that are reserved for Trinitarian Christians, such as the Royal Order of Scotland.

Members of these orders, however, can point out that both their orders' Christian character and their coexistence with the Masonic grand lodges go back well into the mid-1700s, and that the right to free association should allow for specialized subgroups among Masons.

In any event, there is no single authoritative ruling on this question and no single authoritative body that might give it. Once again, Freemasonry's decentralized nature prevents any single group from controlling it.

The Scottish Rite

The Ancient and Accepted Scottish Rite (AASR)—with its degrees numbered up to 33, its ruling body called the Supreme Council 33°, and a leader called the Sovereign Grand Commander—would seem to be the very embodiment of pomp and power. The Scottish Rite's emblem, a double-headed eagle, is redolent of European royalty: the same dual-headed bird graced the coat of arms of the Hapsburg Holy Roman Empire and the Russian royal family, although there is no direct connection between the AASR and those royal lines. The headquarters of the Scottish Rite (Southern Jurisdiction) in Washington, D.C., called the House of the Temple, is an impressive structure, modeled on the mausoleum at Halicarnassus, one of the seven wonders of the ancient world. A succession of three, five, seven, and nine steps leads up to its entrance, which is flanked by a pair of sphinxes.

Given all these trappings of power, it's not really surprising that conspiracy theorists have assumed that the Scottish Rite must be the spider in the middle of the Masonic web. However, as always, appearances can be deceiving, and whatever power the Scottish Rite really wields is limited to its own organizational structure.

Unlike the York Rite degrees, which are largely of British origin, the Scottish Rite's degrees originated in France in the mid-1700s. Masonry on the Continent became fashionable in aristocratic circles, as we saw earlier, and this affected the composition of "higher" degrees there. While the York Rite rituals are largely biblical in their time and place and cast of characters, the Scottish Rite's rituals draw upon a variety of eras, and the cultural and geographical scope is wider.

The titles of the degrees are also more extravagant. The most grandly named degree in the York Rite is probably Super Excellent Master, which sounds like an honorific invented by Bill and Ted. But that can't hold a candle to Scottish Rite titles such as Prince of Jerusalem (16°), Grand Pontiff (19°), Knight of the Brazen Serpent (25°), and Master (or Prince) of the Royal Secret (32°).

But perhaps the biggest difference between the York and Scottish Rites is how the degree rituals are performed. The York Rite bodies commonly hold their meetings in local blue-lodge buildings, and the degrees are performed as participatory rituals in much the same fashion as the three craft degrees— within the three-dimensional space of the lodge room.[18]

The Scottish Rite, on the other hand, evolved during the course of the 19th century into an organization with its own theater-equipped

Insignia of the Ancient and Accepted Scottish Rite: a double-headed eagle, similar to—but not related to—the emblems of European and Russian monarchies

buildings wherein the degrees were presented as full-blown stage dramas, with sets, props, backdrops, and elaborate costumes. Candidates for the degrees would gather as a "class" to watch the degrees, which were typically performed over the course of several months at the rate of one or two each week.[19]

At least that was the approach back before motion pictures and television transformed how people spent their evenings. Clearly it took an enormous amount of coordination and a sizable expenditure of time and energy on the part of dozens of men to provide this series of teaching dramas. And it should be noted that even at the peak of such diligent activity, in the early decades of the 20th century, some degrees were merely "communicated" (i.e., given as a verbal summary) rather than presented in full form.

The picture today is a bit more austere. While there are a few Scottish Rite "Valleys" (i.e., local units) in the Southern Jurisdiction that still perform all or most of the degrees (either in the course of a year or in a four-day marathon), it is increasingly common for candidates to be part of a weekend class where the five "mandatory" degrees are performed (of which one is the 32nd degree) and the remaining twenty-four are verbally communicated in summary form.

In short, over the course of a day or two, a Master Mason goes from the Scottish Rite's 4th degree to the 32nd, by dint of skipping most steps in between. This may be disappointing news to those readers who have cherished the notion that rising to the ranks of the 32nd degree is the result of years of hard work and an attainment of great distinction. However, if we wish to gain a realistic view of Masonry, we need to see it as it really is, not as some might wish it to be.[20]

But, what of the fabled 33rd degree? Some anti-Masons seem convinced that the possessors of this degree must be the real kingpins of Masonry. Such ideas are usually held by armchair theorists who have never met an actual 33rd-degree Mason. To put things in perspective, we need to briefly touch on the Scottish Rite's organizational structure.

First of all, the AASR in the United States is actually divided into two distinct organizations: the AASR-NMJ (Northern Masonic Jurisdiction) and the AASR-SJ (Southern Jurisdiction). This division stems back to the earliest days of the Scottish Rite at the start of the

1800s, though as the century progressed the territorial division came to roughly resemble that of the Civil War's North-South division. The AASR-NMJ has its headquarters and Supreme Council in Lexington, Massachusetts, and administers the Scottish Rite degrees in the states east of the Mississippi and north of the Ohio River and the Mason-Dixon line. The AASR-SJ has its headquarters in Washington, D.C., where its Supreme Council meets, and administers the Scottish Rite degrees in the states west of the Mississippi and south of the Mason-Dixon line.

This is important to note as both Scottish Rites have their own Sovereign Grand Commanders and their own governing Supreme Councils made up of "active" 33rds (called Sovereign Grand Inspector Generals [SGIGs] in the Southern Jurisdiction). Roughly speaking, each state (or "Orient") in the Southern Jurisdiction has its own SGIG who sits on the Supreme Council and oversees the Scottish Rite in his state. By contrast, each state in the Scottish Rite–Northern Masonic Jurisdiction may have as many as five "active" 33rds, but only one of them represents the state as a "deputy" to the Supreme Council of the NMJ.[21]

At one further step down the ladder, the SGIGs or active 33rds designate "Personal Representatives" at each of the local Scottish Rite Valleys. The Personal Representatives, in conference with their SGIG or active 33rd, can nominate local AASR members to receive an *honorary* 33rd degree as a distinction for their public service or service to the Craft. This 33rd degree is not administrative but honorary, the only "active 33rds" being those who serve on the Supreme Council.

An intermediate honor between the 32nd and 33rd degrees, in the Southern Jurisdiction, is the Knight Commander of the Court of Honor (KCCH), also given for service to the Craft or one's community. The highest honor, in the AASR-SJ, is to receive the "Grand Cross," but none of these honors grants more palpable power or secret knowledge, except in the imaginations of the conspiracy theorists. (The "active" 33rds do hold considerable power over the affairs of the Scottish Rite Valleys in their respective states, and collegially over their Supreme Council, but this power is again limited to administering the Scottish Rite.)

Yet misunderstandings of Masonic powers persist. After all, doesn't the AASR-SJ's Supreme Council call itself "the Mother Council of the World"?

Indeed it does, but that has a specific, narrow meaning that is not apparent at first glance. The Supreme Council of the Southern Jurisdiction happened to be the first AASR body to organize itself into a Supreme Council back in 1801. The charters for all subsequent Scottish Rite Supreme Councils in other countries derived, either directly or indirectly, from this "Mother Council," but as any parent will testify, merely having had offspring doesn't guarantee control of one's children. And as was previously discussed, the Scottish Rite leadership has no jurisdiction over any part of Masonry besides the Scottish Rite itself.

I Want to Take You Higher

It should by now be clear that although there is a consecutive order to the sequence of higher degrees in both the York Rite and the Scottish Rite, higher numbers or fancier titles are not indicators of rank in Masonry at large. In general, the additional degrees either amplify some details of the three craft degrees or teach further lessons of an ethical or philosophical nature. Those who take these degrees may gain some insights into their own lives and into the fraternity, but doing so largely depends on their own efforts to understand what they have seen or experienced.

However, this is not to say that issues of hierarchy and rank are nonexistent in Masonry, no matter how much some idealistic Masons would like that to be the case. There may be no single overarching hierarchy monopolizing power, but there is an almost infinite supply of hierarchies spread across the Masonic landscape.

Not only does every blue lodge have its line of officers, but so does every grand lodge. Every local York Rite body (Chapter, Council, or Commandery) has its own line of officers, and above that are state grand bodies, such as Grand Chapters, with their officers as well. At the national level, in the York Rite, there is the General Grand Chapter of Royal Arch Masons, the Grand Encampment of the Knights Templar, and so on. Again, each of these administrative bodies has its own officers' line. Local Scottish Rite Valleys are composed of four subbodies, each with their own officers. And on and on. The Shrine? Plenty of officers to go around. The Eastern Star? The same. Indeed, every Masonic organization under the sun is fitted out with officers at multiple levels.

As Masonry shrinks, in some groups practically every active member is an officer of one sort or another. And the most active Masons are often officers in several groups simultaneously. This overlap of leadership can lead to a certain consolidation of power and influence, but it is almost always of a local and insular sort.

In truth, most Masonic groups—be they lodges, chapters, councils, commanderies, valleys, or orders—amount to social groups where the members who stick around and stay active do so because they enjoy each other's company or have found a small pond in which to be a large frog. Inevitably there are instances of organizational politics or power plays, but remarkably few reverberate beyond the Masonic milieu into the world at large.

Birds of a Feather

Nevertheless, there is one annual occasion in the Washington, D.C., area that might appear to the casual observer to confirm the impression of there being an elite clique of jewel-bedecked worthies within Freemasonry. I refer to what is known as "Masonic Week," a four-day stretch in the dead of winter that centers on an anonymous hotel not far from the George Washington Masonic National Monument in Alexandria, Virginia. Beginning on Wednesday, the hotel lobby and bar begin to fill with an assortment of mostly graying men in suits, sporting the medals and lapel pins of at least a dozen obscure Masonic orders, councils, side degrees, and rites. Until recently, when antismoking laws became pervasive, the air was thick with cigar smoke, for these are men who enjoy living the Masonic archetype of a backroom operator.

In fact, what is going on is a series of closely scheduled annual meetings and banquets of many of the lesser-known invitational societies within Freemasonry. These are groups with names like Sovereign Order of Knights Preceptor (SOKP), the Masonic Societas Rosicruciana in Civitatibus Foederatis (MSRICF, the Masonic Rosicrucian Society in the United States), the Holy Royal Arch Knights Templar Priests (HRAKTP), the Knights of the York Cross of Honour (KYCH), the Chevaliers Bienfaisant de la Cité Sainte (CBCS, the Knights Beneficent of the Holy City), the Allied Masonic Degrees (AMD), and lest we forget, the Masonic Order of the Bath (MOB) and Ye Antiente Order of Corks (YAOC), the latter presided over by the Grand Bung for the Americas. Most of these groups are "appendant" orders or side degrees to the York Rite, and the great overlap in membership between the groups makes an annual get-together a matter of convenience.

Many of these orders are open only by invitation to presiding officers (or past presiding officers) of York Rite bodies. For instance, the Holy Royal Arch Knights Templar Priests requires prospective invitees be Past Commanders of Knight Templar commanderies, while the Knights of the York Cross of Honour is for invitees who are honored for having been the presiding officer of a blue lodge, a Royal Arch chapter, a Cryptic council, and a Knights Templar commandery. In order to take the "fun" side degree of Ye Antiente Order of Corks, one must be a member of the Allied Masonic Degrees, which is open only by invitation to Royal Arch Masons, and so on.

In addition to these worthy attendees, there are also dozens of Masonic authors, researchers, and pundits who have come for the meetings and banquets of Masonic research societies such as the Society of Blue Friars (invitational society for Masonic authors), the Philalethes Society (an international society of Masonic researchers), and the Grand College of Rites of the USA, this last a group dedicated to preserving and publishing the rituals of now-defunct orders and degrees.

Incredibly enough, at least six of the groups that hold meetings during Masonic Week were the brainstorm of one J. Raymond Shute II, who launched all six in a four-year spree, including three groups (the Allied Masonic Degrees, Grand College of Rites, and Society of Blue Friars) between April 16 and July 1, 1932.[22] This tradition of cross-affiliation and leadership is still upheld today: at a recent Masonic Week, one participant was simultaneously Grand Master of a state grand lodge, Grand Preceptor of the SOKP, Grand Master General of the KYCH, Grand Chancellor of the CBCS, and Commander General of the MOB. One might think that this would make him the veritable

King of Masonry, but it is doubtful that more than a small percentage of American Masons would recognize his name or be affected by his influence.

In the course of the long weekend, hospitality suites proliferate all over the hotel, and the feelings of good fellowship and elevated spirits are conspicuously present. There is even some Masonic politicking going on, with flyers posted by the elevators for some candidates running for office in various York Rite bodies.

For many years there was little official Scottish Rite presence at Masonic Week, but beginning in 2004, the new Sovereign Grand Commanders of both Scottish Rite jurisdictions began to attend as part of an effort to promote Masonic unity and lessen the feelings of competition that some Masons have felt between the Scottish and York Rites.

Masonry is a network of networks, and Masonic Week is a networker's dream. Two informal lunches during the week bring together Masons who share membership on e-mail lists and who know each other from their online contact. Local D.C.-area lodges also hold special banquets and events to attract the visiting Masons. If one wants to command or already commands a leadership position in certain Masonic circles, Masonic Week is the place to be.

Still, if plans are being hatched in those annual meetings and hospitality suites, they are not plans for world domination or for the worship of alien gods. They are the intraorganizational plans of the most active Masons, who love their fraternity and worry that it may be too old-fashioned for a hurry-up world. They are plans for the upcoming year within specific Masonic groups, not marching orders for the world economy.

The men here may constitute a formidable old-boy network of York Rite leaders who enjoy the prestige of their inclusion in exclusive groups. But it is a status earned by years of leadership in meetings, rituals, charities, and projects. Without their efforts, the actual treasures that Freemasonry *does* protect—the emotional power of its degrees, the mystery that unfolds for its initiates, the intellectual stimulation of its symbols and mythos—might well have been lost during Masonry's leanest years.

Shortly before his death, Martin Luther King Jr. gave a sermon on what he called "the drum major instinct," the all-pervasive human need for recognition and distinction. In the sermon, King—who was the son of a Prince Hall Mason—made a telling observation:

> Now the presence of the drum major instinct is why so many people are "joiners." You know, there are some people who just join everything. And it's really a quest for attention and recognition and importance. And they get names that give them that impression. So you get your groups, and they become the "Grand Patron," and the little fellow who is henpecked at home needs a chance to be the "Most Worthy of the Most Worthy" of something.[23]

In King's view the drum-major instinct wasn't inherently bad, but it needed to be shaped and redirected away from purely selfish ends and toward a striving for greatness in love, generosity, and moral excellence. One could best achieve greatness in the act of serving others. At the same time that King was teasing the Masons present in his congregation that day, he was also reminding them to stay true to values that Masonry encourages:[24] To lead is to serve. Don't just seek the lofty title, but shoulder the responsibility that comes with it.

The Masonic Knights Templar no longer hold public processions through major urban thoroughfares, and it may be just as well. This is not a historic juncture at which it is helpful or advisable to publicly emulate those earlier Western crusaders who occupied the Temple Mount in Jerusalem and fought pitched battles with Muslim foes. Where the Masonic Templar leadership *can* still play a leading role, as can the leadership across the whole panoply of Masonic orders and rites, is in helping guide and protect those pilgrims making their *symbolic* journey to the East—in this case, Masons wending their way toward the interior temple at the heart of the Craft. It is to this journey embodied in Freemasonry's rituals that we will now turn our attention.

From Darkness to Light, *a color print from 1908, published by the M. W. Hazen Company of New York. The scenes and symbols depicted here are mostly referred to in the three Masonic degree rituals, with a couple of extras thrown in for good measure, such as the two angels.*

6

Secret Rites and Rituals

What Do Masons Do?

N o matter how much one delves into the questions surrounding the origins of Masonry or studies the endless details of Masonic history, the answer to the question of what Masons actually *do* is likely to remain elusive to anyone who isn't a Mason.

Typically, Masons are happy to brag about their charities or earnestly assert that they "take good men and make them better"—a rather smug motto that alludes to Masonry's character-building virtues. But when the subject is raised as to what goes on behind the closed doors of the lodge room, things can get a little . . . vague.

"It's a secret" is not a very satisfying answer, nor is "I can't tell you"—not least because neither is really true. The Masonic penchant for secrecy—originally rooted in medieval customs of protecting trade secrets—evolved in the speculative era into an amorphous "secrecy for secrecy's sake." This secrecy may have been crucial in periods when Masons were attacked by the Inquisition or the Nazis, but its purpose has been less clear in open societies such as North America's.

Many Masons, not being sure of what is supposed to be secret and what isn't, have simply clammed up altogether. This mystique of secrecy has led many anti-Masons of a paranoid bent to assume that behind those doors Masons are performing diabolical rituals and conniving together to enact a New World Order for their own benefit.

Such suspicions are hard to allay, as many Masons have discovered to their chagrin when they've tried to explain that nothing nefarious is actually taking place.

"Oh, that just means that you don't have access to what's *really* going on," their critics insist. "The Masonic big shots keep average Masons like you in the dark."

In order to head off such fruitless exchanges, one San Francisco Mason of my acquaintance has taken to laughing fiendishly whenever someone tells him that the Masons are secretly running the world: "Heh, heh, heh! How *did* you find out? Care to join us?"

This same Mason, who likes to dress in a dapper black suit, black shirt, and black fedora, once had another strange encounter of a Masonic kind.

One evening he stopped by his favorite watering hole, dressed in his usual attire, and took a spot near the end of the bar. He soon became aware of an old Italian gentleman at a table farther back giving him a sustained hostile stare, for no apparent reason. Soon after, the old man got up to leave and in walking past muttered loudly, "You don't know so much!"

He then stopped to talk with a friend of the Mason's farther down the bar. A few minutes later, the Mason felt a right hand come snaking around his shoulder to shake his hand. It was the old man.

"Our friend tells me you're a Mason," the gent said. "I'm Mafiosi. Same t'ing."

Momentarily struck speechless, the Mason shook his hand and began to explain, "No, they're really *not* the same thing." But the old man cut him off with a conspiratorial grin. "You know what I mean," he insisted, and then left, disappearing into the night.

Once again we find ourselves at the recurring nexus of secrecy and power. Even if the kinship between the Masons and the Mafia was a figment of the imagination of an isolated wise guy—and I would argue that it was—the fact that they both take a vow of secrecy and of group loyalty is bound to raise suspicions. And it has, as we've already seen.

This brings us to the heart of the Masonic puzzle: why all the secrecy? With organized crime or intelligence agencies or terrorist cells, secrecy is essential to allow clandestine activities to proceed without exposure. Is it entirely a surprise, then, if similar motives are attributed to Masonry?

Masonic leaders are usually at pains to clarify that "Freemasonry is not a secret society—it is a society with secrets," a distinction that will be lost on most people. Alternatively, they suggest that it should be viewed as merely a "private" society. This suggestion is not without merit as the actual day-in, day-out secrecy required of Masons is considerably less than that required of an average employee at a large corporate facility.

Masons don't have to wear photo IDs around their necks, punch in number codes to enter their lodge rooms, or shred confidential documents. The Tyler—the man who guards the lodge-room door with a sword—is largely symbolic; he is invariably a longtime member of the lodge, probably in his seventies or eighties, and his sword of office would be hard-pressed to even cut cheese cubes.

And yet, a vow of secrecy does lie at the heart of the "obligation" to which every Mason swears as he goes through the degree rituals. This warrants some investigation.

Professor Hugh Urban, in analyzing American Freemasonry, has suggested that its secrecy has less to do with the *content* of its secrets than with the status conferred by having a secret in the first place, both in its own subculture and in the culture at large. For Urban, Masonic secrets constitute a kind of "symbolic capital"—"a rare, scarce and highly valued commodity." The possession of these secrets serves both to differentiate the Mason from the outsider and to locate the Mason within an organizational pecking order—with the "higher" degrees of Masonic bodies such as the Scottish Rite supposedly having more status than the three basic degrees conferred at the local blue lodge.[1]

This is an intriguing analysis, but it misses the boat in several ways. First, an emphasis on secrecy was part of operative masonic custom even in the 1500s, long before there were "higher" degrees and even before there was apparently much in the way of philosophical or symbolic knowledge to possess within Masonry. Secrecy on the part of operative masons protected their trade secrets, and the secret "Mason's Word," taught only to initiates, served to winnow out interlopers, particularly "cowans"—stonemasons who had not gone through the customary guild channels—who would stand out by not knowing the word when challenged to give it.

Second, the idea that the higher degrees (and the supposed knowledge they impart) hoist their possessor higher up a hierarchical totem pole is largely mistaken. Hierarchies there may be in present-day Masonry, but they are not predictably linear or centralized, as we've seen.

And last, the possession of secrets confers status in the world at large only if the world considers those secrets to be valuable or desirable. The sausage maker may possess the secret of what goes into a sausage, but that's a secret that most of us would rather not know.

However, I would suggest that the secrecy within Masonry, at this point, serves a different purpose altogether—one that will become clearer if we first return to our original question: what do Masons do? In order to answer that, I will briefly take the reader through the process of becoming a Mason and receiving the degrees—the same process that I, and millions like me, have undergone.

Three Knocks at the Door

What might a would-be Mason find in first encountering Freemasonry? It is a little-known fact that Masons are forbidden to solicit new members. This seems like a curious policy for *any* organization, much less one that has seen its numbers shrink in recent decades to less than half of what they once were. The official reason for this policy is that new members are supposed to join "of their own free will and accord," as Masonic ritual phrases it. Freemasonry considers itself a potentially lifetime commitment and not something to be entered into lightly or because of someone's cajoling.[2]

In its heyday, interest in Masonry spread through word of mouth, and there was rarely a lack of applicants. In more recent times, with membership declining, the strictness of the "no solicitation" rule has been loosened in many locales to allow grand lodges to advertise and encourage inquiries. Nevertheless, anyone who harbors a grudge that they've never been invited to join has things backward. The interested applicant must make the first step.

Voluntarily applying ("petitioning") for membership is only the first of several requirements. All candidates must also believe in a supreme being (although their specific religion is usually not an issue) and in an afterlife. This requirement of a belief in Deity is optional in some European lodges such as the Grand Orient of France, but it is considered essential in British and American grand lodges. Masonry, while not overtly religious, does assume a generic nonsectarian spiritual outlook, and outright atheists or agnostics would soon find themselves at odds with the statements, prayers, and biblical references that are a part of traditional Masonic rituals.

Other requirements screen out applicants with a criminal record, those under eighteen (or under twenty-one in some jurisdictions), those in serious financial straits, and those whose spouses object to Masonry. In many states, an applicant (and his wife, if he is married) will be visited by as many as three lodge members (either together or separately) who are prepared to answer any questions the prospective member may have and who come equipped with a list of questions of their own. As one vintage manual for members of such investigating committees put it:

If the applicant is received into Masonry, it is a favor bestowed. No man has a right to become a Freemason. Only honorable men should be made Masons, and only those worthy of the friendship of yourself and your family.[3]

This all may seem quaintly stringent and possibly elitist, but the practical reason for such caution is that Masonry basically takes in men who are often strangers to each other and tries to encourage a sense of brotherhood and cooperation between them. Trust is central to this effort, and a lodge wants to be sure of the honesty and stability of its potential members.

If a candidate receives a favorable report from the investigating committee, his application will be voted on by the lodge in a secret ballot. If it is accepted by unanimous vote, the candidate will move on to the next stage: receiving the three degrees.

As mentioned earlier, these degrees parallel those of the medieval guilds, and are called by similar names: Entered Apprentice (first degree), Fellow Craft (second degree), and Master Mason (third degree). Each degree features a specific ritual through which the candidate is led. The rituals, which can be quite moving, impart lessons or teachings that build on each other to provide an orientation in Masonry. Each ritual includes an obligation that the candidate must willingly swear to. These obligations largely consist of vows of confidentiality and of a stated intent to abide by Masonic ideals. Symbolic penalties are invoked should the vows be violated, but the only real penalty for behavior "unbecoming a Mason" is to be expelled from the order.

The penalties referred to in each degree have been the object of considerable misunderstanding among critics of Masonry, who take them to be punishments enacted upon Masons who break their oaths. Rather, they are a slightly more graphic equivalent of vowing "Cross my heart and hope to die"—a symbol of the seriousness of one's vow, *not* a penalty that will actually have to be paid. A similar promise can be found in Psalm 138:5–6. "If I forget you, O Jerusalem, let my right hand wither, let my tongue cleave to the roof of my mouth, if I do not remember you. . . ."

The rituals do something more than merely impart lessons or underscore commitment, however. When properly performed, they provide an initiatory experience that can have deep ramifications within the unconscious psyche of the candidate.

The Ritual

Ritual is, unfortunately, a word that has been rendered suspect in this day and age. Those who fail to see its value are happy to refer to "mindless" or "meaningless" ritual, as if anything that is done repeatedly in the same way is inevitably empty and boring. Others, who ascribe too much power to the word, mutter about "ritual abuse"—linking ritual with paranoid notions of satanic rites or child abuse. Both approaches totally miss the mark.

A ritual is nothing more or less than a ceremony of symbolic actions that has meaning for those who participate in it or witness it. Cultural anthropologists point to "rites of passage"—such as weddings, bar mitzvahs, and christenings—that mark transition points in people's lives. The Masonic degree rituals serve as rites of passage for men who are ready to move from the chronic isolation and fragmentation of modern life into a community based on "brotherly love, relief, and truth," as one version of the third-degree ritual puts it. As initiations, they mark a new beginning that is symbolically deepened with each degree ritual.[4]

Each of the three degrees is performed in the lodge room—a room especially arranged for ritual purposes. The scholar Mircea Eliade, in his book *The Sacred and the Profane*, describes the recurring features found in "men's houses" in New Guinea, and in the sacred lodges among the Algonquin and Sioux Indians. He notes:

> Their sacred lodge, where initiations are performed, represents the universe. The roof symbolizes the dome of the sky, the floor represents earth, the four walls the four directions of cosmic space. . . . In extremely varied cultural contexts, we constantly find the same cosmological schema and the same ritual scenario.[5]

Interestingly enough, the Masonic lodge room matches this pattern almost exactly, including the ceiling as sky, and the four cosmic directions proceeding out from the center of the room. The mythic model for the Masonic lodge room is the Temple of Solomon—the archetypal sacred temple of the Most High. This temple was originally built to house the sanctum sanctorum, or holy of holies—the dwelling place of the Most High.

Although the Masons make no official claim such as this for their own lodges, the psychological effect of such a meeting place is that of a "sacred space" set apart from the "profane" daily world of commerce and mundane matters. Words that are spoken in such a space are amplified in their effect upon the candidate, and upon the minds of the members joining in the ritual.[6]

One possible interpretation of this combined effect of lodge, special space, and ritual is that it creates a subconscious template of Solomon's Temple within the candidate's psyche. In first going through the rituals, and in later helping to perform them for other candidates, the Mason is reminded that within him is a kind of holy of holies—a point of potential contact with the sacred. Although the motif is that of a biblical temple, it works sufficiently well as a universal symbol to speak to men of any religion.

The Journey Begins

The candidate starts his symbolic journey at the entrance to the lodge in the West and finally arrives, with the assistance of his guide, in the East—the place of the rising sun, the source of light. For the Mason, light is the great symbol of knowledge: a greater awareness of the sacred and of oneself.

This prominence of light as a recurring Masonic symbol has led some fundamentalist critics to accuse Masonry of worshipping the sun or Lucifer, and of substituting the light of Masonry for Jesus Christ, "the light of the world." But this ignores the frequent use of light as a more generalized symbol of knowledge and goodness throughout history and all over the globe. Moreover, there is nothing to prevent a Christian Mason from interpreting "light" as referring to Jesus Christ if he so wishes.

Traditionally, before a new member can proceed from one degree to the next, he must commit to memory a catechism reviewing the movements, lessons, and vows of the ritual he has just undergone. He often memorizes this with the help of another lodge member who serves as a coach and with whom he meets for oral instruction, as most of the ritual is still not allowed to be written or printed.

Such secrecy might seem silly or irrelevant—the rituals have, in fact, seen print in numerous "exposures" over the years—but the effect of this emphasis on memorization is to fix the rituals even deeper in the candidate's unconscious mind. Typically, a candidate must demonstrate to the lodge his "proficiency" in the catechism before moving on to the next degree.

In some Masonic jurisdictions, "cipher books" may be used as aids to memorization. These usually employ a set of abbreviations and symbols to transcribe the ritual in encoded form. In British Masonry and other non-U.S. lodges, much more of the ritual may be found in printed "monitors" than is common in U.S. lodges. Requirements of memorization vary considerably from grand lodge to grand lodge. Increasingly, such requirements are being minimized or, in some cases, eliminated altogether. By contrast, in some European lodges, a candidate must write a paper on some aspect of the degree he has just taken, demonstrating some understanding of what he has undergone, before he is allowed to continue.

The values that Masonry inculcates in its degrees border on the cliché—such old-fashioned virtues as faith, hope, and charity; brotherly love, relief, and truth; temperance, fortitude, prudence, and justice. These are not really any different from the moral virtues advocated by most religions. But through their ritual repetition in regularly performed degrees and through the heightened impact of their inculcation within the sacred space of the lodge, these ideals may stand a better chance of bearing fruit in a Mason's life.

Inside the Lodge

When I first considered applying to become a Mason, I read everything that I could find about what to expect. Between the Internet and published books, I found plenty, including detailed descriptions of the three degree rituals by Christopher Knight and Robert Lomas in their bestseller, *The Hiram Key,* and word-for-word scripts for the degrees in exposures reprinted from the 19th century, such as *Duncan's Ritual of Freemasonry.*[7] I didn't want to undergo anything that I would find objectionable, so some prior research seemed in order. Yet when I took the degrees, I found that they differed in certain details from what I had read—especially from the accounts of Knight and Lomas. What was going on?

Eventually I discovered a curious but little-known fact: there are literally dozens of variations on the basic three degree rituals in use around the world. Knight and Lomas's account, for instance, described the degrees as performed in English lodges using one of the six ritual versions approved by the United Grand Lodge of England. The rituals that I underwent were those approved by the Grand Lodge of California—a different Masonic jurisdiction and a different ritual.

This kind of variation is the end result of an oral tradition wherein ritual wording was memorized and passed from mouth to ear instead of being officially written down. As with the telephone game, if you have enough oral intermediaries, the final message can vary considerably from the original. In light of this phenomenon, it is impressive that the core rituals of each degree, as preserved in dozens of grand lodges, have retained as many elements in common as they have.

The following summary of the degrees draws upon the rituals as performed in one particular grand lodge, and so, as with any such account, it is not a precise template of Masonic ritual everywhere, nor is it meant to be.[8]

The Journey from West to East

Prior to each degree ritual, the candidate is placed in a preparation room adjacent to the lodge room. He is told to dress in the special ritual garb that is provided, to remove any metal objects from his body, such as rings and watches, and to wait there until summoned.

When the candidate is thus prepared and the officers in the lodge room have finished the ritual opening of the lodge, the Stewards (the two most junior officers of the lodge) are sent to accompany the candidate as he knocks three times on the door to the lodge room. The candidate is blindfolded ("hoodwinked" in Masonic jargon), both to heighten the ritual experience and to minimize his view of an open lodge should he change his mind in the middle of the ritual. He also has a ropelike cord (called a "cable-tow") tied around his body, in a different location for each degree, which symbolizes his new ties to the fraternity.

Upon hearing the knocks, the Worshipful Master (the presiding officer of the lodge) directs the Senior Deacon to see who is at the door. Following a series of questions directed to the candidate, which are answered with the aid of the Senior Steward, the candidate is admitted to the lodge room.

What follows is roughly the same in each degree with only slight variations: the Senior Deacon accompanies and guides the blindfolded candidate in circumambulating the lodge room as a biblical passage is read. The candidate and Senior Deacon then appear before the three main lodge officers (Junior Warden, Senior Warden, and Master), who address their own set of questions to the candidate.

Diagram of lodge room, officers, and general pattern of candidate's circumambulation during degrees: (1, 2, 3, 4) stages of the journey; (5) preparation room; (6) anteroom; (11) altar; (12) Treasurer; (13) Secretary; (14) Senior Deacon; (15) Worshipful Master; (16) Junior Warden; (17, 18) Junior and Senior Stewards; (19) Senior Warden; (20) Junior Deacon; (21) Tyler

The candidate is then taught a few symbolic movements and stances related to the particular degree he is taking. Finally, the candidate is brought to the altar in the middle of the room to take his "obligation" (a vow of confidentiality and responsibility), which he does while kneeling, with his hands upon the holy scriptures of his faith. This is similar to swearing on a Bible to tell the truth in a courtroom.

Once he has done this, his blindfold and cable-tow are removed, and he is taught the "sign" (gesture), "grip" (handshake), and password of the degree. The candidate is tested by the Junior and Senior Wardens to make sure that he has learned the movements and signs correctly.

Next, the candidate is taught how to wear his apron in a fashion indicating whether he is an Entered Apprentice, Fellow Craft, or Master Mason. (The apron, commonly made of white lambskin, harks back to stonemasons' aprons, worn to protect their clothes while working.) He then receives a brief explanation of the symbolic meaning of the "working tools" for this degree.

Once all this has been completed, the candidate is directed back to the preparation room to remove the ritual garb and to dress again in his street clothes. In the first and second degrees, he is then brought back into the lodge, where he receives lectures on Masonic symbolism and on the meaning and significance of various parts of the ritual. These are followed by a "charge"—a brief exhortation to live up to the lodge's standards and to follow the teachings that he has been given.

In the third degree, the candidate returns to the lodge room, where he participates in a short drama that reenacts the story of the tragic death of the Grand Master Hiram Abiff—a mythic figure said to have overseen the building of King Solomon's Temple in ancient Jerusalem.

In this drama, the candidate takes on the role of Hiram Abiff, who is confronted by three disgruntled temple workmen (known as the "ruffians"), who try to get him to reveal "the secrets of a Master Mason," which he refuses to do. He is then symbolically slain, buried, rediscovered, and "raised" to his feet again. Once the candidate has assumed his own identity, he learns that the "Master's Word" is now lost, due to Hiram Abiff's untimely death, and he is given a substitute word in its place, as the password of this degree.[9]

That's It?

Described in this fashion, the degree rituals may sound rather hokey and repetitive and much ado about nothing. And to be perfectly honest, if the rituals are performed in a halfhearted or incompetent manner, the effect can be underwhelming. On the other hand, when well performed, with each officer knowing his part by heart, the rituals can take on an almost timeless quality that is deeply affecting. The actual "experience" of the degrees, both by the candidate and by the performing officers, is not captured in any summary or even in the reading of a full ritual exposure.

It was my good fortune to join a lodge that prided itself on performing excellent ritual, and there was something very touching in realizing that these men, some of whom had been Masons for as long as fifty years, had gone to the trouble of practicing these rituals and delivering whole lectures from memory, all for the sake of giving candidates—including me—a memorable initiation. Further, the realization that generation after generation of Masons had been doing this for some three hundred years or more established a palpable link with the past, a sense of roots that is scarce in today's attention-deficient culture.

It is an awareness of these subtle qualities attached to the initiatory degrees of Masonry that has caused many Masons to decline to discuss them publicly. Oaths of secrecy aside, the experience of initiation into the Brotherhood has an ineffable aspect that simply cannot be described.

No doubt there will be Masons who feel that I've already said too much, but my intention here is neither to break my obligations (which I don't believe I have done) nor to spoil the experience for those who might wish to become Masons. My goal is to provide the reader with an overview sufficient to gain an understanding of Freemasonry as a

The third ruffian dispatching Grand Master Hiram Abiff as depicted in an "exposure" of the Masonic rituals

whole. With that in mind, let's consider the mythic character in the third-degree ritual: Grand Master Hiram Abiff.

Calling All Hirams

Through his participation in the third-degree ritual, every candidate symbolically becomes, for a short span, Hiram Abiff, the grand master of all the masons working to build the great Temple of Solomon. It is doubtful that there was ever such a person, historically speaking, but as with most mythic stories, literal history is hardly the point. Hiram represents a kind of exemplar of a Mason who has honed his own skills and developed his potential to the fullest, becoming, in this case, the greatest Mason overseeing the construction of the holiest temple ever built.[10]

According to the degree's story, Hiram is one of three leaders collaborating on the building of the Temple, the other two being King Solomon and King Hiram of Tyre. All three together possess the Master's Word, but it can be communicated only when all three are present. At this juncture, it is not exactly clear what function the Master's Word serves, but it is seemingly at the heart of "the secrets of a Master Mason."

To make things even more mysterious, according to the degree's story line, there are fifteen disgruntled fellow craft workers on the Temple who plot to wrest those secrets from Hiram—ostensibly so that they can receive the higher wages of a master mason when traveling in foreign countries, although it is pretty apparent that money is not the main issue here. Three of the fifteen fellow crafts, three ruffians named Jubela, Jubelo, and Jubelum, successively waylay Hiram at the south, west, and east gates of the Temple as he tries to leave the premises after offering a noontime prayer. Failing to gain the secrets, each ruffian attempts to kill Hiram, and Jubelum, the roughest of the lot, finally dispatches Hiram with a blow to the head from a setting maul—a mason's hammer used to set stones in place.

Eventually the ruffians bury Hiram in a shallow grave on Mount Moriah and flee. In due course, a search party finds the grave, the culprits are brought to justice, and the two kings try to "raise" (or lift) Hiram from his grave so that the body can be reburied in a more suitable place. On the third attempt they succeed, and once the candidate is pulled to a standing position, he assumes his own identity and is taught the substitute word for the lost Master's Word.

Much can be read into this ritually enacted story, and numerous Masonic books and articles have analyzed it from every possible angle. No official Masonic interpretation of the parable is offered, and each Mason's meditation on its possible meanings is part of his Masonic "work." Anti-Masonic Christians have been sure that Hiram's death and "raising" are a tawdry Masonic replacement for the Easter story of Christ's death and resurrection. Alternative historians Knight and Lomas suggested that the story memorializes in veiled form the murder of an ancient Egyptian king, Seqenenre Tao II, although they later seem to have switched to a theory that Hiram actually represents James, the brother of Jesus.[11]

However, there is no certain indication in Masonic records that the Hiram story was part of the degree rituals before the founding of the premier Grand Lodge in 1717, and it may not have appeared for another dozen or so years after that. Trying to track down the Hiram ritual's origins flings us into endless speculation; thus it will be more worthwhile to make some observations about its effect upon the candidate and that effect's relationship to secrecy.[12]

As a psychodrama, the Hiram portion of the third degree places the candidate in the shoes of the most accomplished and upright Mason—one who possesses "the secrets of a Master Mason" and who withdraws to pray alone in the sanctum sanctorum each day[13]—and then has him repeatedly refuse to divulge those secrets (whatever they may be) to the unworthy, even to the point of death.

Just as the sacred space of the lodge furnishes a template for the candidate's "inner temple," so does his assumption of the identity and courage of the mythic grand master provide a template for his highest self, the "builder" of that inner sanctum within.

In a generic and nondenominational manner, the first two degrees launch the candidate upon a path of spiritual growth by underscoring the ideals of self-restraint, forthright behavior, and compassion toward others. The third degree then drives it home by giving the new Mason a ritual trial run in staying true to his ideals and his inner life, even if it means dying for those principles.

Is this reading too much into the Hiram story? Especially if it was first formulated and promulgated during the heyday of the Enlightenment—a time often thought of as one challenging religion and championing science? Perhaps. Yet both the Renaissance and the Enlightenment encouraged and affirmed the integrity of the individual's quest for knowledge and spiritual authenticity. The rituals of Freemasonry appear to reinforce this quest and make it something that can be experienced by everyday men.

In doing this, Freemasonry is not setting itself up as a rival religion as much as it is trying to provide an additional affirmation of the essential spiritual impulse that might be said to reside in everyone.

It may well be that Freemasonry's endurance through the centuries derives from its allegiance to this impulse, no matter how formularized or veiled by metaphor. The initiation it provides is not into a new religious belief system or set of dogmas, but into a quest for self-discipline and self-knowledge—qualities necessary for any spiritual path. Perhaps this inner work, and the integrity that it requires, make up the true "secrets of a Master Mason" that others are unable to steal and that the Mason should not betray. If so, this would provide one answer to the question of why Freemasonry has made such an issue of maintaining its secrecy: it provides a protected space in which men can risk the kind of vulnerability that comes from trying to care about and support each other as brothers.

An engraved certificate, suitable for framing, presented to a 32nd-degree member of the Ancient and Accepted Scottish Rite (Northern Masonic Jurisdiction) in 1907. While this looks impressive, one should keep in mind that nearly every Mason who joined the Scottish Rite became a 32nd° and received one of these. Such certificates are no longer issued, and old ones have become collectors' items.

7

Out of the Blue

A Look at the "Higher" Degrees

asonry's greatest mystery—the one at the very heart of the Master Mason ritual of the third degree—revolves around the death of Grand Master Hiram Abiff. As we just saw, the mythic story recounts his treacherous murder at the hands of three fellow craft ruffians, their burial of his body in a shallow grave on nearby Mount Moriah, and the ruffians' flight into hiding. A search party discovers the body and happens upon the ruffians, capturing them and returning them to King Solomon for judgment.

The tale concludes with three attempts by King Solomon and King Hiram of Tyre to "raise" or lift Hiram Abiff from the shallow grave so that he can be more properly buried at the Temple. The first two attempts fail, but the kings succeed on the third attempt, and, since the Master's Word is now lost, a substitute word is given to the new Master Mason, supposedly consisting of the first word (or words) spoken upon Hiram's raising.

This substitute, of which there are numerous variations, is not a recognizable word in any known language, but rather an enunciation of two or three syllables that some scholars have hypothesized is a corruption of a Hebrew phrase meaning "The builder is smitten."[1]

This would seem to be a very odd way for the story to end, and herein lies the mystery. Why go through the whole drama of having the candidate portray Hiram Abiff defending "the secrets of a Master Mason" when, at the drama's conclusion, he is not given any secrets worth defending—just a substitute for the Master's Word?

The degree ends with Hiram dead, the Temple unfinished, and the Master's Word lost. Given the preceding buildup, that's very anticlimactic. Dramatically speaking, the third degree cries out for a sequel or some kind of completion that will tie up these loose ends. It should not be surprising, then, that Masonry has come up with at least two responses to the third degree's abrupt ending.

The first is the suggestion that the rest of the Freemason's journey after he takes the third degree—his search for "more light"—is an ongoing work of completion. Solomon's Temple still needs finishing, and in working on himself ("learning to keep his passions within due bounds," as one lecture describes it), the Mason is taking up where Hiram Abiff left off. As the conclusion of one version of the third-degree lecture urges, in grand rhetorical fashion:

> Hence, my brother, how important it is that we should endeavor to imitate [Grand Master Hiram Abiff] in his truly exalted and exemplary character, in his unfeigned piety to God, and in his inflexible fidelity to his trust, that we may be prepared to welcome death, not as a grim tyrant, but as a kind messenger sent to translate us from this imperfect, to that all perfect, glorious, and celestial Lodge above, where the Supreme Grand Master of the Universe forever presides.[2]

The second response to the unfinished tale—one not as homiletic—has been to "complete" the myth with additional degrees that dramatize finding the lost Word and that supply additional details of the Temple story. In this way, the very nature of the third degree—its sudden ending and the tragic loss of its crucial secret (or secrets)—can be said to have inspired the creation of further degrees.

One informed estimate has put the number of additional Masonic degrees at 1,100, most of them invented over the course of the 18th century.[3] French and German Masons were particularly prone to this pastime, and the traditions and symbols of Rosicrucianism, alchemy, Kabbalah, and every other esoteric and mystical system under the sun were plundered in an effort to give the "higher" degrees some secrets worth finding.

A good number of these degrees—some of which had accompanying rituals, and some of which did not—were probably never actually performed and merely led a paper existence. For instance, one higher-degree order, the Rite of Mizraim, had as many as ninety degrees. But you can be sure that the members of the rite who sported a 90° after their name found neither the time nor the participants to enact all ninety degree rituals along the way. Rather, they likely paid their initiation fee, received a diploma and title as a 90°, and perhaps, if they were lucky, received a written copy of the rituals to read at their leisure.[4]

We'll have more to say about such Masonic diploma mills, but for now let's look at the actual degrees of the York and Scottish Rites, starting with the most celebrated of the York Rite's degrees, the Royal Arch.

The Royal Arch

It is still a matter of considerable dispute as to how old the Royal Arch degree really is. The first printed reference to it as a distinct degree appears in 1743, more than twenty-five years after the founding of the premier Grand Lodge in 1717.[5] However, this was also a decade *before* the creation of the Antients' Grand Lodge circa 1751–53, so there may be some substance to the Antients' position that in promoting this fourth degree they were actually preserving earlier Masonic traditions from neglect by the "Moderns."[6]

One theory that has been bandied about posits that the Royal Arch was originally part of a more complete third-degree ritual but was severed from it at some point and thereafter conferred as a separate degree. This seems unlikely, however, as not only is the Royal Arch ritual drama set in a wholly different era from that of the Hiram story, but the combined length of the Hiram and Royal Arch dramas would have taxed the endurance of both the candidates and the officers performing the ritual.

In brief summary, the Royal Arch degree takes place at the time of Zerubbabel's rebuilding of the Jewish Temple circa 500 BCE in Jerusalem, nearly five hundred years after the time of King Solomon and

Hiram Abiff. The degree ritual calls for three candidates, who depict three Hebrew stonemasons who have been released from captivity in Babylon and make a long and arduous journey back to Jerusalem in order to offer their services in rebuilding King Solomon's Temple.

Upon reaching Jerusalem, they come to the Hebrew Tabernacle, where they must pass through a series of four veils, each with its own guardian and passwords, in order to reach the grand council in the inner sanctum. Eventually, their services are accepted and they are set to work. In clearing the ruins of the old Temple they come upon a half-buried stone that serves as the capstone (or keystone) for an underground arched vault. They remove it and take it back to the grand council, which identifies it as the keystone of an arch built by Hiram Abiff.

The three workmen return to the rubble and forge an entrance into the vault. The first worker who descends into it finds three artifacts, which the grand council identifies as the jewels of the three original grand masters (King Solomon, King Hiram of Tyre, and Hiram Abiff). Again descending into the vault, another worker discovers a strange ornate box resting upon a pedestal, which the grand council is initially unable to identify. This box contains several artifacts, including a pot of manna, Aaron's rod, and a scroll comprising the long-lost sacred Book of the Law (Torah). After some consideration, the grand council decides that this curious box is a copy of the original Ark of the Covenant.[7]

Retrieving the replica of the Ark of the Covenant in the Royal Arch degree as cavalierly depicted in a Masonic "exposure" of the early 1800s. Some Royal Arch chapters utilized trapdoors and lower chambers to emulate the experience of the story. Most did not.

Atop the Ark is a triangle of gold in which is inscribed in Hebrew the Ineffable Name of the deity. This is the Master's Word that had been lost with the death of Hiram Abiff and has now been recovered.[8] (Another degree in the York Rite, that of Select Master, explains that these treasures, including the Master's Word, were originally hidden in the secret chamber beneath the First Temple before Hiram's murder, to safeguard them should tragedy befall the Temple or its builders.)

The three candidates are then taught a method for saying the Master's Word, which can be done only by three individuals gathered together, each saying in turn one syllable of the Word. This explains in retrospect why the Word was considered lost when Hiram Abiff was killed. The remaining two grand masters (King Solomon and Hiram, King of Tyre) could not utter the complete Word on their own.

Again, as with any summary of a ritual or drama, this description absolutely fails to capture the dramatic impact or psychological experience of undergoing the degree itself. Yet we can see several ways in which the Royal Arch degree provides a form of completion for the third degree.

First, the formerly solo candidate is now one of three companions undergoing the degree. This underscores the sense that he is now part of a group undertaking a challenging journey together, which helps anchor his experience of brotherhood.

Second, the companions are allowed, step by step, veil by veil, to enter the inner chamber of the tabernacle—a possibility that was only hinted at in previous degrees.

And third, the lost Word is recovered. However, this doesn't exactly wrap things up in a tidy little package. The recovered Word is, in many ways, as ambiguous and puzzling as the substitute Word given at the end of the Hiram drama, as we shall see.

In the Beginning Was the Word

The legend on which the Royal Arch degree is based appears to date back to a story recorded by a fourth-century Greek Christian named Philostorgius, from whom it was passed down through various church histories, and in a number of variations, to the 17th century. Interestingly enough, in one version of Philostorgius's tale, the story's activities take place in the fourth century CE, when Julian the Apostate gives the Jews permission to rebuild their temple in Jerusalem.

In this version, the workman lowered into the excavated chamber discovers a marvelously preserved book resting on top of a pillar. Upon the book's being brought up and opened, its first words are found to be "In the beginning was the Word, and the Word was with God, and the Word was God." This is, of course, the opening verse of the Gospel of John, and the book turns out to contain the entire Gospel. This miraculous discovery provides a rather pointed Christian rejoinder to the plans to rebuild the Temple.[9]

It seems almost certain that the authors of the Royal Arch ritual derived much of their inspiration from the Philostorgius tale, a version of which was published in London in 1659 in Samuel Lee's *Orbis Miraculum; or, The Temple of Solomon*.[10]

According to Masonic scholar Bernard E. Jones, the phrase "In the beginning was the Word" was "in the early days [of the Royal Arch] the words on the scroll found by the Candidate in the vault," according to old rituals preserved at a lodge in Taunton, U.K.[11] This would suggest that for some Masons the recovered Master's Word was identified with the "Word" of the Gospel of John—that is, Jesus Christ as Logos.[12]

Be that as it may, the recovered Master's Word as currently given in the Royal Arch is a sacred Hebrew name of God, the Tetragrammaton, often romanized as "Yahweh" or "Jehovah." In Jewish tradition, such sacred names are considered too powerful to be pronounced aloud, except under special conditions, and a substitute name is usually employed, such as "Adonai."

In following this pattern, the giving of a substitute word in the Masonic third degree is not so much a cheap trick as it is a possible allusion to this practice of pious substitution. Or at least that is what the Royal Arch drama implies: the "lost" Word was, all along, waiting to be found, having been presciently hidden under the Temple before Grand Master Hiram's death. It was lost and a substitute given because the original conditions for its disclosure were destroyed. Now, under new conditions created by the diligence of the three companions, the Word is once again found.

Yet even this "completion" is paradoxical, for the value of the possession of an unutterable Word—a Sacred Name so holy that it can be spoken only by three men, with each taking a different syllable[13]—is far from clear. The ritual and the degree lecture are mute on this point, merely congratulating the new Royal Arch companions on their recovery of that which was lost. As one version of the lecture puts it, "You have labored long and faithfully and the discovery of the Master's Word is your reward."

It seems unlikely that this Master's Word is the same as the famous "Mason's Word" by which Scottish operative masons recognized each other, especially since the method of conveying the word that is taught in the Royal Arch degree precludes its use by fewer than three men. Indeed, early exposures and catechisms suggest that the Mason's Word used by Scottish Masons for mutual recognition was the word substituted for the Master's Word now associated with the Hiram story.

What, one might ask, does this whole business of words and names and arks hidden beneath the Temple have to do with a bunch of stonemasons, anyhow? *Not much* is the most logical answer, not only because there is no evidence of the Royal Arch dating back to the era of operative masonry, but because the likelihood of stonemasons caring about such matters is slim. Who *would* have cared about them, however, would have been the esoterically minded gentlemen and antiquarians who seem to have been instrumental in shaping speculative Masonry.

A League of Gentlemen

The 17th century in England was marked by intellectual elite circles intrigued with alchemy and Kabbalah (of both Jewish and Christian varieties). A fascination with the trope of Solomon's Temple was also present in such circles. Talmudic commentary and Kabbalistic legends have long spoken of the Ark of the Covenant (and other treasures) supposedly buried beneath the site of the Temple.[14] And one variety of Kabbalistic teachings puts an emphasis on the spiritually potent power of sacred names.[15]

As we've seen before, it is almost impossible to try to make sense of Freemasonry's history and preoccupations without falling prey to speculations and theories based on circumstantial evidence. And even as I note the conjunction of these ideas in 17th-century England, I am forced to admit that there is no clear line of transmission from that century to the 18th, which is when the Hiramic legend and the Royal Arch first appeared in ritual.

It is tempting to hypothesize that just as a circle of esoteric German Protestants in the early 17th century apparently devised the legends of Christian Rozenkreutz, the reputed 15th-century founder of Rosicrucianism, and successfully seeded certain spiritual and political ideas into European culture through the intriguing ruse of issuing manifestos from a mythical society of Rosicrucians, a circle of esoteric Englishmen—fascinated and inspired by the Rosicrucian gambit—might have devised another set of legends involving builders in order to seed a further crop of ideas within the culture.

If this were so—and it is a big *if*—it might account for the great Masonic emphasis on secrecy: it was emphasized not because the secrets were terribly profound or special, but because secrecy is itself fascinating. The Rosicrucian myth seized the imagination of the European elite, in part because the Rosicrucians were ostensibly a hidden order operating in secret. How better to attract the interest of Freemasonry's target audience—which was certainly no longer stonemasons but the aristocracy and the rising bourgeoisie—than to play up the secrecy of the Craft?

The main drawback of this technique is that if you use secrecy to attract members and heighten your image, they're going to expect some decent secrets if and when they join. A gaggle of handshakes and passwords hardly passes muster as secrets worth having. And, at first glance, having the third degree conclude with the loss of "the secrets of a Master Mason" seems like some kind of practical joke.

But what if that was merely a test? "We'll hand the guy a MacGuffin and see how he reacts."[16] Those who took the degrees expecting a big payoff of some kind would decide that there was "no there there," as Gertrude Stein once said of Oakland, and go inactive or seek their treasure elsewhere. But those who "got it," even if they sought no degrees beyond the third, would be those who saw that the initiatory experience and the ideas and values conveyed were what was important and that the secrecy was secondary at best.

In a way, the Royal Arch confirms this perspective, for while it delivers a big helping of Kabbalistic symbolism in addition to the penultimate "secret" of the Sacred Name, it does so in an oblique manner that is like another layer of bafflement: "Now let's hand the guy an Ineffable Name and see how he reacts."

*Two examples of the use of the Tetragrammaton in 17th-century alchemical illustrations.
(Left) Detail from the title page of Oswald Croll's* Basilica Chymica, *1608. The triangle as
the Trinity is surrounded by the celestial hierarchy of angels, archangels, cherubim, and so
on. (Right) Detail from the title page of Andreas Libavius's* Alchymia, *1606. The Ineffable
Name radiating light is crowned by two angels, with the moon and the sun on either side.*

To put it another way, even the recovered Master's Word—a Sacred
Name of God—is just another substitute for the divine reality that it
represents, and a not very secret one at that. Any number of Masonic
medallions, aprons, engravings, and banners have displayed the
Tetragrammaton in a blazing triangle, and at the time of speculative
Masonry's inception, the glyph was commonly found in the mystical
engravings and diagrams of 17th-century esotericists such as Athanasius Kircher, Robert Fludd, and Jacob Böhme.

It seems to me that, in offering the Sacred Name as the now-found
Lost Word, the devisers of the Royal Arch were offering a secret that
could function on two levels. Since the vast majority of Masons taking
the degree could hardly be expected to undertake Kabbalistic studies
that would do the Name justice, the Master's Word could function for
them as a token of the wondrous and awe-inspiring nature of God. In
this way, a cursory receiving of the degree could still point an average
recipient toward attending to his spiritual and ethical life.

For the smaller minority of more esoterically inclined Masons, the
Word and the other symbolism of the degree could serve as confirmation of their mystical orientation and a spur to further study.

As a counterpoint to my suggestion of secrecy as a marketing
device, it should be noted that Kabbalistic tradition underscored the

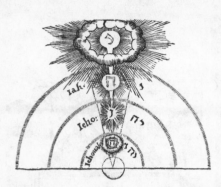

The light of the Divine Name projected into the material depths. (Left) *A Kabbalistic dia-gram from Robert Fludd's* History of the Macrocosm and Microcosm *(1621). In it the Tet-ragrammaton, the Ineffable Name, unfolds through the four worlds.* (Right) *Symbolic design for the Select Master degree of the York Rite. The Ineffable Name casts light down through the nine arches into the crypt containing the Name engraved on a plate of gold.* (The engraving is *from* Cryptic Masonry: A Manual of the Council, *by Albert Mackey [1867].)*

value—indeed, the necessity—of secrecy regarding such powerful mat-ters as Sacred Names. According to this perspective, a Name such as the Tetragrammaton was to be accorded the most profound respect and circumspection, as it was an aperture into sacred realms of unimagi-nable intensity and holiness. If a degree such as the Royal Arch was informed by Kabbalistic principles, secrecy regarding its most essen-tial component would have been intrinsic.

Unfortunately, since we do not know who originally authored the Royal Arch ritual, much less what their intentions may have been, we are left trying to guess causes from effects.

Laurence Dermott, who was instrumental in the founding of the An-tients' Grand Lodge in England and served as its Grand Secretary for many years, called the Royal Arch the "Root, Heart and Marrow of Free Masonry," which reflects the esteem accorded the degree by the Antients. But it is un-certain whether the Antients fully grasped just what they were preserving.

Certain components of the degree (the Sacred Name, the veils, etc.) suggest a strong Kabbalistic influence, but this would almost certainly have been interpreted in a Christian Kabbalistic manner. Subsequent revisions to the ritual, for the purpose of more thoroughly universal-izing it, likely obscured that original orientation.

As far as its later exponents go, it is reasonably clear that Thomas

Smith Webb, the American ritualist most responsible for fashioning the collection of higher degrees in the York Rite into an organized system at the turn of the 19th century, was not inclined toward esoteric or Kabbalistic matters that we know of.

Thus the York degrees in their present form, while little changed since Webb's day, two hundred years ago, may have undergone untracked changes, additions, and deletions while passing through various hands before they came to Webb. Such uncertainty and hidden roots are part of the Masonic inheritance, virtually guaranteeing that no single "correct" interpretation or history will ever win everyone's agreement.

The Rest of the York Degrees

The Royal Arch, as important as it is, is only one of the ten degrees in the York Rite. Most of the remaining degrees flesh out and explain other details of the Hiram and Temple story.

Thus the *Mark Master degree,* which is the first of the York Rite's "higher" degrees, is considered a "completion" of the Fellow Craft degree (the second in the blue lodge). It gives a dramatized illustration of the kind of craftsmanship that would have been expected of operative fellow crafts and completes the promise of wages for work well done that is first broached in the second degree.

The degree derives its name from the practice of operative stonemasons "signing" their work (i.e., carefully chiseled building stones) with individual identifying "marks" unique to each worker. (See accompanying picture on page 136.)

At the completion of the degree, the newly initiated Mark Master is requested to devise his own mark, which is then entered into the records of his Royal Arch Chapter.

In England, the Mark Master degree is deemed sufficiently important that it has its own administrative body, the Mark Grand Lodge, while in Scotland and Ireland, the Mark Master degree is conferred in local blue lodges as an additional degree under the jurisdiction of the grand lodges of those countries.

In the United States, the Mark Master is the first of the four degrees conferred in a Royal Arch Chapter, followed by the Past Master

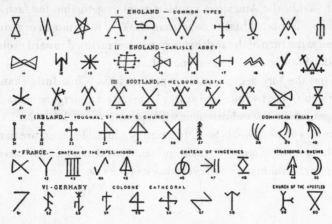

Masons' marks found in various cathedrals, abbeys, and castles. Stonemasons used their marks as personal identifiers to "sign" their work.

degree, the Most Excellent Master degree, and, only once those three have been taken, the Royal Arch degree.

The *Past Master degree*, sometimes referred to as the "virtual" Past Master degree, is a relatively brief degree that goes through the motions of installing the candidate as the Worshipful Master of a lodge. In it the inductee is formally seated "in the East," presented with a gavel, and taught the significance of the gavel knocks with which the Master of a lodge brings the brethren to order at lodge meetings, as well as certain principles of leadership.

In the earliest days of speculative Freemasonry, the only members given the title of Master Mason were those who served as the Worshipful Master of his lodge. His installation as lodge Master generally entailed a short private ritual enacted by other current Masters or Past Masters (i.e., those who previously served as Master). It was only once a Mason had served a term as Worshipful Master that he became eligible to receive the Royal Arch degree. However, this custom gradually fell by the wayside as the number of eligible Past Masters couldn't keep up with the number needed to satisfactorily propagate the Royal Arch. The solution was the (virtual) Past Master degree, which satisfied the formal requirement but could be conferred without the candidate having to actually serve a term as Worshipful Master of a lodge.

The *Most Excellent Master degree,* the third Chapter degree, returns to the time of King Solomon and depicts the completion and dedication of the Temple following the death of Grand Master Hiram Abiff. This brings closure to the interruption in the work on the Temple caused by Hiram's murder. This degree is usually attributed to Thomas Smith Webb, the American ritualist, but it is based on similar degrees in Scotland and England that also served as prerequisites to taking the Royal Arch.[17]

Tales from the Crypt

The next sequence of degrees in the York Rite are the degrees of the Council of Royal and Select Masters, sometimes called the Council of Cryptic Masons. *Cryptic* here refers not to obscure or puzzling, but to the underground crypt(s) referred to in the council's two main degrees.

The degree of *Royal Master* takes the candidate back to when Hiram Abiff was still alive and the Temple under construction. In it, Hiram tells a trusted workman, Adoniram, that he will bury the Master's Word beneath the altar for safekeeping in case anything should befall him before the Temple can be completed.

The degree of *Select Master* follows upon this, allowing the candidate, after tests and challenges, to witness the burial of the reproduction of the Ark, and its accompanying treasures and Master's Word, within the vault or crypt beneath the sanctum sanctorum. This retroactively sets the stage for their discovery in the Royal Arch degree. Were the degrees conferred in a strictly linear timeline, these would have come between the second and third degrees in the blue lodge. However, to do so would have blunted the impact and mystery of Hiram's tragic story in the third degree and undercut the wonder of the discovery in the Royal Arch. As they are presented here, they fill in holes in the story, rounding it out to a satisfying whole.

A third degree, that of *Super Excellent Master,* is also given by the Cryptic Council, but it is often treated as an optional side degree, as it has no direct connection with the other two Council degrees and requires a large cast and considerable stagecraft. It depicts the period when Jerusalem was under siege by King Nebuchadnezzar and the subsequent captivity of the Jews in Babylon.

Sequentially, this would precede the main action in the Royal Arch, which commences with three Jewish companions traveling back from Babylon to Jerusalem to offer their services in rebuilding the Temple.

Following Orders

The last three degrees of the York Rite, conferred within a Knights Templar Commandery, are technically not degrees but "orders" into which the candidate is installed. However, this is a fine point of detail, and for all intents and purposes these follow the same form of ritual found in other degrees.

The first order, the *Illustrious Order of the Red Cross*, forms a bridge between the preceding biblical-era degrees of the Chapter and Council and the chivalric/military orders that follow. In it the candidate portrays Zarubbabel, whose efforts to rebuild the Temple have been impeded. He sets out to try to reach the king of Persia, who had previously promised to enable the rebuilding to proceed. After several challenges, he succeeds in gaining the king's favor and not only obtains his aid for the rebuilding but is inducted into a new knightly order, the Illustrious Order of the Red Cross.

This is, of course, entirely anachronistic, as knights enter the historical stream only millennia later.

Next is the *Order of Malta*, a latter-day re-creation of the crusading order of the Knights Hospitaller. This mostly involves a formal dubbing, an obligation, and a history lecture about the original knights.

Last is the *Order of the Temple*, where the candidate is inducted into the Masonic version of the Knights Templar. This entails a symbolic portrayal of seven years spent as a pilgrim, warrior, and penitent, a scriptural reading of the ordeal of Jesus Christ's last days, memorial libations, and, finally, a dubbing as a Knight Templar. Curiously enough, while the Knights Templar degree is the summit in the American York Rite, with the Order of Malta preceding it, this order is reversed in England. There, the Order of Malta is an invitational honor given only to some Knights Templar.

The Scottish Rite

The degrees of the Scottish Rite parallel, in many instances, those of the York Rite. Just as the York degrees are divided into and overseen by several related bodies (the Chapters, Councils, and Commanderies), so are Scottish Rite degrees overseen by four bodies, although the names of the bodies and the specific degrees they oversee vary between the Northern and Southern Jurisdictions.

In both jurisdictions, nevertheless, the 4th through 14th degrees (known as the Ineffable Degrees) are under the aegis of a body called the Lodge of Perfection. Those eleven degrees are roughly equivalent in subject and teaching to the York Rite's Chapter and Council degrees— that is, they expand upon the Hiram/Solomon myth and provide their own version of the Royal Arch story, culminating in the 13th degree with the recovery of the lost Master's Word, the Ineffable Name of God.

The main difference between the York Rite and Scottish Rite versions of the Royal Arch story is that the Scottish Rite's version refers back to the work on the First Temple, shortly after the death of Hiram Abiff, while the York Rite's version occurs during the building of the Second Temple.

In the Scottish Rite version, while clearing rubble from ancient ruins near the Temple site, three workmen discover a stone with a ring set in it, which when lifted from its place reveals an arched chamber underground. Further exploration reveals a series of nine arched chambers, each going deeper than the last, until within the ninth they find a large agate cube to which is affixed a golden triangle inscribed with the Ineffable Name of God in Hebrew.

This, it turns out, was hidden in the earth by the prophet Enoch, an ancestor of Noah's, following a vision he had of the Name. The workmen take the cube and Name to King Solomon and are rewarded for their bravery and diligence with the knowledge that the inscription on the gold plate is the Lost Word now found.

The 14th degree largely anchors this discovery with a ritual of purification and initiation symbolically taking place within a sacred vault that Solomon has built beneath the Temple in which to house the gold plate and cube. This caps the Solomonic degrees of the Lodge of Perfection.

The next four Scottish Rite degrees are handled differently by the Northern and Southern Jurisdictions. Within the Northern, the 15th and 16th are conferred by the Council of Princes of Jerusalem, while the 17th and 18th are conferred by the Chapter Rose Croix. In the Southern Jurisdiction, all four degrees fall under the control of the Chapter Rose Croix. As far as the degrees themselves go, there is again some similarity to those of the York Rite. The 15th and 16th degrees tell the story of Zerubbabel journeying back to Babylon to seek permission and assistance in

Officers of the Yerba Buena Lodge of Perfection no. 1, circa 1898, San Francisco (founded 1868). A Lodge of Perfection was the Scottish Rite body responsible for overseeing the 4th through 14th degrees. The members shown here were dressed in costumes used in those degrees.

rebuilding the Temple—the same story that is covered by the Illustrious Order of the Red Cross in the York Rite Knights Templar Commandery.

This advances the time sequence of the degrees up to the time of the Second Temple. Another leap in time occurs with the 17th and 18th degrees, which move things up, symbolically, to the Christian Era. The 18th or Rose Croix degree ponders the universal symbolism of the cross and imparts a further significant Word. It would seem, judging from earlier versions of the Rose Croix ritual, that this was originally a specifically Christian degree, and it remains so in England and some other countries. However, the Scottish Rite in the United States, in its commitment to keeping its membership open to men of all faiths, revised and universalized its degrees early in the 19th century, retaining much of the prior symbolism but loosening its interpretation.

The next twelve degrees (the 19th through the 30th), within the Southern Jurisdiction, are conferred by the Council of Kadosh, with the final two degrees (the 31st and 32nd) conferred by the Consistory of Princes of the Royal Secret. Within the Northern Jurisdiction, all degrees from 19th to 32nd are conferred by the Consistory. These degrees have a potpourri of messages, including the defense of political and religious freedom and freedom of thought, and a survey of various ancient mystery traditions and chivalric traditions. The 30th degree, that of Knight Kadosh, could be considered a Knights Templar degree, with the use of the name *Kadosh* ("holy" in Hebrew) instead of *Templar*. It portrays the tests and trials undergone by a candidate for knighthood.

The 32nd degree, that of Prince (or Master) of the Royal Secret, when done in full form, reviews the lessons of all the preceding degrees, aided by representatives of the four Scottish Rite bodies gathered in a symbolic "encampment" of all the degrees. However, in practice, local Scottish Rite Valleys have tended to trim out much of the detail in order to shorten a very long degree into something more presentable.

The "Royal Secret" itself is less of a secret, in the usual sense of the word, than a charge or challenge on how to live one's life. As Scottish Rite scholar Rex Hutchens puts it:

The human is ever interlaced with the Divine, perhaps best expressed in man by the divine gift of reason. When mediated by faith, reason creates that harmony which is, in fact, the Royal Secret itself.[18]

Or at least that is how it is characterized in the Scottish Rite—Southern Jurisdiction, whose degree rituals were overhauled and rewritten in the 1860s by Albert Pike, the Sovereign Grand Commander of the AASR-SJ from 1859 until his death in 1892.

Here again we run into the untidy fact that there is no single uniform Masonry. The 32nd degree and its ritual are distinctly different in the two Scottish Rite jurisdictions, and that goes for all of the AASR degrees. What's more, the staging and scripts of the degrees have been revised and edited—usually to shorten the degrees—in many local Valleys. Hence, Scottish Rite candidates in different Valleys may experience the degrees in radically different ways.[19]

This also means that anti-Masonic critics who rely on "exposures" of Scottish Rite rituals in order to understand the higher degrees are likely wasting their time. For instance, the most prominent such exposure, *Scotch* [sic] *Rite Masonry Illustrated,* actually consists of transcripts of the degrees of the so-called Cerneau Scottish Rite, an irregular rival to the AASR-NMJ that was mainly active in the first half of the 19th century.[20] The rituals there exposed match neither of those used by the two present Scottish Rite jurisdictions in the United States. They may, however, bear some resemblance to the state of the AASR rituals prior to Albert Pike's revisions of them for the Southern Jurisdiction. In a pamphlet, Pike described the state of those rituals thus:

> I have said that the rituals of the degrees of the Ancient and Accepted Scottish Rite, and those of the Rite of Perfection, when I received them, were worthless. I repeat it, excepting the Rose Croix only. They taught a man nothing that he did not know before. They were not impressive in any way. No man of intellect and knowledge could regard them, as literary productions, with any respect. They were trivial, insipid, without originality, contemptible as literary productions, mere collections of flat, dull, commonplace . . .[21]

Elsewhere, he elaborated further:

> The jargon of some of the degrees was as unintelligible as that of the Alchemists, convincing me that their real meaning had been communicated orally and that the rituals were purposefully framed to mislead those into whose hands they might unlawfully fall.[22]

Pike made a mighty effort to rewrite the degrees into something resembling a higher education in comparative religion, philosophy, and ethics, supplemented with a healthy dose of esoteric symbolism and musings. He might have succeeded all too well. His first draft, submitted to the Supreme Council 33° of the AASR-SJ in 1857, was rejected as too abstruse. Subsequent revisions better hit the mark, and Pike was able to funnel some of the degree lectures from his first draft into his formidable compendium *Morals and Dogma,* where they served as additional commentaries upon the degrees.

Morals and Dogma

First published in 1871, *Morals and Dogma* bears the distinction of being the most widely circulated book in Masonic history. From 1872 until 1974, a copy of *M&D,* as it is familiarly known, was given to each member of the Scottish Rite (Southern Jurisdiction). This amounted to well over a million copies in circulation. Though perhaps *given* is not quite the right word, since for much of that time the books bore a notice on the title page saying, in bold capital letters: "ESOTERIC BOOK, FOR SCOTTISH RITE USE ONLY; TO BE RETURNED UPON WITHDRAWAL OR DEATH OF RECIPIENT."

This amounted to a rather forlorn wish on the part of the Scottish Rite that the volume would be restricted to its members only, since it was bound to stir confusion among nonmembers. Unfortunately, this wish was to be doubly defeated, as the book inevitably leaked into the world at large and stirred confusion not only among nonmembers but among members as well.

Morals and Dogma is, by any measure, a difficult book. For years I used to run across copies in used-book stores, where I'd pick it up, read a paragraph, grimace, and put it back on the shelf. I finally broke down sometime in my late twenties and bought a copy for all of $8.50. It then sat on my own shelf for years, where I'd pick it up, read a paragraph, grimace, and put it back on the shelf.

What I didn't understand was that not only were the chapters (one for each degree of the Scottish Rite) almost impossible to grasp without having experienced the degrees, but they consisted of a jambalaya of unattributed quotes from unidentified sources intermixed with Pike's own unwieldy Victorian prose.

Albert Pike

Pike admitted as much in the book's preface, where he claimed for himself "little of the merit of authorship" and stated that he (in the third person) had "not cared to distinguish his own from that which he has taken from other sources, being quite willing that every portion of the book, in turn, may be regarded as borrowed from some old and better writer."[23]

Most anti-Masons have ignored this confession (as did I), and consequently they have had a grand old time tarring Freemasonry in general with the brush of Pike's eccentric selection of quotes, which make up "quite half its contents."[24] These quotes derive from sources as varied as the French occultist Eliphas Lévi, the British antiquarian Godfrey Higgins, and a Latin translation of portions of the Zohar, the most important Kabbalistic text. Removed from their original context, many of these quotes almost beg misinterpretation—a drawback that Pike appears to not have foreseen since he was familiar with the totality of his own sources.

Pike also committed a serious gaffe in titling the compendium *Morals and Dogma*, thus lending it the air of holy writ. Again, he tried to clarify matters in the preface by asserting:

> The Ancient and Accepted Scottish Rite uses the word "Dogma" in its true sense, of doctrine, or teaching; and is not dogmatic in the odious sense of that term. Every one is entirely free to reject and dissent from whatsoever herein may seem to him to be untrue or unsound. It is only required of him that he shall weigh what is taught, and give it fair hearing and unprejudiced judgment. Of course, the ancient theosophic and philosophic speculations are not embodied as part of the doctrines of the Rite; but because it is of interest and profit to know what the Ancient Intellect thought upon these subjects.[25]

Of course, in tossing in for consideration what he believed to be the teachings of the ancients, Pike ran the risk of sparking the ire of Christian fundamentalists who considered any wisdom outside of the Judeo-Christian canon as "pagan" or, worse still, satanic. Pike was himself a Christian, but one of a sufficiently liberal temper that he was intrigued by the possibility of tracking down that primordial faith that mythographers such as Godfrey Higgins presumed was the common heritage of post-Noah humanity. He was also intrigued by other possible early sources for Masonic symbols, such as Hermeticism, Kabbalah, and alchemy.

These topics and many more were introduced into *Morals and Dogma*'s strange mix of erudition and credulity, insight and pontification. It is hard to say just what your average Mason must have made of it. For some it undoubtedly opened doors to a larger universe of philosophical speculation—and that was certainly Pike's hope. But for most, I suspect, it likely sat unread on the shelf, an 861-page behemoth eliciting bafflement and awe.

Because of the AASR-SJ's high respect for Pike, the book continued to be given to all initiates until the early 1970s, by which time it had long since become an expensive-to-reprint artifact of Victorian scholarship. These days, a far more accessible book, *A Bridge to Light*, by Rex Hutchens, is given to each initiate. It offers well-informed glosses on the degrees and their symbolism, as well as pertinent quotes from *Morals and Dogma*.

Nevertheless, whatever its status in the Scottish Rite, *Morals and Dogma* has served as a favorite whipping boy for anti-Masonic critics who have elevated Albert Pike to the status of a Masonic pope and treated *M&D* as if it were holy writ for Masons. Passages that Pike had himself wrenched out of context from other sources and copied without attribution into the book are seized upon by anti-Masons as telling clues to Masonry's hidden diabolical nature.

This has been particularly troublesome in the case of two passages discussing Lucifer that Pike, in fact, lifted from Eliphas Lévi's *History of Magic*, where they were part of a lofty and abstract discussion about the nature of God, good and evil, and the devil.[26] Pike tackles the same topics and, in using Lévi's words—the meaning of which was ambiguous to begin with—muddles things even further. If one considers as a whole the chapter of *Morals and Dogma* in which these passages appear, however, it is clear that Pike is not expounding a Luciferian doctrine.[27]

The association of Lucifer with Pike was unfortunately compounded by Léo Taxil's dissemination of a bogus speech he credited to Pike, which was replete with statements such as "Lucifer is God" and "The Masonic religion should be, by all of us initiates of the high degrees, maintained in the purity of the Luciferian doctrine." This hoax speech was swallowed whole by a French anti-Masonic author, Abel Clarin de la Rive, in 1894, and picked up and disseminated further by Lady Queenborough in *Occult Theocrasy* [sic]. It lives on in numerous contemporary anti-Masonic books and on anti-Masonic Web sites.[28]

The Higher Degrees in Perspective

The Scottish Rite sometimes refers to itself as "the University of Freemasonry," implying that it offers a higher education in Masonry. In a sense this is true, as its additional degrees do provide lessons and ideals that supplement those of blue-lodge Masonry. However, more often than not the only degrees given in many Scottish Rite Valleys are a handful of obligatory degrees over the course of a weekend or a few weeks. Many members never see the degree rituals again, although all are welcome—old members as well as candidates—at the conferrals.

While some Valleys may offer degree-reading study groups to enable members to read the degrees that aren't performed, such efforts are merely a drop in the bucket. One such study group I'm aware of draws at best two dozen participants out of a Valley membership of two thousand.

Many Valleys have amassed impressive Masonic libraries over the past century filled with books delving into Masonic history, symbolism, philosophy, and related subjects. But more often than not, the libraries are unused by an aging membership that no longer reads. If the Scottish Rite is indeed a "university" of sorts, its opportunities for study are, of necessity, largely self-directed.

Sadly, the situation with the York Rite is no better—and possibly worse. As blue lodges have shrunk and consolidated, so have the York Rite bodies that have traditionally met in their buildings. Far less visible than the Scottish Rite, and without the Scottish Rite's centralized infrastructure, the York Rite has struggled just to stay viable.

This situation was worsened in 2000 when the Shrine (the Shriners) ended its 128-year-old tradition of requiring that its applicants be either a 32nd° in the Scottish Rite or a Knight Templar in the York Rite; now one has only to be a Master Mason to join. The Shrine had debated taking this step (or possibly the even more radical step of eliminating a Masonic requirement altogether) for a number of years, as its own numbers fell along with those of the rest of Masonry. By lowering the requirement to that of Master Mason only, the Shrine suddenly doubled its pool of potential members.

This change sent a shock wave through the leadership of the York and Scottish Rites, for the previous requirement had assured that any Mason who wanted to enter the Shrine also had to join and maintain his membership in one or the other of the appendant bodies. Now that incentive was gone. The "higher" bodies now had to attract new members—and keep them—largely on those bodies' own merits rather than just serving as handy springboards to the Shrine.

Ironically, even as the Shrine was enacting this change, it received a potentially fatal blow in the form of 9/11 and the increased militancy of Islamist fundamentalists. The tongue-in-cheek practice of dressing up in fezzes and Ottoman garb and driving little cars in public parades was suddenly not so funny. Shrine temples became nervous as they began to receive calls from both Muslims and anti-Muslims wondering just what they were about. The very real possibility that they might be caught betwixt a rock and a hard place began to dawn.

Whether the Shrine eventually scuttles its pseudo–Middle Eastern trappings altogether in a final bid for members and acceptability remains to be seen. Conferring no degrees, and with its main claim to a Masonic pedigree being its charitable hospitals for children, there is probably nothing to stop the Shrine from cutting its ties with Masonry entirely, changing its name, and reinventing itself with a new non-Masonic and non-Orientalist image.

As for the "higher" degrees, their future survival is tied to that of blue-lodge Masonry. And we'll return to a consideration of that at the book's conclusion.

Frontispiece to Athanasius Kircher's Arithmologia (Rome, 1665). Although not a Masonic drawing per se, it contains a number of symbols and motifs that reappear in Masonry. Note the Eye in the Triangle, representing God, surrounded by the three interlaced triangles representing the nine orders of angels in three divisions (three times three). The two men represent a Jewish scholar (note the pentagram and hexagram in his book) and Pythagoras teaching the 47th Problem of Euclid.

8

Veiled in Symbol and Allegory

Deciphering Masonic Symbolism

Among the many mysteries and confusions that surround Free-masonry, its use of symbols is, for many people, the most fascinating. Masonry is a veritable cornucopia of symbols: stonemason's tools, ladders, winding stairs, middle chambers, pillars, beehives, anchors, hourglasses—you name it, and it has probably been used as a Masonic symbol at one time or another. Like a philosophical pawnshop, Masonry has acquired a vast and confounding collection of symbolic objects and images—all of which represent something besides themselves, although just what that something is, is often part of the mystery.

Those who believe that Masonry guards some secret knowledge—whether for good or for ill—typically assume that this secret knowledge must be hidden in Masonic symbols in coded form. If you can break the code, you'll get the secrets.

This brings to mind an incident that happened to me a couple of years ago when I was attending an art show opening at a San Francisco gallery. I ran into an old friend there whom I hadn't seen in several years. Thirty years before, she had been a dedicated scene maker at all the local punk shows, but she had eventually married a musician with whom she had a child, and now she was dressed in a tasteful cocktail dress—another middle-aged patron of the arts.

What had I been up to, she wondered. Knowing that it would get some kind of rise out of her, I mentioned that I'd become a Mason several years before. She edged backward slightly and looked at me with a raised eyebrow, as if I'd casually noted that I'd taken up vivisection as a hobby.

After a few minutes of trying to get me to admit that there was something dark and dangerous at the heart of Masonry, she played her trump card. Some time before, she'd gained access to a Masonic lodge, and right there, on the wall of the lodge room, was a giant inverted pentagram. So explain that, Mr. Smarty Pants!

Here we go again, I thought to myself, and patiently pointed out that this wasn't a satanic symbol at all, but the emblem of the Order of the Eastern Star, the rather stodgy Masonic women's organization. However, try as I might, she wasn't buying it. It was much more excitingly spooky to believe that this symbol gave the game away: Masons were satanists, and she'd seen the evidence with her very own eyes.

If nothing else, this proves the power of symbols to spark the imagination, and it also illustrates the dangers of misinterpretation. We'll examine the truth behind the Order of the Eastern Star's pentagram shortly, but let's return to the notion that Masonry's secrets are hidden in its symbols.

This is not an entirely ridiculous assumption, since we know that mid-17th-century Masons such as Elias Ashmole and Robert Moray were fascinated by subjects like alchemy and Rosicrucianism, and it's an accepted fact that both alchemists and Rosicrucians used allegories and symbols to veil their secrets.[1] Ashmole, whose diary notes that he "was made a Freemason" on October 16, 1646, published translations of alchemical manuscripts in 1648 and 1652, and his 1652 book, *Theatrum Chemicum Britannicum*, included richly detailed engravings in this symbolic vein.[2]

As pointed out earlier, the rise of speculative Masonry seems to have been accompanied by an influx of gentlemen and nonoperatives into lodges and circles formerly dominated by stonemasons. If alchemy and Rosicrucianism were in the air, and some of those joining Masonry were students of those teachings, might not some of their secrets—and their methods of concealment—have found their way into Masonic symbolism?

It is questions like this that have inspired many Masons to delve more deeply into the symbolism of their own traditions. And where Masons have gone, their anti-Masonic critics have not been far behind, nipping at their heels and offering hostile counterinterpretations.

Secrets, Symbols, and Suspicions

There is a passage in the obligations to which each Mason swears during the degree rituals that binds him to "never reveal any part . . . of the secrets or mysteries of . . . Masonry," or words to that effect.[3] Exactly which "secrets or mysteries" these might be has never been precisely defined, although the consensus seems to be that they refer to the modes of recognition between Masons (which consist of certain grips [or handshakes], words, and signs [or gestures]), to the exact wording of unprinted portions of ritual, and to personal secrets given in confidence between individual Masons. The symbols themselves have hardly been kept secret, as they have been plastered all over the place: on aprons, badges, medals, posters, paintings, watch fobs, and even auto decals.

In light of this, the whole realm of Masonic symbols has typically been fair game for discussion in print, and there have been numerous books by Masons discussing possible interpretations of their own symbols. That these discussions even exist and can be read by non-Masons suggests at least two things:

First, it suggests that Masonry itself—in its rituals, lectures, and other official material—doesn't provide a definitive interpretation of its own symbols. Elementary didactic interpretations are indeed given, but every Mason is allowed the freedom to devise alternate interpretations if he wishes. As Masonic authors Arturo de Hoyos and S. Brent Morris note, "Because Freemasonry values free thought so highly, grand lodges as a rule neither endorse nor condemn ideas. That decision is left to individual Masons."[4]

Second, if there really is a coherent body of secret knowledge in Masonry "veiled in allegory and illustrated by symbols," it has been so well hidden by its original creators that institutional Masonry, on the whole, has failed to recognize its existence or pass this knowledge on to its members. This would account for the cottage industry of Masons trying to discover some thread of hidden wisdom within their own heritage of symbols and ritual forms.

There is, however, another possibility that deserves consideration: that those Masons who devised Masonry's symbols, rituals, and myths consciously designed them in such a way that their deeper meanings and significance would be revealed to a brother Mason only through diligent study and inquiry into the esoteric and mystical ideas being discussed at the time of speculative Masonry's emergence (i.e., the 17th and 18th centuries). Were this the case, institutional Masonry and its traditions would mainly serve as the carrier of symbols and forms whose meanings remained latent until decoded by insightful recipients of the symbolic bundle. J. D. Buck, a Mason and a Theosophist, expressed his belief in this notion over a hundred years ago when he declared: "It is in the ancient symbols of Freemasonry that its real secrets lie concealed, and these are as densely veiled to the Mason as to any other, unless he has studied the science of symbolism in general, and Masonic symbols in particular."[5]

Objections can be raised to each of these possibilities, but before we consider them, we should investigate just how Masonic symbolism works.

The Symbolic Mix

On the most basic level, a symbol can be defined as something (an image or object) that stands for or refers to something else. Symbols in this sense are often fairly straightforward things.[6] A heart symbolizes love; a big bag of coins symbolizes wealth.

At first glance, most Masonic symbols seem to operate in this manner. For instance, in the second-degree ritual, the new Fellow Craft is taught that the plumb, the stonemason's tool for determining true perpendiculars, symbolizes that he should walk upright before God and man. The plumb also serves as the identifying jewel of the Junior Warden, so it does double duty, symbolizing both upright behavior and a specific officer of the lodge. In either case, there seems little in the way of concealment or complexity going on.

Similarly, the square (a flat metal working tool in the shape of a ninety-degree angle, or "L") symbolizes virtue and morality, and is the jewel of the Worshipful Master, the leading officer of the lodge. In

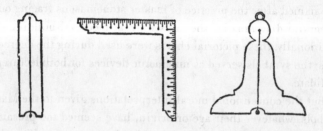

The symbolic "Working Tools" of a Fellow Craft: the plumb, square, and level

the same way that a stonemason would use a square to make sure that the sides of a block of stone were square with each other, the symbol of the square is supposed to remind the Masonic initiate to maintain a high standard of integrity—to "square his actions," as a ritual phrase states it.

Likewise, the level (a working tool that helps determine true horizontals and level surfaces) symbolizes equality between Masons under God; it is the jewel of the second senior officer—the Senior Warden. One version of the ritual for closing a lodge meeting includes a reminder that Masons should meet "on the level," act "by the plumb," and part "upon the square."

Masonry extends this kind of symbolism of moral and ethical ideals to virtually all of the stonemasons' tools. Similar qualities are associated with symbols derived from architectural features such as the "Three Great Pillars" of a lodge, which are said to represent wisdom, strength, and beauty. Other symbols have a biblical source, such as Jacob's Ladder, whose three principal rounds (or rungs) symbolize faith, hope, and charity. And finally there are a potpourri of seemingly random symbols such as a beehive (symbolizing industriousness and working together) and a sword pointing to a naked heart (symbolizing justice). (See the tables of the degree symbols at the end of this chapter, pages 169–171.)

A good number of these symbols appear to go back to the earliest days of speculative Freemasonry and in some cases earlier still to operative masonry. Others seem to have been added along the way in the 18th and 19th centuries as Freemasonry grew and evolved.[7] The symbols have been traditionally imparted through pictorial charts or paintings called "tracing boards" (or sometimes "trestleboards") that were named after the practice of master stonemasons tracing out architectural diagrams for the day's work at medieval building sites.[8] Traditionally, these pictorial charts were used during the degree lectures; the symbols served as mnemonic devices for both lecturer and candidate.

But the conventional moral interpretations given to the Masonic symbols, whatever their age or origin, have seemed too prosaic and underwhelming to those in search of hidden meanings. It's as if one had laboriously climbed a steep mountain in order to ask a holy man the secret of life, only to be handed a child's book of ABCs.

Beneath the Surface

Unwilling to accept that Masonry may really just be "a peculiar system of Morality, veiled in allegory and illustrated by symbols,"[9] Masons and anti-Masons alike have been determined to find another layer of meaning within Masonic symbolism. Masons of a mystical bent have typically drawn upon the Kabbalah, Rosicrucianism, Christian mysticism, sacred geometry, and numerous other traditions in their efforts to plumb the depths of Masonic profundity. Meanwhile, anti-Masons—many of whom exhibit a zealous glee in assigning the worst possible interpretations to anything Masonic—have sought to prove that Masonic symbols and rituals conceal (or reveal) a writhing mass of satanic, heretical depravities, guaranteeing all participants eternal damnation. In this enterprise both parties have been aided by the ambiguous and open-ended nature of the symbols themselves.

Any symbol worth its salt will lend itself to multiple interpretations—some moral, others philosophical, psychological, literary, religious, or political—and, depending on one's predisposition, these can be given a positive or negative spin. Further, as with Rorschach's famous inkblot test, such interpretations often say more about the person doing the interpreting than about the symbol itself.

But there is another way of working with symbols besides simply interpreting them. This involves living with them over an extended period of time: using them, meditating upon them, and experiencing them—as Masons do, both when they undergo the degree rituals and later when they help perform them for others.

In this way, one discovers that certain symbols begin to associate themselves with certain emotions or feelings, or with inner states that elude a verbal description.

Psychologists know that only a small portion of human awareness is truly conscious at any given time. The greater portion resides in what they call the unconscious (or subconscious) mind. The unconscious often has important things to tell us about aspects of our lives that need changing or rebalancing in order for us to become more fully alive. And the most common way that the unconscious communicates with us is through symbols.

Anyone who has kept a dream diary knows that, over time, certain motifs recur, as do locales, types of people, interactions, and objects. The dramas that we undergo in dreams—or at least some of them—are our unconscious speaking to us in symbolic form. If we are dissatisfied with our lives (or perhaps too smugly satisfied), it pays to take heed of recurring symbols emerging from the unconscious. They can be warnings of impending crack-ups if we let bad habits prevail or fail to deal with self-destructive patterns. Conversely, if we are taking our life in a positive direction, our unconscious may encourage us with dreams expressing happiness and beauty.

However, our interaction with our unconscious is a two-way street. The direction of our lives is also affected by what we *put into* our unconscious. Many spiritual traditions emphasize the repetition of prayers, the reading of mystical poetry or scriptures (which invariably speak in symbols), and the regular commitment of charitable or altruistic acts—all of which help feed the unconscious with images of wholeness and harmony. Spiritual disciplines, such as Sufism, that teach their students to expand their inner awareness in meditation speak of a process of "purification," in which the student loosens the grip of negative emotions and fixations through just such repetitive (and ritual) practices. Over time the capacity develops to quiet the mind's incessant ruminations, opening the way for experiences of pure consciousness that can have a refreshing and transformative effect.[10]

It is indicative of the overwrought anxiety of certain anti-Masons that they regard such meditative calm as fraught with danger. According to one critic:

> [C]entering, deep relaxation, or meditation is what a Christian would regard as a descent into the void of the self or the void of nothingness. Once this empty mental state is reached, those lurking demons of the Adversary rush in to fill the void, giving the practitioner a sense of self-deification by altering his thought patterns.[11]

In any event, all of these traditions of inner growth and spiritual awareness developed long before the concepts and terminology of modern psychology had been formulated. Yet they managed to evolve sophisticated systems of inner work that have proven effective over the centuries. It seems fair to suggest that the men who handed down the Masonic symbols and rituals through the years must have had a similar working knowledge of how symbols can serve to teach and inspire, and how ritual repetition can anchor ideas and values in the human psyche. But did they intend for Freemasonry to be a full-blown system leading to mystical awareness? This was one of the questions that I kept coming back to as I unraveled the Masonic myth.

The Blazing Star

There isn't room in a book of this size (or possibly in a lifetime) to fully explore every symbol that Freemasonry utilizes. To do so is the work of a Mason as he pursues his symbolic journey to the East, and no one can do it for him—or you. Nevertheless, an in-depth look at one of the most controversial Masonic symbols will illustrate the challenges facing anyone in search of deeper meanings.

The symbol in question is the Blazing Star, a symbol that has attracted any number of contradictory readings—some inspired, some hostile.

Traditional Masonic lectures describe the Blazing Star as being at the center of the lodge, and old pictures of Masonic lodges sometimes show a star depicted in the center of the floor or the ceiling or on the east wall of the lodge room.

For many Christian Masons, starting in the late 18th century, the symbol of the Blazing Star represented "the star which led the wise men to Bethlehem, proclaiming to mankind the nativity of the Son of God."[12] Another

One version of the Blazing Star. The Blazing Star is sometimes depicted as a simple pentagram.

reading associated it with the "period when the Almighty delivered the two tables of stone, containing the ten commandments, to His faithful servant Moses on Mount Sinai, when the rays of His divine glory shone so bright that none could behold it without fear and trembling."[13] Other readings simply identified it as a symbol for God ("the Great Architect of the Universe") or for the virtue of prudence.

The Blazing Star is most often depicted as a five-pointed star emitting rays of light (sometimes with the letter *G* in its middle, which stands for "God" in this context). In the first-degree ritual it is identified as one of the "ornaments" of a lodge and is commonly interpreted to represent "Divine Providence," Whose glory radiates infinite goodness.

This seems an innocent enough equation: star = divine light = goodness. Masons are supposed to seek "more light," which means that they are encouraged to seek a greater understanding of the world, of themselves, and of spiritual matters. The influential sixth-century Christian theologian Pseudo-Dionysius the Areopagite, a great defender of the use of symbols and metaphors, interprets light as a symbol of the goodness of God:

> Light comes from the Good, and light is an image of this archetypal Good. Thus the Good is also praised by the name "Light," just as an archetype is revealed in its image. The goodness of the transcendent God . . . gives light to everything capable of receiving it, it creates them, keeps them alive, preserves and perfects

them. Everything looks to it for measure, eternity, number, order. It is the power which embraces the universe. It is the Cause of the universe and its end.

The great, shining, ever-lighting sun is the apparent image of the divine goodness, a distant echo of the Good.[14]

That the star is commonly drawn with five points would seem unremarkable, given that stars on flags, coats of arms, and military insignia, and in numerous other traditional uses, are typically five pointed. It's a rare child who hasn't learned to draw a five-pointed star by the time that he or she enters kindergarten.

But to note this fails to reckon with the negative readings that can be given to five-pointed stars.

As luck would have it, one version of a five-pointed star, the pentagram (drawn with five crisscrossing lines), has become associated in the modern era with two "alternative" religions that carry spooky connotations for much of the population: Wicca (witchcraft) and satanism.

Wicca uses an upward-pointing pentagram within a circle as its most prominent symbol. Satanism, at least as represented by the Church of Satan founded by Anton LaVey in 1963, employs the opposite: a downward-pointing pentagram within a circle. Shortly after its emergence, this latter symbol was co-opted by numerous heavy metal bands and their fans as a surefire way to exasperate parents.

According to certain anti-Masonic critics, Masonry's use of a star symbol reveals its diabolical nature. Even more damning in their eyes is the use of a multicolored upside-down star as the signet or insignia of the Order of the Eastern Star, the Masonic-related women's order. What further proof is needed of Freemasonry's nefarious intent?

However, this instance of guilt by association begins to disintegrate as soon as one investigates the actual facts.

The Masonic Blazing Star dates back to at least 1730, and in many cases it is depicted as a star with more than five points—or with no points at all, but instead a "glory" of radiating lines indicating brightness. In short, the salient element of this Masonic symbol is "light" or "divine goodness," not the number of points.[15]

The Order of the Eastern Star (OES) was first initiated in 1850 by

The signet of the Order of the Eastern Star (OES), the Masonic appendant order for female relatives of Masons. The use by the OES of a five-pointed star, whether pointing up or down, predates the later use of pentagrams as Wiccan or satanic symbols and has no connection to them.

Rob Morris, a pious Mason who was intent on encouraging a form of Masonry for the wives and other women in Masons' families.[16] Early publications of the organization show the OES star depicted in either of two positions—a single point up or down—suggesting that the ultimate positioning of the points was somewhat arbitrary.

Although pentagrams were used with a variety of meanings in numerous cultures, the interpretation of an inverted pentagram as a malevolent sign seems to have originated in the writings of Eliphas Lévi (born Alphonse-Louis Constant), an influential French participant in the "occult revival" of the latter half of the 19th century. Lévi declared in his 1856 book *Dogmas and Rituals of High Magic:*

> The Pentagram with two points in the ascendant represents Satan as the goat of the Sabbath; when one point is in the ascendant, it is the sign of the Saviour. The Pentagram is the figure of the human body, having the four limbs and a single point representing the head. A human figure head downwards naturally represents a demon—that is, intellectual subversion, disorder or madness.[17]

It is true that the pentagram had been used in medieval Christianity to refer to Christ—symbolizing, in part, his five wounds—and was also associated with the human body, as Lévi notes.[18] However, the negative interpretation of the "upside-down" pentagram seems to be

Lévi's brainstorm: historians have failed to find examples, prior to Lévi's take on it, as a malevolent emblem. Early Christians are said to have posted it in their catacombs as a potent symbol to *repel* evil, but it is only since Lévi's day that a symbol that was formerly considered a protection *against* evil has seen its meaning flipped to the opposite: an emblem *of* evil.

But most relevant to the issue at hand is the fact that Rob Morris's invention of the OES emblem predates Lévi's published musings about inverted pentagrams. Moreover, Morris loaded the OES signet with all sorts of biblical connotations: each point of the star, for instance, represents a biblical woman associated with a particular "womanly" virtue. (Ruth is associated with constancy; Martha, with faith; and so on.) The motto accompanying the emblem on OES banners is a quote from the Gospel of Matthew (2:2): "We have seen his star in the east, and are come to worship him." The explanation of the OES for the downward-pointing star is that it represents the point where God's grace comes into the soul from "above." In any case, it is likely that, had Morris had any inkling that over one hundred years after he founded the OES, anti-Masonic conspiracy theorists would try to link the OES emblem with satanism, he would have chosen a different symbol—one less likely to become controversial.[19]

Two sets of figures from the engraving The Magical Calendar, *by Johann Baptista Grosschedel von Aicha (Frankfurt, 1620), a synthesis of Christian, Hermetic, and numerical symbolism. Shown here are two aspects of the Trinity: God the Father represented by a hexagram (on which are placed the six letters of the sacred name Adonai), and Jesus Christ represented by a pentagram (on which the sacred name of God, the Tetragrammaton—the four letters YHVH in Hebrew—is transformed into five syllables to coincide with the five letters of Jesus's name (IESVS), which surround it. The interlaced hexagram and pentagram later appeared in Royal Arch imagery, quite possibly with similar meanings originally intended.*

As for Wicca, a nature religion of benign disposition largely systematized by Gerald Gardner circa 1950, I could find no evidence of a

Wiccan use of the pentagram and circle as an identifying symbol prior to Gardner's employment of it.[20] It is even possible that Gardner, who was reportedly an initiate of a small co-ed fringe Masonic order, might have borrowed the pentagram from Masonry, just as he appropriated its three-degree structure and some ritual components.[21] Then again, Gardner could well have borrowed the upward-pointing pentagram from its use in post–Eliphas Lévi magical orders, with which he was familiar.[22]

In short, the use by Masonry and the OES of the pentagram or five-pointed star precedes the star's later associations with Wicca and satanism, in some cases by centuries.

More Light

To return to our investigation of the Blazing Star, Masonic tradition locates the Blazing Star at the center of the lodge, and if we recall that Masonic lodges are said to replicate the layout of Solomon's Temple, this center could symbolize the inner chamber in which the Ark of the Covenant was supposed to rest. The Ark, of course, was said to be the dwelling of the Most High; thus the Blazing Star could be a symbol of God (perceived as a blinding blaze of glory) occupying a central point in Masonic doings and awareness.[23]

In most American lodges, the center of the lodge-room floor is occupied by an altar, on which rests the "Volume of Sacred Law" (VSL), most commonly the Bible. So the guidance provided by scripture could be yet another symbolic meaning of the Blazing Star.

Yet another interpretation of the Blazing Star could see its light as representing the light of knowledge. A new Mason is encouraged to seek "more light," which he does in a lodge illuminated by the Blazing Star.

As with all such interpretations, these are purely speculative on my part, but they serve to demonstrate how the complex of Masonic symbols can build upon itself, one symbol interacting with another, spatial locations suggesting one thing, mythic figures suggesting another, visual symbols yet another.

"G" Is for Geometry

While Masonry has a wealth of visual symbols represented by the pictures on its tracing boards and charts, there is another kind of symbolism that may hold certain keys to the deeper aspects of the Craft.

In the middle-chamber lecture of the second degree, Masons are urged to study the seven liberal arts—grammar, rhetoric, logic, arithmetic, geometry, music, and astronomy—the most important of which, we are told, is geometry. Indeed, geometry is one of the meanings commonly associated with the letter G, which is usually placed within the symbol of the square and compasses. (The other meaning of the letter G is said to be either "God" or the Masonic metaphor for God: "the Great (or Grand) Architect of the Universe.")

If speculative Freemasonry is truly a descendant of operative masonry, the importance of geometry makes sense. There would have been few things more important than the use of geometry in designing, planning, and constructing cathedrals and other great structures. What may be less obvious, but no less significant, is that there is a long-standing tradition of sacred geometry, wherein certain numbers, proportions, ratios, angles, and other mathematical components have symbolic meanings discernable to "those with eyes to see," quite apart from their practical applications.

My own background as an artist and writer predisposed me to give prominence to visual and mythic-literary symbols, but I had to grant that some of the "hidden mysteries of Masonry" might reside in the realm of geometry.

While pulling together material for this book, I came upon chapters from an unpublished book written by a Mason, Lee Miller, that made a strong case for considering geometrical symbolism as central to the Masonic quest for "more light." Miller alerted me to a telling passage in the Masonic second-degree lecture written circa 1772 by William Preston, perhaps the most influential author of ritual lectures in the 18th century.

In this lecture, Preston lauds geometry as a science from which "we can trace the nature and measure of an asymptotic space which is a species of knowledge at once wonderful and comprehensive, for while it displays the mighty powers of the Great Architect of the Universe, it equally exhibits the spiritual nature of the soul of Man." He goes on to define *asymptotic space* as consisting of "an extension, actually infinite, comprehended between a right line and a curve, which though continually approaching each other never meet."[24]

The significance of this, according to Preston, was

[t]hat Man by the light of the "mind" can penetrate beyond infinity and can discover what no sensible experience can bring to his knowledge. It proves to his firm conviction that besides his material faculties of perception and imagination, which proceed from the organs of the body, there is in Man a power independent of these, separate from matter and by no means deriving in its origin from the body, whence he is enabled to judge, reason and determine.

Perhaps for most readers, as for me, this borders on the incomprehensible, but it does suggest that one of the primary speculative Masons of the 1700s located profound symbolic and philosophical meanings in geometric and mathematical concepts. Dating back to Pythagoras and to Greek and Hebrew gematria, numbers themselves and the letters of the alphabet with numerical equivalents provide additional layers of interpretation.[25]

This stream of mathematical symbolism can be found in the recurrence of references in Masonic ritual to such numerical sums as the three great lights, the three lesser lights, the three steps in the East of the lodge, the Triple Tau in the Royal Arch degree, and so on.

Of course, the question remains as to whether all this accretion of symbolism and interpretation actually leads to some form of wisdom and self-knowledge or whether it amounts to an esoteric chess match that goes on forever. Preston's references to "the light of the mind" and "reason" could be taken as indicators that he assumed that rational thought was sufficient to "penetrate beyond infinity."

However, I'd argue that Preston, who seems to have gotten much of his discussion of geometry from Pythagoras, Plato, Euclid, and other ancient philosophers, was harking back to the original Greek meanings of mind (*nous*) and reason (*logos*). These refer to an inherent human capacity to resonate with the divine order of things, where

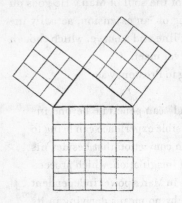

Symbolic representation of the 47th Problem of Euclid. According to Masonic tradition, geometry is the first and noblest of the seven liberal arts.

the intelligent order of the universe (the laws of nature, if you will) and its playing out in our lives can be intuited by us but ultimately elude our "material faculties of perception and imagination."

In urging the new Mason to give special attention to geometry, Preston was echoing Plato, who wrote in his *Republic* that "the knowledge at which geometry aims is knowledge of the eternal . . . geometry will draw the soul towards truth, and create the spirit of philosophy, and raise up that which is now unhappily allowed to fall down."[26]

Besides the letter *G* and the references to geometry in the second-degree lecture and charge, a further hint of the significance of geometry can be found in the inclusion of the so-called 47th Problem of Euclid in the symbols associated with the third degree. In the accompanying lecture, this geometric principle is attributed to Pythagoras, and it serves as a reminder once again to study geometry.

The 47th Problem (which reads, "In every right angled triangle the square on the hypotenuse is equal to the sum of the squares on the other two sides," and is usually depicted by a right triangle with sides of three, four, and five units respectively) might be metaphorically seen as the mere tip of a geometric iceberg awaiting further investigation.

From Symbol to the Symbolized?

I raised the question earlier of whether the men responsible for the Masonic symbols and rituals intended for Freemasonry to be a full-blown system leading to mystical awareness. (And by *mystical awareness* I refer to a lived experience, either momentary or ongoing, of one's true relationship to God, the order of the universe, and the totality of life.) Whether or not one believes that such an awareness is possible is beside the point. What is important to recognize is that numerous mystics down through the ages, in a variety of religions and spiritual traditions, have reported mystical experiences, and some esoteric traditions, such as Yoga, Sufism, Kabbalah, and so on, have set about systematizing practices to encourage such experiences in their students.

In trying to determine whether speculative Masonry was intended as a mystical system, I reviewed the claims and intentions of the esoteric seekers who preceded speculative Masonry and who in some cases joined Masonry as it began to form itself into a new brotherhood.

The alchemists of the late Middle Ages and the Renaissance, when they weren't being sidetracked by efforts to make gold, seemed to believe that their workings led to such an awareness. The magi such as Giordano Bruno, Trithemius, and Giorgio certainly assumed that their ritual and symbolic interactions with the higher worlds would bear fruit in a greater appreciation and experience of the divine. The same goes for the Kabbalists (both Jewish and Christian) and the pursuers of the Rosicrucian vision.

Nevertheless, it has been my observation that few people are capable of developing a system to get to a place where they've not already been. To use a mundane example, the American transcontinental railroad wasn't built by simply starting on the East Coast and blindly heading west. It entailed men reaching the West Coast by other means, surveying the best route in between, and then building back from the West Coast toward the East Coast and vice versa until the tracks, advancing from both directions, met somewhere in the middle.

The bona fide mystics, such as Jacob Böhme and St. John of the Cross, who tried to systematize their expanded consciousness in order to share glimpses of it with others, did so only after having achieved it themselves.

Yet, try as I might, I could find few if any indications that the nonoperative gentlemen and other worthies who transformed Masonry into a philosophical and moral brotherhood were coming from a state of mystical awareness or creating a coherent path back to that state for others to follow.[27] It seemed evident that some proponents of Kabbalah, Hermeticism, and Rosicrucianism, such as Robert Fludd and Thomas Vaughan, achieved a higher consciousness of an elevated order; but they had no discernable connection to Freemasonry.

While the Eye in the Triangle—often called the Eye of Providence—is frequently considered a Masonic symbol, it is also found in other contexts, such as the reverse of the Great Seal of the United States (left) and this Roman Catholic holy card from Italy (right). Symbols such as this are often shared and used by a variety of groups and are not the exclusive property of just one.

The Scottish historian David Stevenson suggested that a reference to "the Arte and Science of Memorie" in one of the early Masonic documents, the Schaw Statues of 1598, indicated an injection into the Craft of one technique of Renaissance Hermeticists, the Art of Memory advocated by Giordano Bruno.[28] But even were this so, that art, by itself, is merely a technique of mental discipline, not a full-blown spiritual path. Moreover, there was no indication of such an art being passed along, after that time, in the Masonic tradition. There *is* a strong emphasis in Masonry on the memorization of the rituals and lectures, but such rote memorization is a far cry from the Art of Memory as advocated by Bruno and others.

Whatever the early brethren were doing with their rudimentary rituals in the upstairs rooms of pubs, it was intermixed with too much ale, punch, and comestibles to qualify as a mystical order. One suspects that Hogarth's comic engraving of a drunken Mason stumbling home at the tail end of a lodge night was not too much of an exaggeration, at least for many lodges.

My present hypothesis—and it is subject to change by subsequent investigations—is that speculative Masonry, as it evolved from the mid- to late 17th century into the mid-19th century, by which time it was effectively frozen by Grand Lecturers and ritual standardization, reflected the intellectual trends of each era's speculations. Perhaps it was not called "speculative" without reason.

Beginning with an understructure derived from operative masonry's myths and rituals, it absorbed a smattering of Hermetic, Kabbalistic, and Rosicrucian symbols, took on many of the values of the Enlightenment, and then became a playing field for the projections of antiquarian mythographers and the imaginations of would-be chivalric knights.

By the time that Albert Mackey, Grand Secretary of the Scottish Rite (Southern Jurisdiction), gave Albert Pike the task of rewriting that particular rite's "higher" degrees into a more coherent progression of meaningful rituals (c. 1856), Pike, as a well-read mid-19th-century mythographer, turned his branch of Masonry into a summation of his predecessors' speculations in comparative mythology and religion, tempered by a set of political and moral principles appropriate to a Southern lawyer thrust into the tensions and contradictions that led to the Civil War.

Thus, depending on which portion of the Masonic totality one chooses to focus on, one can view a snapshot of a different era's preoccupations and resolutions. The three degrees of blue-lodge Masonry preserve the links with a late-medieval and Renaissance mythos (capped by the Royal Arch degree); the further degrees of the York Rite preserve the concerns of the last half of the 18th century; and the Scottish Rite's further degrees, at least as revised by Pike, provide a summation of speculative mythography up through the middle of the 19th century.

If this is so, it quashes the hopes of alternative historians, such as Knight and Lomas, that somehow finding the earliest versions of Masonic rituals will succeed in capturing the "real" Masonic secrets. What this historical evolution implies is that those supposed secrets, at any given time, were the evolving reflections of that era's suppositions about Masonry's own past and mankind's spiritual roots.

Operative masons—the builders of cathedrals and monasteries—were inextricably anchored in a Christian (in fact, Catholic) worldview, which took on Protestant characteristics as the political and religious landscape altered over the course of the 16th and 17th centuries in Britain. Arising in the wake of the religious conflicts of the English civil war and the Stuart/Hanover struggle, speculative Masonry sought a nonsectarian basis for a universal brotherhood of believers: men of good will who consciously chose not to judge the fine points of each other's beliefs.

This avoidance of conflict was best maintained by fixing the loci of initiation in the Old Testament stories of Temple building and re-building—a pious enterprise that sidestepped the contentious issues of Christian theology and authority.

It is intriguing that the advocates of a new science coming to the fore as the Enlightenment began, such as Francis Bacon and Isaac Newton, often spoke of the advance of human learning as the erection of a new House of Solomon. Given that the experimental scientist John Theophilus Desaguliers—an associate of Newton's and a member of the Royal Society—was a driving force in the premier Grand Lodge, it is possible that the Temple of Solomon motif was able to kill two birds with one stone. To the intellectual cognoscenti it symbolized a hopeful future of knowledge and brotherhood. To simpler, more conventional men of faith, it symbolized a righteous homage to the Almighty: "Holi-ness to the Lord," in the words of the Antients' Grand Lodge motto.

Once again we can see the multifaceted nature of symbols and the futility of trying to consider any single interpretation as definitive. Any symbol worth its salt is bound to mean different things to different people, which helps explain both Freemasonry's universal appeal and the hostility it receives from fundamentalist anti-Masons who consider more than one possible meaning for anything to be a sign of duplicity.

As I experienced the various degrees of blue-lodge Masonry and the additional degrees offered by the Scottish and York Rites, and as I delved into the numerous and varied interpretations that those de-grees and symbols have inspired, I gradually came to a paradoxical conclusion: if there is any single key to Masonic symbolism, it is that there is no single key. Wisdom comes—if it comes at all—from an open-ended consideration of multiple possibilities. Perhaps the confusion and indeterminacy surrounding Masonic symbols is a virtue, not a curse. (Or as the software programmers' joke goes, "It's not a bug; it's a feature.")

SYMBOLS OF
THE FIRST DEGREE
RITUAL & LECTURE

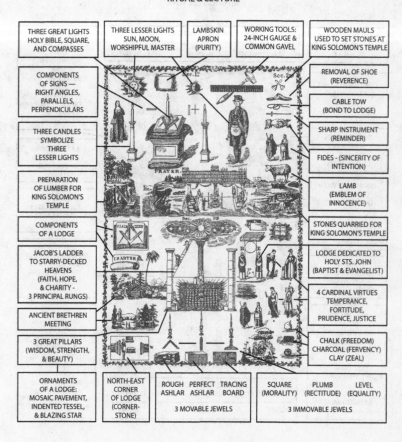

THREE GREAT LIGHTS
HOLY BIBLE, SQUARE,
AND COMPASSES

THREE LESSER LIGHTS
SUN, MOON,
WORSHIPFUL MASTER

LAMBSKIN
APRON
(PURITY)

WORKING TOOLS:
24-INCH GAUGE &
COMMON GAVEL

WOODEN MAULS
USED TO SET STONES AT
KING SOLOMON'S TEMPLE

COMPONENTS
OF SIGNS —
RIGHT ANGLES,
PARALLELS,
PERPENDICULARS

REMOVAL OF SHOE
(REVERENCE)

CABLE TOW
(BOND TO LODGE)

THREE CANDLES
SYMBOLIZE
THREE
LESSER LIGHTS

SHARP INSTRUMENT
(REMINDER)

FIDES - (SINCERITY OF
INTENTION)

PREPARATION
OF LUMBER FOR
KING SOLOMON'S
TEMPLE

LAMB
(EMBLEM OF
INNOCENCE)

COMPONENTS
OF A LODGE

STONES QUARRIED FOR
KING SOLOMON'S TEMPLE

JACOB'S LADDER
TO STARRY-DECKED
HEAVENS
(FAITH, HOPE,
& CHARITY -
3 PRINCIPAL RUNGS)

LODGE DEDICATED TO
HOLY STS. JOHN
(BAPTIST & EVANGELIST)

4 CARDINAL VIRTUES
TEMPERANCE,
FORTITUDE,
PRUDENCE, JUSTICE

ANCIENT BRETHREN
MEETING

3 GREAT PILLARS
(WISDOM, STRENGTH,
& BEAUTY)

CHALK (FREEDOM)
CHARCOAL (FERVENCY)
CLAY (ZEAL)

ORNAMENTS
OF A LODGE:
MOSAIC PAVEMENT,
INDENTED TESSEL,
& BLAZING STAR

NORTH-EAST
CORNER
OF LODGE
(CORNER-
STONE)

ROUGH   PERFECT   TRACING
ASHLAR   ASHLAR   BOARD

3 MOVABLE JEWELS

SQUARE   PLUMB   LEVEL
(MORALITY)   (RECTITUDE)   (EQUALITY)

3 IMMOVABLE JEWELS

SYMBOLS OF
THE SECOND DEGREE
RITUAL & LECTURE

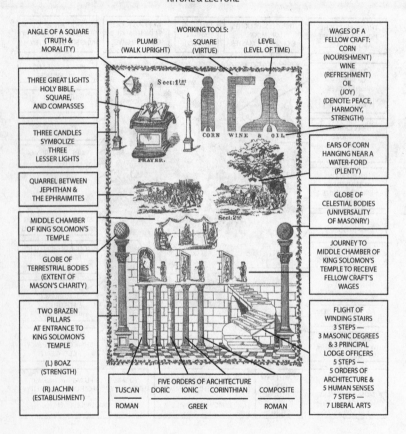

ANGLE OF A SQUARE
(TRUTH &
MORALITY)

WORKING TOOLS:

PLUMB
(WALK UPRIGHT)

SQUARE
(VIRTUE)

LEVEL
(LEVEL OF TIME)

WAGES OF A
FELLOW CRAFT:
CORN
(NOURISHMENT)
WINE
(REFRESHMENT)
OIL
(JOY)
(DENOTE: PEACE,
HARMONY,
STRENGTH)

THREE GREAT LIGHTS
HOLY BIBLE,
SQUARE,
AND COMPASSES

THREE CANDLES
SYMBOLIZE
THREE
LESSER LIGHTS

QUARREL BETWEEN
JEPHTHAN &
THE EPHRAIMITES

MIDDLE CHAMBER
OF KING SOLOMON'S
TEMPLE

GLOBE OF
TERRESTRIAL BODIES
(EXTENT OF
MASON'S CHARITY)

TWO BRAZEN
PILLARS
AT ENTRANCE TO
KING SOLOMON'S
TEMPLE

(L) BOAZ
(STRENGTH)

(R) JACHIN
(ESTABLISHMENT)

EARS OF CORN
HANGING NEAR A
WATER-FORD
(PLENTY)

GLOBE OF
CELESTIAL BODIES
(UNIVERSALITY
OF MASONRY)

JOURNEY TO
MIDDLE CHAMBER OF
KING SOLOMON'S
TEMPLE TO RECEIVE
FELLOW CRAFT'S
WAGES

FLIGHT OF
WINDING STAIRS
3 STEPS —
3 MASONIC DEGREES
& 3 PRINCIPAL
LODGE OFFICERS
5 STEPS —
5 ORDERS OF
ARCHITECTURE &
5 HUMAN SENSES
7 STEPS —
7 LIBERAL ARTS

FIVE ORDERS OF ARCHITECTURE				
TUSCAN	DORIC	IONIC	CORINTHIAN	COMPOSITE
ROMAN		GREEK		ROMAN

SYMBOLS OF
THE THIRD DEGREE
RITUAL & LECTURE

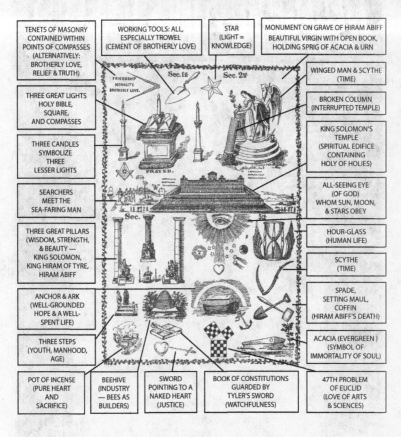

TENETS OF MASONRY CONTAINED WITHIN POINTS OF COMPASSES (ALTERNATIVELY: BROTHERLY LOVE, RELIEF & TRUTH)

WORKING TOOLS: ALL, ESPECIALLY TROWEL (CEMENT OF BROTHERLY LOVE)

STAR (LIGHT = KNOWLEDGE)

MONUMENT ON GRAVE OF HIRAM ABIFF BEAUTIFUL VIRGIN WITH OPEN BOOK, HOLDING SPRIG OF ACACIA & URN

THREE GREAT LIGHTS HOLY BIBLE, SQUARE, AND COMPASSES

THREE CANDLES SYMBOLIZE THREE LESSER LIGHTS

SEARCHERS MEET THE SEA-FARING MAN

THREE GREAT PILLARS (WISDOM, STRENGTH, & BEAUTY — KING SOLOMON, KING HIRAM OF TYRE, HIRAM ABIFF

ANCHOR & ARK (WELL-GROUNDED HOPE & A WELL-SPENT LIFE)

THREE STEPS (YOUTH, MANHOOD, AGE)

POT OF INCENSE (PURE HEART AND SACRIFICE)

BEEHIVE (INDUSTRY — BEES AS BUILDERS)

SWORD POINTING TO A NAKED HEART (JUSTICE)

BOOK OF CONSTITUTIONS GUARDED BY TYLER'S SWORD (WATCHFULNESS)

47TH PROBLEM OF EUCLID (LOVE OF ARTS & SCIENCES)

WINGED MAN & SCYTHE (TIME)

BROKEN COLUMN (INTERRUPTED TEMPLE)

KING SOLOMON'S TEMPLE (SPIRITUAL EDIFICE CONTAINING HOLY OF HOLIES)

ALL-SEEING EYE (OF GOD) WHOM SUN, MOON, & STARS OBEY

HOUR-GLASS (HUMAN LIFE)

SCYTHE (TIME)

SPADE, SETTING MAUL, COFFIN (HIRAM ABIFF'S DEATH)

ACACIA (EVERGREEN) (SYMBOL OF IMMORTALITY OF SOUL)

ILLUMINATI
THE GAME OF CONSPIRACY

DELUXE EDITION

David Martin

STEVE JACKSON GAMES

The fable of the survival of the Illuminati as the grand conspirators running the world down to the present continues in the form of tongue-in-cheek card games such as this popular game.

9

The Illuminati Factor

Does a Hidden Order Rule the World?

In the early 1970s, authors Robert Anton Wilson and Robert Shea published the *Illuminatus!* trilogy, a madcap fictional tour of a world in which all conspiracy theories are true and a host of conspiratorial elites battle it out as the world merrily hurtles toward "the immanentization of the Eschaton"—the end of history.

The trilogy's title referred to the Illuminati, a short-lived Bavarian secret order of the 1780s that, some conspiracy theorists claim, has actually survived to the present and is a secret cabal shaping world events. Wilson and Shea had great fun with this notion, as did author Dan Brown in his bestselling suspense novel *Angels and Demons*. In that book, the supposed Illuminati return to battle the Vatican and nearly succeed in taking out the present-day Vatican City with a colossal bomb. Such tales are clearly meant as entertainment, but there have been others who have taken the Illuminati quite seriously.

I came face-to-face with this fact one day in 1975 in San Francisco. I was twenty-five at the time and pursuing research on political extremism that eventually saw print in a number of publications.[1] I had found a listing in the city phone book for an American Opinion Bookstore, one of a number of "patriotic" bookshops then being run by the John Birch Society. In its day, the JBS was the most famous ultraconservative organization on the right, and a purveyor of its own conspiracy theory regarding "the Insiders." Its publishing arm was responsible for a steady stream of alarmist books that circulated in far-right circles but were rarely seen in conventional book outlets. In order to better understand that side of the political spectrum, I was interested in acquiring more examples of its literature.

Tracking down the address listed in the phone book, I found that the "bookstore" was an ordinary house located in the Outer Sunset district, a stuccoed, middle-class, residential neighborhood. I rang the front doorbell and was let in cautiously by a graying woman. The bookstore? It was a little two-shelf bookcase in the front hall.

Just what was I interested in? the woman asked. Oh, information and books on the way things are *really* run. You know, the Council on Foreign Relations, the Rockefellers—stuff like that, I answered, trusting that I had used the right buzzwords to justify my presence.

Squatting in the hallway, I looked through the meager selection of paperbacks and pamphlets reprinted from old *American Opinion* magazines and chose a few of the more promising ones.

By now, apparently convinced of my sincere interest, my hostess took me into her confidence. You can't be too careful in battling the Insiders, she warned. Why, her neighbors in the house next door used to have regular nighttime meetings—mysterious gatherings of men who'd arrive by car and meet behind closed drapes, doing *what,* God only knew! You can imagine how shocked her husband and she were

The original paperback covers of the popular Illuminatus! trilogy, by Robert Anton Wilson and Robert Shea, which poked fun at Illuminati-centered conspiracy theories.

to discover that the Illuminati—yes, *the Illuminati*—were holding meetings right next door!

Well! They wasted little time in informing their neighbors that they knew who they *really* were, and by George if it wasn't just a few months later that their neighbors sold their house and moved away!

Somewhat taken aback by this astounding tale of an informed citizenry at work, I offered my congratulations on this small victory against the Conspiracy and left shortly after, clutching my newly purchased literature.

Paranoia Strikes Deep

The world of conspiracy theories and theorists is a peculiar place. Most of its inhabitants live under a permanent Red Alert, certain that our destinies are being shaped by hidden forces behind the scenes. Researchers amass mountains of data in support of their theories, but in most cases this research is conducted from the safe environs of their armchairs and laptop computers, unsullied by actual contact with the targets of their theories.

Pursuing conspiracies is not, in and of itself, a bad thing. Investigative journalists do it as a matter of course, and it can be argued that every case of political corruption, corporate malfeasance, organized crime, or terrorism involves a conspiracy deserving to be unmasked. However, journalists, like legitimate historians, are supposed to hold themselves to professional standards of inquiry, requiring credible and reliable sources for facts and, in the case of whistle blowers or leakers, determining whether a given source is indeed in a position to know what is claimed.

Sadly, most conspiracy theorists show far less rigor in gathering data. If a thirdhand source says something that fits their theory, in it goes, without further ado. If a firsthand source contradicts the theory, that must be proof of a cover-up. Too often the goal becomes the preservation of one's theory at all costs, the truth be damned.

For much of the modern era, a preoccupation with conspiracies has been a fringe phenomenon indulged in by the population at large only during times of upheaval and heightened social anxiety. However, these days one can barely turn around without running into the trope of conspiracies.

David Lynch and Mark Frost's cult TV series *Twin Peaks* toyed with a snowballing mystery leading inexorably toward a hidden "Black Lodge." *The X-Files* capitalized on the popularity of numerous conspiracy theories, ranging from alien abductions to covert intelligence manipulations. Dan Brown's novels—and the even more wildly popular Harry Potter series—all involve battling conspiracies.

With the advent of the Internet, fevered cranks who would previously have been limited to wearing sandwich boards and hawking leaflets now have the opportunity to create Web sites filled with their overheated accusations. With a good search engine and the right key words, one can find a virtually endless supply of rants and raves. The Web, in its role as the great leveler, has rendered any site as more or less equal to any other site, undermining the former barriers and distinctions between "official" and "alternative" realities. This has contributed to the present juncture's unique psychological state in the population at large—a mixture of expectation and dread that might be characterized as the mainstreaming of paranoia.

Consensus reality—that fragile set of myths that hold a society together through the shared narrative it tells itself—was largely held in place up through the mid-'60s by the informal coalition of government, media, popular culture, and social arbiters. But a series of shocks, starting with JFK's assassination (and the subsequent assassinations and near-assassinations of popular leaders) and proceeding through the rise and fall of the counterculture, the traumas of Watergate, the fall of Saigon, the Iran hostage crisis, the Iran-Contra imbroglio, up through the implosion of the Soviet Bloc and the end of the Cold War, severely damaged the shared narrative of consensus reality.

The undercurrents of social anxiety that had been held in check by the static worldview of the Cold War began to bubble to the surface in a new, unfamiliar terrain symbolized by then President George H. W. Bush's ill-phrased invocation of "a new world order" in 1990. By uncanny coincidence, this was the exact code phrase that the conspiracy theorists of the far right had been using for several decades to describe that which they feared the most: a One-World Government imposed from above by a hidden elite (variously described as the Illuminati, the Insiders, the International Bankers, etc.).

This same period of social dislocation and trauma was also marked by the rise of another counterculture groping toward its own consensus reality: the tens of millions of socially conservative evangelical Christians whose favored narrative interprets contemporary upheavals as the fulfillment of the biblical prophecies of the apocalyptic End Times. This worldview is inclined to see the hand of Satan at work behind any events or social manifestations that do not meet its own definitions of virtue or proper conduct.

In addition to these two converging streams of suspicion, mainstream popular culture was slowly penetrated by the growing fascination with dark accusations and unexplained phenomena: crop circles, UFOs, cattle mutilations, claims of alien abduction, "Men in Black," "Area 51," suspected collusion between a secret government and aliens in our midst, mind-control experiments, and ritual child abuse. The meme of diminutive green aliens with big heads and large almond-shaped eyes spread throughout the culture, nearly reaching the ubiquity of the yellow happy face of the '70s.

This agitation in the culture at large rose to a fever pitch in the year leading up to the Y2K millennium. Predictions of a social collapse triggered by computer malfunctions were rife, and survivalists stockpiled dried milk and beef jerky in anticipation of the chaos. The collective sigh of relief that accompanied the turn of the clock on New Year's Eve, when the Y2K hysteria proved unfounded, was short-lived, however, for the very next year saw the unfathomable tragedy of 9/11 and the onset of every paranoid's worst fear: a shadowy network of Them out to get Us.

The Roots of Hysteria

Such examples of social anxiety and pathology would be tangential to the focus of this book except for the unpleasant fact that fear and suspicion of Freemasonry have been a recurring motif among the hypervigilant. Those who live in fear of the advent of a New World Order are sure that the Masons are an arm of the Illuminati. Those who anticipate the imminent arrival of Armageddon are certain that Masons are minions of Satan. And those who perceive an octopuslike foe of aliens, mind controllers, and ritual abusers are convinced that Masons must be involved in one way or the other.

It is tempting to chalk up such fears to sheer paranoia and be done with it. Richard Hofstadter, in his famous 1964 essay "The Paranoid Style in American Politics," applied the label cautiously, noting:

> I call it the paranoid style simply because no other word adequately evokes the sense of heated exaggeration, suspiciousness, and conspiratorial fantasy that I have in mind. In using the expression "paranoid style" I am not speaking in a clinical sense, but borrowing a clinical term for other purposes. I have neither the competence nor the desire to classify any figures of the past or present as certifiable lunatics. In fact, the idea of the paranoid style as a force in politics would have little contemporary relevance or historical value if it were applied only to men with profoundly disturbed minds. It is the use of paranoid modes of expression by more or less normal people that makes the phenomenon significant.[2]

Hofstadter linked the recurring outcroppings of hysteria over conspiracies to feelings of dispossession and frustration in significant sectors of the population.

> Having no access to political bargaining or the making of decisions, they find their original conception that the world of power is sinister and malicious fully confirmed. They see only the consequences of power—and this through distorting lenses—and have no chance to observe its actual machinery.[3]

Hofstadter's insights might help explain certain manifestations of anti-Masonic suspicion such as those found in evangelical circles. Whether justly or not, millions of born-again Christians experience great frustration at living within a heterogeneous culture that falls short of their hopes for a Kingdom of God on earth. Masonry's nonsectarian acceptance of a variety of believers, its puzzling symbolism, its trappings of power, its tradition of secrecy, and, perhaps most irritatingly, its assertion of its own virtuousness make it a perfect scapegoat on which to project one's suspicions.

Incredibly enough, such anti-Masonic suspicions almost predate Freemasonry itself. In 1698, nearly twenty years before the premier grand lodge was even formed, anti-Masonic leaflets were already circulating in London, which warned:

TO ALL GODLY PEOPLE, IN THE CITIE OF LONDON

Having thought it needful to warn you of the Mischiefs and Evils practiced in the Sight of GOD by those called Freed Masons, I say take Care lest their Ceremonies and secret Swearings take hold of you; and be wary that none cause you to err from Godliness. For this devllish Sect of Men are Meeters in secret which swear against all without their Following. They are the Anti Christ which was to come leading Men from Fear of GOD. For how should Men meet in secret Places and with secret Signs taking Care that none observe them to do the Word of GOD; are not these the Ways of Evil-doers?

Knowing how that GOD observeth privilly them that sit in Darkness they shall be smitten and the Secrets of their Hearts layed bare. Mingle not among this corrupt People lest you be found so at the World's Conflagration.[4]

One assumes that had the author of this leaflet been alive in the early Christian era, he would have been picketing the catacombs in which Christians met in secret, accusing them of evildoing as well. Such is the mind-set that fears the worst from others about whom one knows little.

"Unknown Superiors"

The supposition that there is or was a secret order behind Freemasonry (or within it) recurs so frequently that it is worthwhile to investigate what facts are known about the actual historical Illuminati and about the notion of a secret leadership. My inquiries into this topic took me back to the evolution of the Craft on the Continent, and particularly to the flourishing of higher degrees.

Typically, various series of multiple degrees were organized in rites or orders that developed separately from more traditional grand lodges. In some cases, these organizations pulled together degrees from a variety of sources, including other groups. Thus memorable degrees often floated around and wound up in more than one rite or system.

One of the most notable of these rites was a German order called the Rite of Strict Observance, which long had the reputation of being the first Masonic body to claim the Knights Templar as Masonic ancestors. It was also the first to claim a secret leadership of "Unknown Superiors" who were supposedly the source of the exalted wisdom it claimed to impart. This motif of an unidentified leadership—which raised suspense and made things alluringly mysterious—had previously been a feature of the Rosicrucian manifestos of the early 1600s, when a mythic organization of savants and reformers was anonymously announced to the world in Germany. The manifestos had caused a tremendous stir among the intelligentsia in Europe and helped stimulate discussions about religious and political reform, which was seemingly the whole purpose of the hoax.

In the case of the Rite of Strict Observance, the pretence of "Unknown Superiors" was more of a power ploy on the part of the rite's leaders, assuring their positions of power as links to the supposedly hidden leadership. Unfortunately, this situation helped foster a culture of intrigue and manipulation in German Masonry that was soon exploited by the rise of the Illuminati.

The Real Illuminati

The Illuminati were the brainstorm of one Adam Weishaupt, a professor of canon law at Ingolstadt University in Catholic Bavaria. Weishaupt seems to have drunk deeply from the well of Enlightenment ideas, and, taking a page from the book of the Jesuits, from whom he had originally received his education, he conceived a radical plan for a secret order that would transform the political and religious landscape.

On the one hand, Weishaupt put great stock in reason, a natural religion (Deism), and human perfectibility—familiar Enlightenment notions. On the other hand, the secret order that he devised was so supremely manipulative that it reduced its members and the public at large to the status of pawns. Weishaupt stratified the order so that its true intent of social/political revolution was only gradually revealed as members worked their way up the ladder, and members' identities were shielded from one another.

Weishaupt founded the order in 1776 (one of those coincidences of dates that conspiracy theorists would later read much into) and set about attracting members. He soon concluded that Freemasons would make a good recruiting pool and appealed to Masons who were disenchanted with the secrets that the Rite of Strict Observance promised but failed to deliver. The Illuminati would really deliver the goods, they were told, although by the time they were drawn in deep enough, those goods turned out to be a program for social revolution, not personal enlightenment.

The organization's penetration of the Masonic milieu was sufficient to stir up considerable opposition, and the defection of

PROOFS
OF A
CONSPIRACY
AGAINST ALL THE
RELIGIONS AND GOVERNMENTS
OF
EUROPE,
CARRIED ON
IN THE SECRET MEETINGS
OF
FREE MASONS, ILLUMINATI,
AND
READING SOCIETIES.
COLLECTED FROM GOOD AUTHORITIES,
BY JOHN ROBISON, A. M.
PROFESSOR OF NATURAL PHILOSOPHY, AND SECRETARY TO THE
ROYAL SOCIETY OF EDINBURGH.

Nam tua res agitur paries cum proximus ardet.

THE FOURTH EDITION.
TO WHICH IS ADDED, A POSTSCRIPT.

NEW-YORK:
Printed and Sold by George Forman, No. 64, Water-Street,
between Coenties and the Old-Slip.
1798.

Title page of John Robison's influential book Proofs of a Conspiracy, accusing the Illuminati of surviving its dissolution and of being behind the French Revolution. The book remains in print today.

disillusioned members added to the clamor. Employing a blunderbuss approach, the local authorities banned both the Illuminati and Freemasonry in general in 1784 and reiterated the ban the following year.

As far as anyone has been able to determine, that was the last of the Bavarian Illuminati, at least as a formal organization. Some historians, such as James Billington, suggest that some of the Illuminati's ideas continued to influence later radicals, but the idea that the Illuminati continued as a specific organization or merely shifted operations elsewhere is almost universally dismissed.[5]

However, the Illuminati lived on in the works of two influential conspiracy theorists: John Robison, a professor of natural philosophy at the University of Edinburgh; and a Jesuit, the Abbé Barruel. Robison's *Proofs of a Conspiracy Against All the Religions and Governments of Europe, Carried on in the Secret Meetings of Free Masons, Illuminati and Reading Societies* was published in Edinburgh in 1797 and reprinted in the United States the following year. Barruel's four-volume *Memoirs Illustrating the History of Jacobinism* saw print shortly thereafter.[6]

Although there were certain differences between the two men's grand theories, they both saw the Illuminati as a force behind the French Revolution. (Robison added the twist that the Illuminati were, in turn, a tool of the Jesuits—a notion not shared by the Jesuit Barruel.) Robison's book inspired accusations that the Illuminati were now active in the fledgling United States. These allegations were propagated from the pulpit by a famous Boston preacher, Jedidiah Morse, in May 1798. Further agitation was contributed by the president of Yale, Timothy Dwight, who orated, "Shall our sons become the disciples of Voltaire, and the dragoons of Marat; or our daughters the concubines of the Illuminati?"[7]

The conservative Federalists tried to tar Thomas Jefferson and the Democrats with the Illuminist brush, but the tar failed to stick, in part because concrete evidence was not forthcoming. In due course the Illuminati hysteria ran its course, but the idea of a secret order manipulating world history would return over and over, especially as radical republicans in 19th-century Europe and Latin America increased their efforts to rein in or replace monarchies with more democratic governments.

Different Masonries

Before we go any farther, it needs to be pointed out that not all suspicions about Freemasonry were necessarily baseless. The Bavarian
Illuminati *did* succeed in penetrating and using Masonry in Germany, albeit for a relatively brief period. And as we will soon see, *some*
Masons in *some* subsequent situations could be justifiably accused of
contesting the powers of Church and Crown. However, this does not
mean that the conspiracy theorists and Illuminati hunters are bark-
ing up the right tree. This is one of those points where the fog begins
to roll in again, so we need to tread carefully across a landscape strewn
with misconceptions. In order to understand things, a little more history is in order.

As I mentioned previously, Freemasonry in America responded
to the uproar over the Morgan Affair by first keeping its head down
and then, as the turbulence subsided, emphasizing its patriotism and
subscribing to an implicit conservatism. The United States in the 19th
century was already a republic, and Masons were generally inclined
to uphold the status quo. Similarly, Great Britain was a constitutional
monarchy with legislative bodies and a policy of tolerance. Masonry
there was at pains to locate itself on the side of the establishment.

The situations on the Continent and in Central and South America
were another ball of wax altogether. The divine right of monarchies
was still upheld by the Catholic and Eastern Orthodox Churches, and
principles that Americans could take for granted, such as the separa-
tion of Church and State, were considered subversive elsewhere. Insofar as Masonry conveyed certain Enlightenment principles, such as
religious tolerance, scientific inquiry, philosophical debate, and self-
governance, it served as a de facto challenge to regimes that looked
askance at such developments. But there's more to it than just that.

Tensions between Masonry and the powers that be, on the Continent and in Latin America, were further heightened by their grand
lodges allowing discussions of religion and politics in their lodges.
Such discussions were forbidden in the lodges of North America and
the British Empire, but that was not the case elsewhere. This left open
the possibility that lodges might debate social issues and even take

stands, either formally or informally. In France, for instance, the Grand Orient, the dominant grand lodge, explicitly supported efforts to institute "laicism," a policy of eliminating Church influence in government and education.

Italian Masons, meanwhile, were active in republican struggles to unify the patchwork of duchies and papal states into a single nation— a direct challenge to the political power of the Vatican. Spanish and Portuguese colonies in the Americas, where the Inquisition was still in operation throughout the 19th century, sought an independence modeled on that of the United States. Freemasons in those territories— whose ranks included such famous Latin American patriots as Simón Bolívar and José de San Martín—were active in those struggles.

An obvious example of this phenomenon is the internationalist republican Garibaldi, who journeyed to Latin America in the mid-1830s, joined in battles defending the new country of Uruguay, and later returned to Europe and fought in republican struggles in Italy in 1848. Decades later, after the success of the Italian Risorgimento (unification), he was deemed a national hero and accepted the honorary grand mastership of the Grand Orient of Italy.

There is also the curious case of the Order of Memphis, a minor French higher-degree rite of some ninety-six "Egyptian" degrees, originally founded in 1815, which seems to have evolved by some convoluted route into a political secret society of revolutionary republicans by 1848.[8] In the wake of the failure of the 1848 revolutions, French émigrés relocated to Britain, founding a Memphis-chartered Lodge of Philadelphes in London and a number of lodges elsewhere. These seem to have led a quiet existence out of the public eye, though by 1859 the United Grand Lodge of England became sufficiently aware of the problem that it forbade its members from holding any communication with the "spurious" and "irregular" lodges.[9]

Nevertheless, another ten years down the line, matters had seemingly progressed to where the editor of a new Masonic magazine, *The Freemason*, felt obliged to complain:

We grieve to learn, however, that doubtless in ignorance of this caution [i.e., the Grand Secretary's warning in 1859], some members of English lodges have given countenance to the "Philadelphes," by attending their soirees and balls, where, tricked out in fantastic finery, as "Hierophants of the Star of Sirius," "Sovereign Pontiffs of Eleusis" and "Grand Masters of the redoubtable sacred Sadah," these imposters libel the simplicity and purity of our noble Craft. . . . The gravest rumours are also in circulation as to the designs of these intriguing "Philadelphes," the most revolutionary ideas, it is said, have been broached in their mystic assemblies, and Orsini-like conspirators have been seen emerging from their dark and dangerous dens.[10]

I must admit to having a bit of trouble wrapping my mind around revolutionary conspirators in fantastic finery throwing soirees and balls as Hierophants and Sovereign Pontiffs, but with the French, anything is possible.

As circumstances changed in France, the Order of Memphis lodges in England faded out of the picture, their émigré members returning to France. When the order next popped up in England, in 1872, the political components were gone, and it was a largely paper organization under the guardianship of John Yarker, an inveterate collector of rites and propagator of fringe Masonic organizations.[11]

In any event, from the perspective of the pope and the monarchs of Catholic countries, Freemasonry must have looked like a grand conspiracy. Enlightenment values were bad enough, but democratic politics were anathema. Everywhere they cast their gaze, Masons seemed intent on paring back the Church's power, or at least siding with those who were. How could it *not* be a conspiracy?

A Confluence of Forces

Yet I would argue that a scattershot of small conspiracies does not a grand conspiracy make. The tide of history marked by scientific advances, industrialization, and the gradual collapse of monarchies was propelled by innumerable factors, Freemasonry being at best a minor actor.

While it is true that some American Masons applauded from afar the aborted European republican revolutions of 1848, seeing in them an effort to replicate American democracy in the Old World, I could find no evidence that such applause was supplemented by material support or strategic connivance. The balkanized nature of sovereign grand lodges effectively prevented any efforts to coordinate cross-fraternity actions.

Attempts to build a greater unity between American state grand lodges in 1843, as Masonry was regrouping after the devastation of the Morgan Affair, had singularly failed, and there was no single vehicle through which a foreign grand lodge could contact all American grand lodges en masse. Moreover, despite the lofty ideals of universal brotherhood, many of these grand lodges abroad were not "recognized" by U.S. grand lodges nor by each other, with the end result that their respective members were not allowed to associate with one another.

This splintered situation is epitomized by the rift that occurred in 1877 between the Grand Orient of France and the English-speaking grand lodges of the British Empire and the United States.

From the time of the French Revolution on, Masonry in France underwent periods of success or suppression, depending on the regimes in power. Unlike grand lodges in the British Isles and North America, which confined themselves to administering blue lodges performing only three degrees, the Grand Orient of France evolved into an inclusive umbrella of several rites, some conferring only three degrees and others conferring "higher" degrees as well. As a strong exponent of Enlightenment ideals, the Grand Orient took as its own the slogan of the French Revolution, "Liberty, Equality, Fraternity." Throughout the succession of republics, the empire, restorations, and republics again, the Grand Orient took the side of forces pushing for laicism.

It was in this context in 1877, at an annual "convent" (conference) of representatives from the Grand Orient's constituent bodies, as the national struggle over laicism was coming to a head, that a resolution was passed advocating an absolute "freedom of conscience" for its members. Grand Orient Masons were no longer required to profess a belief in a deity, and the presence of the Bible in the lodge room became optional.

We needn't get into the fine points of the controversy that subsequently erupted between the Grand Orient and various English-speaking grand lodges. Suffice it to say that the United Grand Lodge of England (UGLE) and other grand lodges maintained that a belief in God was a crucial "landmark" of the Craft and that in making it optional, the Grand Orient became "irregular" and lost the "recognition" of UGLE and other grand lodges. The French defended their action as being called for by their unique social circumstances, and thus it remains to this day.[12]

The salient point here is that with Freemasonry, as with so many things, to generalize from the particular is to risk incoherence. Notwithstanding its universalist rhetoric, Masonry actually consists of many Masonries, some of which prefer to ignore or even disavow each other. And nowhere is this more obvious than in the case of a final absurd attempt to revive the Illuminati, to which we will now turn our attention.

Illuminist Mirages

Despite the actual demise of the Illuminati in the 1780s, its survival as a bogeyman in conspiracy theories gave the defunct group a kind of perverse cachet among romantic contrarians of the Victorian era. This led to more than one tiny occult order of the late 1800s claiming to be a survival or revival of the Illuminati—an amusing pastime that served the dual function of attracting naive followers while causing hyperventilation among conspiracy theorists.

Although the original Illuminati's goals were rationalist and materialist, its organizational window dressing had been esoteric and mystical. At the same time, its ambiguous name could equally refer to the light of knowledge associated with the Enlightenment or the inner light of spiritual illumination. The romantic occultists of the late 19th century, who claimed to be a new Illuminati, cast aside the old order's radical politics and appropriated its image of an inner Masonic elite. It was a pretentious exercise in smoke and mirrors, with little substance to justify the hoopla, but it provided the conspiracy hunters with further "evidence" of the Illuminati's continued existence and its connection, however slim, to Masonry.

The best example of this phenomenon was the revived Order of the Illuminati in Germany cooked up by Theodor Reuss and Leopold

Engel in the 1890s. Reuss led a checkered career as a concert singer, journalist, and occult entrepreneur, both in his native Germany and in London. For a couple of years in the mid-1880s, he cultivated contacts in William Morris's Socialist League, but was expelled from the league in 1887 on accusations of spying for the Prussian political police.[13]

Prior to all that, Reuss had joined a German-speaking Masonic lodge in London, shortly after his twenty-first birthday in 1876, but was excluded from membership in 1880, possibly owing to nonpayment of dues. It appears that he had little to do with Freemasonry for the next twenty years, during which time he acted as a foreign correspondent for various newspapers and news services.

Reuss would later claim that he first revived the Bavarian Illuminati in Munich in 1880, but there is no evidence for this claim. A more likely date for this "revival" is 1895, when he first met Leopold Engel, an itinerant actor, hypnotist, and naturopathic healer with an interest

in spiritualism and the occult. Engel apparently joined Reuss's Order of the Illuminati in 1896, but broke away to found his own Order of the Illuminati in 1897. According to Reuss, the two orders were reunited in 1899, although it wasn't until 1901 that officers were appointed and meeting minutes recorded.

Reuss and Engel's order—whose relationship to the original Illuminati was created out of whole cloth—claimed the right to make Masons, a rather bold claim considering that the only bona fide Mason in the group was Reuss, and his status as a Mason had lapsed more than twenty years earlier.

Theodor Reuss, German fringe Mason and accused police spy, devised a "revival" of the Bavarian Illuminati before settling on a neo-Templar order, the Order of the Oriental Templars (OTO), as his primary field of operations.

At this point, events accelerated at a furious pace. Within

three months of the 1901 election of officers, the "revived" lodge dropped its official connection with the Order of the Illuminati (i.e., with itself) and rapidly refashioned itself into the Grosse Freimauer Loge für Deutschland, even adding five additional member lodges by the end of 1901.

Meanwhile, Reuss had established contact with John Yarker, the eccentric English Mason who headed innumerable "higher-grade" Masonic orders that mainly led a paper existence and were unrecognized by the United Grand Lodge of England and other mainstream grand lodges. In quick succession in 1902, Reuss received warrants and charters from Yarker to establish German branches of the Rite of Swedenborg, the Ancient and Primitive Rite of Memphis and Mizraim, and the renegade Cerneau version of the Scottish Rite. In the middle of all this activity, Reuss and Engel had a falling out, and Engel went off to refound his own Order of the Illuminati once again.[14]

None of this would be especially notable save for the fact that in due course, possibly as early as 1906 but no later than 1912, Reuss rolled all of his enterprises into the Order of the Oriental Templars, better known as the OTO. In doing so, he allied himself with Aleister Crowley, the self-styled "Great Beast 666," known to tabloid readers as "the wickedest man in the world." The OTO, which admitted both men and women and taught a neo-Tantric sex magic in its higher degrees, had as much to do with the Knights Templar or legitimate mainstream Freemasonry as Reuss's Order of the Illuminati had to do with Adam Weishaupt's Illuminati—that is, nothing.

Crowley, for his part, fanned the flames of mystification with overblown statements such as the following:

Although I was admitted to the thirty-third and last degree of Freemasonry so long ago as 1900, it was not until the summer of 1912 that my suspicion was confirmed. I speak of my belief that behind the frivolities and convivialities of our greatest institution [i.e., Freemasonry] lay in truth a secret ineffable and miraculous, potent to control the forces of Nature, and not only to make men brethren, but to make them divine. But at the time I speak of a man came to me, a man of those mysterious masters of esoteric Freemasonry who are alike its Eyes and its Brains, and who exist

in its midst—unknown, often, even to its acknowledged chiefs.
. . . This man had been watching my occult career for some years,
and deemed me now worthy to partake of the Greater Mysteries.

With these he proceeded to acquaint me, and my life has
since then been devoted principally to their study and practice.[15]

Crowley is here engaging in a combination of sleight of hand and
sales pitch, which it is worthwhile to unpack, as quotes such as these
are like catnip to anti-Masonic critics.

Crowley's claim that he was "admitted to the thirty-third and last
degree of Freemasonry so long ago as 1900" sounds impressive enough
until one realizes that he received this "honor" from a "minuscule irregular Supreme Council" in Mexico, "headed by a claimed descendant
of the Dukes of Medina-Sidonia of Spanish Armada fame."[16] In other
words, his 33rd° carried no standing in mainline Freemasonry and
would have been considered spurious by recognized supreme councils
of the Scottish Rite.

Similarly, Crowley's reference to being contacted by one of "those
mysterious masters of esoteric Freemasonry" loses much of its luster
when one learns that he is here referring to none other than Theodor
Reuss.

As for the "Greater Mysteries" imparted to Crowley by Reuss, one
need only consult Reuss's own claim for the OTO: "Our Order possesses the KEY which embraces all masonic and hermetic secrets. It
relates to sexual magic and this teaching completely explains all Masonic symbolism and religious teachings."[17]

Such a claim takes us right back to the notions of the 18th-century
antiquarians and mythographers: the bright idea that all religion and
all Freemasonry can be traced back to phallus or sun worship. Such
sweeping generalizations are attractive to those in search of simple
answers that explain everything, but reality inevitably has the last
laugh.

To give him his due, it seems that Reuss was introduced by Karl
Kellner, one of his occult associates, to a stream of esoteric teachings
akin to those of Tantric yoga, which taught that sex can serve as a meditative practice leading to higher consciousness.[18] The influential but
little-known occult teacher Paschal Beverley Randolph was a propo-

nent of the spiritual and health benefits, as well as magical power, of simultaneous male/female orgasms. His teachings were promulgated beneath a heavy veil of Victorian verbiage by esoteric orders such as the Hermetic Brotherhood of Luxor (or Light) in the latter half of the 19th century. Thus, there may have been some substance to what Reuss was teaching, but it wasn't a substance derived from Masonry.[19]

After his numerous attempts to get some Masonic enterprise off the ground, Reuss may finally have achieved liftoff with the OTO, which was not in itself Masonic, but purported to explain "all Masonic symbolism and religious teachings." As head of the OTO in England, Crowley had an interest in promoting the conceit.

Whatever else might be said about Crowley, he was brilliant at mirroring back to critics exactly what they accused him of. In his manifesto for the British section of the OTO, Crowley one-upped the conspiracy theorists by insisting that the OTO was the repository of "the wisdom and knowledge" of no less than twenty bodies, including the Gnostic Catholic Church, the Order of the Illuminati, the Order of the Temple (Knights Templar), the Order of the Knights of the Holy Sepulchre, the Hidden Church of the Holy Grail, the Rosicrucian Order, the Order of the Holy Royal Arch of Enoch, the Rite of Memphis (97 degrees), the Rite of Mizraim (90 degrees), the Ancient and Accepted Scottish Rite (33 degrees), the Order of Martinists, and the Hermetic Brotherhood of Light, among others.[20]

It is unfortunate that Crowley failed to include the Barnum and Bailey Circus in his list, as he was clearly an adept of the P. T. Barnum "there's a sucker born every minute" school of marketing. The only thing more amazing than such claims is the phenomenon of some people, anti-Masons among them, taking them seriously.

Meanwhile, Leopold Engel, Reuss's old compatriot, continued to promote his own Illuminati order, which mutated into the World League of Illuminati in 1926. Engel died in 1931, and the league ran afoul of the Gestapo in 1934. However, the organization survived in branches in other countries, most notably Switzerland, eventually coming full circle and merging with the OTO in 1963.[21]

Needless to say, neither Reuss's nor Engel's Illuminati orders—nor the OTO, for that matter—had any influence over mainstream Freemasonry or over the political and economic affairs of the world.

This, however, didn't stop the profoundly clueless Lady Queenborough from alleging in her *Occult Theocrasy* [sic] that the doings of Theodor Reuss proved both the survival of the Illuminati into the 20th century and its intimate relationship with Freemasonry. Queenborough, as you may recall, was a gullible propagator of the Léo Taxil hoax, including the wireless Masonic telephones of 1891, complete with flame-breathing toads. And Queenborough, in turn, has been a recurring source for anti-Masons such as Jack Harris and Ed Decker, as well as anti-Masonic Web sites such as Freemasonry Watch.[22]

Ignorance breeds confusion, which in turn feeds rumors and strange conclusions. Thus, even a seasoned raconteur of the outré like Adam Parfrey inserts foot firmly in mouth with garbled declarations such as the following:

> Scottish Rite Freemasonry, the most popular American Masonic organization, has 33 degrees in its hierarchy. A Mason revealed to me that the top two degrees are known as the "Illuminati." Aleister Crowley's sex-magical OTO organization reputedly swiped its own rituals from the top Masonic initiations. It's no longer such a well-observed secret that the highest degrees of freemasonry involve sex magic.[23]

By now you will have, I hope, read and understood enough to be able to detect the errors in every sentence in the preceding extract, but just in case you haven't, let's run through them.

Calling the Scottish Rite "the most popular American Masonic organization" is misleading but relatively harmless. It indeed has 33 degrees, but they do not constitute a hierarchy. The top two degrees in the Scottish Rite are *not* known as "the Illuminati," and if a Mason really did tell this to Parfrey, he was either pulling Parfrey's leg or was himself deluded.

The Scottish Rite and the OTO are totally unrelated organizations, and if there is any resemblance between the OTO rituals and so-called Masonic initiations, these would have derived from Reuss's or Crowley's fringe Masonic contacts, which could hardly be described as "top."

Finally, and no doubt to widespread disappointment all around, the highest degrees of Freemasonry *do not* involve sex magic. Considering that your average Mason is in his mid-seventies, the notion is patently ridiculous. Flattering, perhaps, but out of the question.

And the same goes for the whole grandiose Illuminati conspiracy. Sorry, but it just isn't happening.

A Matter of Proportion

In the end, the problem with most, if not all, conspiracy theories is that they overreach themselves. It would be foolish not to grant that there are behind-the-scenes players in the world at large: political dirty tricks; covert intelligence operations; organized crime; the underground economy; political and religious fanatics; gift-bearing lobbyists; and the big-money interests that political scientist C. Wright Mills once referred to as "the power elite." All of these affect our lives in ways at which most of us can only guess.[24]

It is even safe to say that various of these players impact each other's spheres of influence and sometimes have interests in common. But it is another thing altogether to hypothesize that the fate of the world is being coordinated behind the scenes by a small cabal of Illuminati. Moreover, it is patently ridiculous to believe, as many anti-Masons seem to, that a shrinking fraternal order, which has trouble simply maintaining its own aging buildings, is a cog in the Illuminati's wheel. Were there really a powerful secret cabal using Masonry as a front, one might at least expect them to maintain the Craft as a well-oiled machine.

The continued existence of the Illuminati is an intriguing myth, but like its first cousin the Elders of Zion canard, it is a dangerous delusion. As we have seen, Freemasonry in some of its manifestations has not been free of manipulation or misuse, but these have invariably been brief deviations from the norm.

Masonry's plethora of thousands of local blue lodges might seem, to the conspiratorial mind, like a network of cells ready to spring into action upon orders from "higher-ups." However, the practical reality is that the last thing that most lodges feel like doing is jumping to someone else's orders, even those from their own grand lodges.

Illustration playing up the mysterious public image of Freemasonry and other secret societies, including secret handshakes and temple buildings covered with symbols and insignia (Illustration by Tennessee Dixon, Gnosis, *no. 6, Winter 1988)*

10

Is Masonry Occult?

And Is Occult *Even a Useful Word?*

One fine Indian summer day, I'm sharing lunch with a couple of fellow Masons in a down-home diner in a small town in Oklahoma. The lunchroom is filled with folks in coveralls and work clothes caught up in their own conversations. We're sharing anecdotes of a Masonic nature, and the brother across from me sports a laconic smile as he recalls a favorite. He's the building engineer for the Scottish Rite temple in town—an imposing structure dominated by a flight of stairs in front leading to giant columns, with handsome stained-glass windows lining the building's sides.

"Then there was the time that this evangelical preacher brought his congregation into town in order to 'exorcise' the Temple. They were marching around the Temple and he was at the head of the line. Every now and then, they'd come to a halt and he'd blow on this giant horn to drive the demons out of the building. What a pain in the neck!

"We just tried to ignore them, but I still wish we had acted on this idea I had to get rid of them once and for all. My idea was to dress up one of the brethren in red long johns with a tail and horns and paint him red. And at a climactic moment, with the reverend blowing his horn, we'd have the brother run lickety-split out of the Temple, across the lawn, and off into the distance. Then we could go out and tell them, 'See? You drove the devil out. Now go home!'"

Once Upon a Time

The word *occult* is one of those ooga-booga words the mere utterance of which can send shivers down the spines of otherwise reasonable people and cause those who are unreasonable to reach for their pitchforks and torches. This is unfortunate, because once upon a time the word had the quite serviceable meaning of "hidden from view" or "covered."

That massive compendium of occult knowledge, the *Oxford English Dictionary,* informs us in its sparkling prose that in the 17th century and before, the word was "[a]pplied in early science or natural philosophy to physical qualities not manifest to direct observation but discoverable only by experiment, or to those whose nature was unknown or unexplained; latent." Thus Isaac Newton, in his *Optics,* writes: "The Aristotelians gave the name of occult qualities . . . to such qualities . . . as they supposed to lie hid in bodies, and to be the unknown causes of manifest effects."[1]

Over time, the term was also applied to "those ancient and mediaeval reputed sciences (or their modern representatives) held to involve the knowledge or use of agencies of a secret and mysterious nature (as magic, alchemy, astrology, theosophy, and the like)."[2]

It is important to remember that these occult "sciences," now generally derided as superstitious hokum, were considered in earlier eras to be on the cutting edge of the investigation of nature. Were it not for alchemy, modern chemistry would never have developed, while for millennia astrology and astronomy were intertwined. As for magic, perhaps the most misunderstood of these fields, its practices ranged from the common folk magic of love charms and herbal remedies to the high magic of attempts to converse with angels and better understand matters divine.

None of this endeared the students of these occult sciences to the Church, of course, as such studies represented an independent sphere of inquiry continually at risk of running up against the limits of the Church's power and knowledge. One might, with the best of intentions, cross a line into heresy and be rewarded with house arrest or a burning at the stake, as Galileo and Giordano Bruno were to learn to their chagrin. Bruno went to the stake in 1600, while Galileo was tried for heresy as late as 1633—both men earning the Church's wrath for advocating versions of Copernicus's heliocentric theories.[3]

Bruno, like other famous figures involved in birthing modern science, such as Francis Bacon, John Dee, and Isaac Newton, saw nothing strange in investigating the hidden laws of nature by experimenting with alchemy, magic, and astrology. God works in mysterious ways, it was believed, and these scientific pioneers felt it proper to expand mankind's appreciation of those mysteries by uncovering His workings. Rather than being the creation of a rather arbitrary divine ruler, nature was increasingly seen as evidence of divine reason and rationality. In attempting to uncover the laws of nature, "natural philosophers" were trying to better understand the laws of God.

Thus by a series of half steps, natural philosophy evolved from its occult roots in the Renaissance to the Enlightenment's advocacy of science and reason. Along the way, the occult was eclipsed by new scientific premises, and the term eventually took on a negative cast with implications of irrationality, superstition, and the supernatural.

Science writer Michael White sees Isaac Newton as a prime example of this process. He notes:

> Ironically, although Newton was largely responsible for the development of the scientific enlightenment which swept away the common belief in magic and mysticism, he created the origins of empirical science and the modern, "rational" world in part by immersing himself in these very practices.[4]

To reiterate, throughout the 17th century and even into the 18th, practices and perspectives that might be labeled "occult" were still looked upon with favor and interest by some of the top educated and inquiring minds of the West. Although sometimes viewed with disfavor by the Church, these "sciences" were seen by their proponents as compatible with Christianity. Indeed, in some cases they were viewed as a synthesis or summation of the combined wisdom of Christianity, Judaism, and the ancients. For instance, according to historian Betty Jo Teeter Dobbs:

> [Isaac Newton thought that] with their understanding of true natural philosophy, the ancients were enabled to create a form of

religious structure and worship that adequately represented to human beings the structure of God's cosmos and suggested the study of nature as a means to satisfy human aspirations for knowledge of God—an extremely rational way of going about things. . . . "So then the first religion was the most rational of all others till the nations corrupted it. For there is no way (without revelation) to come to the knowledge of a Deity but by the frame of nature."[5]

Whether this notion of an uncorrupted primordial wisdom still accessible by investigating nature's secrets via "occult" means was a romantic fantasy or not is beside the point. What is important to note is that the proponents of the occult sciences saw themselves as serving both God and the good of mankind by advancing knowledge and truth. And, in point of fact, in pursuing their studies they *did* have a positive impact. Not only did they make certain experimental breakthroughs that led to modern science, but they did so in an inner-directed manner that also deepened their own faith and spiritual growth.

The Inner Life

In addition to such apparently outer-directed activities as the pursuit of the philosopher's stone in alchemy and charting celestial paths in astrology, students of the occult sciences occupied themselves with that subjective realm of human experience that would now be subsumed under the discipline of psychology. Or, to put it another way, the occult sciences in their heyday were among the precursors of modern psychology.

Psychology is generally considered a "soft" science, as the human psyche is notoriously difficult to pin down in any objective fashion that would lend itself to reproducible scientific measurement and experimentation. Human consciousness varies so widely from person to person, and from moment to moment, that it is hard to identify a baseline "normal" state of mind with specific characteristics upon which all psychologists can agree.

Despite advances in neurological research into the brain, where scientists are beginning to link certain emotions or psychological states with the stimulation of certain neural pathways or lobal areas, there is much that remains mysterious—one might even say occult— about human consciousness.

Psychology, as a systematic field of study, is barely a hundred years old, yet it is easy to forget that what amounted to psychology in the 19th century was a cacophony of arts and "sciences" that would now be dismissed as "occult": mesmerism and the theory of animal magnetism, which gradually evolved into hypnotism; phrenology—the study of bumps on the head; and a mix of "water cures," electrical treatments, and "mental" healings.

These areas of study were relatively scientific for their day in that they attempted, by and large, to find materialist causes and explanations for the various states of the human mind and body. The psychology of the 18th century and before, by contrast, was a mélange of spiritual and natural concepts, with a worldview where the natural order feathered incrementally into a supernatural or divine order. Behind the world of appearances lay an unseen world of beings and energies capable of affecting this world and, perhaps, vice versa.

What would now be considered psychoses were then considered evidence of demonic possession. Prayer, confession, penance, exorcism, and, all too often, torture constituted the psychotherapy of the times, with the Church presuming to monopolize the treatment of psychological fluctuations.

In such a context, the occult sciences were relatively sophisticated systems of psychological exploration, experimentation, and healing. Using symbolic "maps," such as the twelve signs of the zodiac, the four elements (fire, water, earth, and air), the four cardinal directions, and the four worlds and ten sephirot of the Kabbalah, the esotericists cross-categorized the interaction between human consciousness and the natural and supernatural (or unseen) realms.

While we might be tempted to dismiss such efforts as nonsensical products of the imagination having little to do with objective reality, I would suggest that the subjective realm of the human psyche is capable of sustaining a variety of "maps" that "work" for different people. Freud, we should recall, drew upon Greek myths in characterizing psychological complexes, while Jung found inspiration for many of his insights in precisely those symbolic maps previously associated with the occult. In engaging with the unseen realms, the occult sciences provided, in many cases, a means for the practitioner to communicate with his unconscious psyche as well as enter into meditative and contemplative states.

Regarding alchemists' interaction with their psyches and inner spiritual selves, Michael White suggests that

> the spiritual element of the experiment was in fact the key to the true alchemist's philosophy. It is this which has led to the suggestion that, for many alchemists, it was the practical process that was in fact the allegory and their search was really for the elixir or the philosophers' stone within *them:* that, by conducting a seemingly mundane set of tasks, they were following a path to enlightenment—allowing themselves to be transmuted into "gold." This is why the alchemist placed such importance on "purity of spirit" and spent long years in preparation for the task of transmutation before so much as touching a crucible.[6]

Which is all very well, but what exactly does this have to do with Freemasonry? Let us see.

Brethren of the Rosie Cross?

Modern speculative Freemasonry, as we saw earlier, began to take shape during the 17th century, at the cusp between the Renaissance and the Enlightenment. As you'll recall, the two earliest nonoperative Masons on English soil, for whom accounts of Masonic initiation survive, were Robert Moray and Elias Ashmole. Both men were fascinated by "occult" or esoteric subjects such as alchemy and Rosicrucianism, and both men were instrumental in the early days of the Royal Society, the first officially condoned scientific society.

Though there is no record of Moray or Ashmole having any specific impact on Masonry's evolution from an operative to a speculative organization, it is fair to surmise that other men with a similar mix of interests were also attracted to Masonry, with its claims of ancient origins and knowledge. Note that I say "surmise," as this is a supposition that is hard to prove. What little is known about those men who were nonoperative Masons in the 1600s does not give us a handy list of known occultists, by any means. Instead, what we have are extremely circumstantial references to shared interests in such matters.

For instance, the earliest appearance in print of a reference to the "Mason Word" was in *The Muses Threnodie*, by Henry Adamson, published in Edinburgh in

Elias Ashmole, early Freemason and antiquarian

1638. There, in the midst of an account of Perth and its surroundings—rendered in verse, no less—we find the following characterization:

> For what we do presage is not in grosse,
> For we be Brethren of the Rosie Crosse;
> We have the Mason word, and second sight,
> Things for to come we can foretell aright.[7]

Similarly, nearly forty years later, in 1676, a satirical "divertissement" appeared in *Poor Robin's Intelligence* for October 10, 1676, announcing:

These are to give notice that the Modern Green-ribbon'd Caball, together with the Ancient Brother-hood of the Rosy-Cross; the Hermetick Adepti, and the Company of accepted Masons, intend all to Dine together on the 31 of November next, at the Flying-Bull in Wind-Mill-Crown-Street; having already given order for great store of Black-Swan Pies, Poach'd Phoenixes Eggs, Haunches of Unicorns, &c. To be provided on that occasion; All idle people that can spare so much time from the Coffe-house [sic], may repair thither to be spectators of the Solemnity: But are advised to provide themselves Spectacles of Malleable Glass; For otherwise 'tis thought the said Societies will (as hitherto) make their Appearance Invisible.[8]

There is a tongue-in-cheek quality to both these references to Masons, and it is quite possible that all they signify is that the early nonoperative Freemasons were associated, in the public imagination, with the mythic Rosicrucians and assorted "occult" topics, and that they were fit subjects for teasing by their contemporaries. While it is tempting to suppose that these things were not lumped together by random chance, all we can really say is that the trope of Masons and the occult was there in people's minds from the very earliest days of speculative Freemasonry.

My own guess, mentioned earlier, was that, based on some elements in the ritual such as the Lost Word and the Substitute Word in the third degree, and the True Word in the Royal Arch, it seems likely that someone (singular or plural) conversant with Kabbalistic concepts and symbolism contributed to the evolution of the ritual. The Kabbalah began as a form of Jewish mysticism and theurgy, but some of the key figures of the Renaissance, such as Pico della Mirandola, became sufficiently familiar with it to develop a new Christianized Kabbalah (sometimes spelled as "Cabala"). This, in turn, had a significant impact in intellectual circles both on the continent and in Britain during the 16th and 17th centuries.[9]

Certain Kabbalistic practices, such as gematria and notarikon, placed great emphasis on number and letter symbolism, assigning numerical values to the Hebrew alphabet and eliciting additional meanings from scripture by identifying words having numerical affinities to each other. There was, of course, much more to Kabbalah than just this, but my point here is that the Masonic emphasis on words, both lost and found, both secret and discovered, strongly suggests a Kabbalistic influence.

The Kabbalah, of course, along with alchemy and astrology, was part of "occult" studies, so does this mean that Freemasonry is itself "occult"? This is the jackpot question, and it can't be easily answered with just a casual yes or no. It partly depends on how the word *occult* is defined.

The legions of anti-Masons, most of them superstitious believers in the occult as a demon-infested quagmire, hasten to shout "yes" and shiver dramatically as they hawk their books and videos denouncing the fraternity. Meanwhile, the vast majority of Masons, knowing full well that nothing that they would consider occult goes on in their lodges, confidently answer "no."

Neither camp, however, is likely to be able to provide a reasonable answer as to what it would entail for Freemasonry to be occult. That Masonic rituals and lectures share some symbols and motifs with Kabbalah and alchemy does not turn Freemasonry into an occult organization any more than its having some symbols and motifs in common with medieval stonemasons turns it into an architectural firm.

Fundamentalist anti-Masons, operating with an either/or logic according to which you are either Us or Them, determine that Freemasonry is not a strictly Christian group and hence is a tool of the devil. This kind of paranoia is compounded by their simplistic approach to symbol interpretation in which some symbol that has been identified as "bad" (e.g., the sun, since a sun symbol must surely connote pagan sun worship) takes on a radioactive quality that contaminates everything in its vicinity.

This brand of thinking has, from the early days of organized anti-Masonry, been mixed with a not-too-subtle anti-Semitism that considers Jews as part of the dreaded "Them." If one legacy of the Renaissance was an increased interest in and openness to Jewish mysticism (Kabbalah) and Jewish scriptural interpretation (Talmud and Midrash) among Christian scholars, an interest that also seems to have influenced Masonic motifs, this also engendered a reactionary backlash that saw such advances as evidence of a creeping pollution. One can see such thinking at work in this quote from the *Anti-Masonic Review* at the height of the American anti-Masonic movement in 1829:

> The degrees of Free Masonry above the degree of Master Mason, came to this country [i.e., the United States] from a company of Voltaire's associates, by the hand of the sons of those who in their madness exclaimed; "*his blood be upon us and upon our children!*" Jews, also received it here, and passed it down to you. And

as revealed, it contains both the guile and the venom of the old Serpent.[10]

What is being demonized here is the role played by some Jewish Masons in establishing the Scottish Rite degrees in America. (Several of the founding members of the first Supreme Council of the AASR, established in 1801 in Charleston, South Carolina, were Jewish.)

Similarly, nearly one hundred years later in Munich, in 1927, General Erich Ludendorff, a Nazi fellow traveler, accused Masonry of making "artificially created Jews" through its propagation of Solomonic and Noachite motifs and its Kabbalistic symbols.[11]

This is as if one were to confuse attending a screening of the film *Man of La Mancha*—a movie already twice removed from Cervantes's allegorical novel *Don Quixote*—with becoming a chivalric knight.

It is difficult for many of Masonry's opponents to differentiate between their fear of the occult and their fear of "Kabbalistic Jews." It never occurs to them that their images of both are inaccurate and their fears of both are overexaggerated.

Masonic Occultists

Nevertheless, it also needs pointing out that some of those arguing that Freemasonry *is* occult (in some fashion or other) have been Masons. Some of these, such as our old friend Theodor Reuss, the French occultist Papus, and the Theosophical Co-Mason Charles W. Leadbeater, have been leaders of unrecognized and "irregular" Masonic orders so far from the Masonic mainstream that one might barely call them Masons at all. (Leadbeater was active in the Order of Universal Co-Freemasonry, led by the Theosophist Annie Besant, which admitted both men and women and promulgated a more esoterically oriented version of the Craft.)

Leadbeater's writings on Masonry, such as *The Hidden Life in Freemasonry* and *Freemasonry and Its Ancient Mystic Rites*, interpret the Craft within the framework of the Theosophical teachings of Madame Blavatsky, Annie Besant, and Leadbeater himself, with particular reference to Leadbeater's clairvoyant readings of ancient history. Thus, when he informs his readers that his clairvoyant investigations have determined that Masonry is "a direct descendant of the Mysteries of Egypt ∴ and its purpose is still to serve as a gateway to the true Mysteries of the Great White Lodge," it must be kept in mind that such revelations are as likely to derive from a fecund imagination as they are to be accurate readings of the akashic records.[12]

W. L. Wilmshurst and J. D. Buck were also Theosophists who brought their esoteric perspectives with them into the Craft, although in their cases they joined mainstream Masonry and tried to find acceptance for their perspectives there. They had mild success in the form of publishing several books, one of which, Wilmshurst's *The Meaning of Freemasonry*, is still in print as a thoughtful, nondogmatic mystical approach to Masonry.

Ironically, one of the writers on Masonry most quoted by anti-Masons, Manly Palmer Hall, produced the bulk of his fanciful writings about Masonry in the 1920s, decades before he ever actually became a Mason. Hall shared most of the tenets of Besant's and Leadbeater's Theosophy, but he promulgated them independently through his own Los Angeles–based Philosophical Research Society.

Like Leadbeater, Hall championed notions such as the existence on higher spiritual planes of a Masonic hierarchy, a "concealed brotherhood" who guide humanity's spiritual progress.[13] This was part and parcel of the trope of hidden masters or

C. W. Leadbeater, Theosophical leader and clairvoyant, in Co-Masonic regalia. Separating fact from fantasy is always a problem with psychic visions.

Manly P. Hall in midlife. Although Hall didn't become a Mason until 1949, much of his writing on Masonry was published decades earlier, well before he actually had a real experience of the Craft.

adepts first propagated in the Rosicrucian manifestos, which recurred as "unknown superiors" in the 18th century Rite of Strict Observance in Germany, reappeared in the 19th century with Madame Blavatsky's elusive mahatmas and the Hermetic Order of the Golden Dawn's "secret chiefs," and blossomed in the 20th century into vast pantheons of "ascended masters" and other channeled entities such as Seth and Ramtha.

Foster Bailey, the author of *The Spirit of Masonry* (1957), was married to Alice A. Bailey, a breakaway Theosophist who channeled voluminous cosmological teachings from "the Tibetan" (supposedly one of Madame Blavatsky's mahatmas, the Master Djwhal Khul). In his book Bailey refers to the three Masonic degrees as encapsulating the supposed history of the Lemurian, Atlantean, and Aryan races, among other things.[14] This novel interpretation draws upon the esoteric crypto-history shared by Theosophy and his wife's outpourings. Yet Foster Bailey makes no up-front admission of this context, leaving the naive reader to take his pronouncements at face value.

Not surprisingly, the vast majority of Masons have been oblivious to such assertions, and those who have run across them have usually consigned them to the category of "wacko." Since Freemasonry, in its inclusive approach to brotherhood, accepts men of a variety of faiths, it has generally let any member have his own interpretation of the Craft, its history, and its symbols, and Masonic publishers have been all too happy to publish whatever they think might sell.

But the primary consumers of the Masonic occultists' productions have been fundamentalist (and often paranoid) anti-Masonic critics who have taken the same literalist approach to these channeled revelations and improbable assertions that they have taken to the Bible. In assuming that the Masonic occultists are respected "authorities," they presume that they are revealing the hidden teachings of Masonry, and that those revelations either are literally true or at least indicate what the innermost circle of Masons believe. Given such false premises, everything that follows in the anti-Masons' intricate critiques comes to naught.

The Lingering Question

Still, even if we put aside the Theosophy-tinged assertions of the Masonic occultists and the fear-stricken rantings of the anti-Masons, the question of Masonry's relationship to the occult remains. There are symbols and elements in the ritual that echo motifs from the Kabbalah and Rosicrucianism, and there is the recurring trope of the Knights Templar, but these do not amount to a hidden occult doctrine or teaching. After all, given all the various contributors, both known and unknown, to the Masonic corpus over the centuries, it might simply be that Masonry has collected an eclectic hodgepodge of metaphors and allegories from all over the place, threaded together into nothing more than a "system of morality," as one description of Masonry puts it.

But there seemed to me to be more going on here than merely that. At the risk of succumbing to the temptation to invent yet another theory about Freemasonry, I tried to find a pattern that would encompass all the disparate elements. The best historical evidence seems to indicate the following:

- beginnings in operative lodges that had simple rituals of initiation and obligation and that maintained secrecy for tradecraft reasons;
- a gradual influx of nonoperative members, some of whom were intrigued with occult or esoteric studies;
- the development of a speculative Masonry disengaged from any lingering trade purposes and seemingly imbued with Enlightenment values and some symbols and motifs possibly influenced by the Kabbalah and so forth;
- an incremental increase, over the course of the 18th century, in the complexity of rituals and the number of degrees;
- a further injection of occult or esoteric symbols and motifs within "higher" degrees on the Continent in the latter half of the 18th century;
- a consolidation and systematization of rituals around the turn of the 19th century (1798–1813), more or less

"freezing" the three blue-lodge degree rituals (and the higher degrees of the York Rite) in the forms still used today in the United States.

If we trace the path of this trajectory, it becomes apparent that between, say, 1640 and 1810 there were a variety of inputs and influences shaping Masonry, many of them considerably distant from each other. Hence, rather than being the product of a single author or planning committee, speculative Freemasonry as a whole was the product of a discontinuous collective effort spread over a century and a half.

Since the premise shared by most of those contributors was the one found in the traditional history of the Old Charges and Anderson's Constitutions—that Masonry dated back to the most ancient times—it appears likely that they projected ancient origins onto the bare-bones structure that they inherited from the operative lodges preceding them.

The progressive initiation by degrees, while rooted in the guild customs of the Middle Ages, echoed what little was known about the progressive initiation of the ancient mystery schools. The Mason's Word, used by Scottish operative masons as a means of identification, was seemingly transmuted by the speculative Masons into a secret sacred name of God, while the catechism and oaths, at least partly derived from the operatives, became the structural equivalents of the trials and tests that were part of ancient initiatory rites. The ideal of a brotherhood of man spanning all nations, races, and religions—which was the hallmark of speculative Freemasonry—harked back to the mythic unity of humanity prior to the Tower of Babel.

Yet, while granting Masonry's piecemeal evolution over time, it seems to me that some key men among the earliest developers of speculative Masonry must have consciously set out to found what might be described as a new kind of do-it-yourself mystery school: a nondenominational, philosophical, initiatory order dedicated to Enlightenment values and self-improvement. Their genius was that they created what amounted to a sparsely furnished organizational shell into which each member could move his own philosophical and spiritual furniture. Yet, by banning discussions of religion and politics in the lodge, each member's furniture was invisible to the others.

That some of the sparse furnishings—some symbols and some ritual components—may have invited Kabbalistic or astrological interpretations was largely due to those "sciences" providing a symbolic vocabulary that was shared by certain early Masonic devisers. These elements provided some of the structure and some of the decor, but they were not really the content. And remarkably enough, in a certain sense there *was* no content. A bunch of marching around and banging of gavels and a Master's Word—whether lost or found—do not constitute the secret wisdom of the ages. Beyond a certain point, the initiate had to supply his own content, so to speak.

The Masonic mystery school that came to be, it seems to me, may have been loosely modeled on the mystery schools of the ancients insofar as there were stages of initiation, the progressive disclosure of secrets, and a symbolic death and rebirth. But the mysteries into which the initiate was inducted were not some secret pagan revelation. Rather, they were the vision of a brotherhood of civilized men enjoying "true friendship among persons that must [otherwise] have remain'd at a perpetual distance," as Anderson's Constitutions put it.

There was a spiritual and moral component to this, to be sure, but of as generic and nonsectarian a nature as men of that era could imagine. The intent of the Masonic project was not to usurp its members' religious beliefs or practices, and certainly not to create a rival religion, as many anti-Masons have feared. Nor was it a front for some sort of occult training or to recruit members for an even more secret inner order.

Rather, what Masonry offered—and still offers—was an opportunity for men to come together as brothers, to experience a shared rite of passage into adulthood, and to be of service to each other and their communities. Last but not least, it furnished a template for a path of self-directed spiritual inquiry and growth.

Just Say No

After looking at all the evidence, it seemed to me that the answer to the question of whether Freemasonry is occult was a carefully qualified no. Anyone expecting to find a coherent occult doctrine concealed within its rituals is going to be sorely disappointed, unless, like the aforementioned Masonic occultists, they bring their own doctrine along with them and project it onto Masonry.

I suppose that if one were to categorize as "occult" anything having to do with the inner life of an individual's consciousness, or with the use of symbolic "maps" derived from such sources as Kabbalah and alchemy, the term might superficially apply to the Craft. However, using such a broad definition, one could also label psychotherapy, Chinese Medicine, and folk singing as "occult." Better to just discard the term—which has become trivialized and stigmatized through misuse—and use instead a more accurate term such as "transformative."

The possibility of a careful and positive self-transformation is implied in one of Masonry's most fundamental symbols associated with the first degree. That is the symbol of the "rough ashlar" (quarried stone), which through chiseling and polishing can become the square-cornered "smooth ashlar," fit for the builder's use. This process, the Entered Apprentice is told, symbolizes "divesting our hearts and consciences of all the vices and superfluities of life, thereby fitting our minds, as living stones, for that spiritual building—that house not made with hands—eternal in the heavens."

The wording is typical Masonic oratory, perhaps a bit rich for present tastes, and a trifle obscure. The phrase, in fact, quotes Paul in 2 Corinthians 5:1, where he writes: "For we know that if the earthly tent we live in is destroyed, we have a building from God, a house not made with hands, eternal in the heavens." By "earthly tent" (or tabernacle), Paul is referring to the body, and the "house not made with hands" is the soul.

And this, I think, takes us to the heart of the speculative Masonic project. The original operative masons built actual physical temples and cathedrals, but the temple that the new breed of speculative Masons were intent on elevating was the soul.

The early speculative Masons were a mix of Protestants, Catholics, Deists, and, within a few decades of 1717, Jews. I doubt that they were trying to make subtle theological points as they began to develop their rituals. Fundamentalist critics have taken Masonry to task for supposedly suggesting in passages such as this that merely following Masonry's tenets will save one's soul. However, that imputes to Masonry a role that it explicitly disavowed. James Anderson, the author of the founding Constitutions of 1723 and 1738, was a Presbyterian minister at a London church throughout his Masonic career. He was not in the business of starting some new quasi religion.

The purpose of Freemasonry as a generic mystery school wasn't religious in a doctrinal sense, and it wasn't occult in a practical sense. Rather, it seems to have been an attempt to create a nucleus of men of goodwill, over and above fractious religious conflicts, using the motifs and symbols of temple building as "working tools" both for deepening the individual soul and for building an archetypal temple to the Most High in the collective imagination of humanity.

Of course, Freemasonry wasn't *only* that. It was also an opportunity for feasting, toasting, and the exchange of ideas, and an early provider of a social safety net. I doubt that most Masons thought of the Craft as a mystery school, and it is quite possible that in calling it that I am unwittingly joining the ranks of the alternative historians. The Masonic myth is like that: if you follow the twists and turns of Masonic minutiae long enough, you end up spinning theories to fill in the holes.

We may never be sure what the fraternity's early devisers thought they were really doing, but they must have done something right for it to last this long and to have had such an impact on so many men. What the future may hold, however, is the final mystery.

Examples of a new breed of professionally designed promotional literature, in this case from the Grand Lodge of California, F&AM. The success of Freemasonry's efforts to update itself and adapt to the 21st century will depend on whether it actually meets the needs and captures the imagination of a new generation of men.

11

Back to the Future

Is Freemasonry Doomed?

I n the ever-smiling realm of Masonic public relations, the order
is inevitably portrayed in the best possible light. Its virtues as an
international brotherhood, a support network, an opportunity for
community service, and a source of spiritual and ethical inspiration
are put front and center. Color brochures issued by grand lodges feature photos of clean-cut young men in polo shirts and slacks looking
mighty pleased to be Masons. In this happy universe, Freemasonry is a
vital organization going places and doing things.

There is nothing wrong, exactly, with this rosy portrayal. After all,
playing up the positive is a time-honored technique in advertising and
PR. But, as with all marketing, it tells only part of the story. The rest
of the story reveals itself only as one becomes familiar with the Craft
from the inside.

Future Shock

For at least the past thirty years, Masonic publications have regularly
featured think pieces with titles such as "What Is to Be Done?"; "Does
Masonry Have a Future?"; and "How Do We Turn Things Around?"
Like canaries in a coal mine, the authors have warned of impending

disaster as the Craft's membership figures continue to fall. They have had good reason to worry.

Masonry brags that it is the world's oldest and largest fraternal order, but if present trends continue, it may soon be the world's *only* fraternal order, and a severely shrunken one at that. The fraternal boom of the 19th century that brought us the Odd Fellows, the Elks, the Moose, the Eagles, the Knights of Pythias, the Improved Order of Redmen, and dozens more has long since subsided. Most of these orders either have gone under or barely hang on as mere shadows of their former selves.

For many of the fraternal orders—especially those whose primary function was selling insurance or whose personas were patently ridiculous—the decline set in nearly a century ago. Exactly why Masonry was able to rebound and postpone its decline until the 1960s is mostly a matter of conjecture. Its two boom decades in the 20th century, the '20s and the '50s, each followed traumatic world wars, and it is likely that the prospect of networking and mutual support associated with Masonry made it attractive for men who were heading off into the unknown of war and later trying to start new postwar lives and families. However, changes to the social landscape from the '60s on virtually guaranteed that fewer men would find the time to be Masons.

To cite only the most obvious obstacles:

- *The demographic decline of nuclear families, marked by a working father, housewife mother, and kids attending a neighborhood school.* This stable structure provided sufficient room for a regular "lodge night" out. The present mix of single-parent families, or families where both spouses work, has reshaped how men can expect to spend their evenings.
- *The gradual disappearance of separate men's and women's social spheres.* Perhaps in response to issues raised by the women's movement of the '70s, long-standing gender roles have broadened and shifted, moving the center of social gravity toward group activities that include both men and women.
- *The time demands on working men.* The serious increase

in hours worked per dollars earned, combined with a
dilution of corporate employee benefits, has meant that
many workers, both white- and blue-collar, must work
longer and later in order to approach the equivalent
income levels of their parents' generation. Spare time has
become a scarcity.

- *The progressive informalization of society.* If nothing else,
  Masonry is a bastion of formality in its meetings and
  rituals. This flies in the face of a culture in which the
  casual has become the norm. Once upon a time, men
  wore suits, ties, and bowler hats to baseball games. That
  era is long gone.

- *A decrease in eligible believers.* A belief in a Supreme
  Being remains a core requirement for Masonic candidates. While the American population remains one of
  the most religious on the planet, recent decades have
  seen a growth in evangelical churches and a decline in
  mainstream denominations. Evangelical churches—
  especially those that wish to monopolize their members'
  time and attention—tend to see Masonry as a rival
  religion. The distortions and misunderstandings of anti-
  Masonic ministers and authors are especially widespread
  in such church circles.

- *The Balkanization of age groups.* The rise of a separatist
  youth counterculture in the '60s was short-lived, but it
  left a legacy of generational apartheid in its wake. Age
  groups may mix in the workplace, but they are less likely
  to do so in extracurricular social activities.

The result of these shifts and changes has been a much smaller
pool of men who would consider joining the Craft—assuming they were
even aware of its existence.

Many of these factors are not particular to Masonry alone. As
Robert Putnam has pointed out in his book *Bowling Alone,* the entire
strata of social groupings, from hobby clubs and bowling leagues to
fraternal orders and service clubs, has nearly disappeared from civil
society.

With the exception of support groups such as AA and NA, which have experienced phenomenal growth in recent decades, most Americans have privatized their social contacts through cocooning with friends and family in home theaters, hanging out in online social networks, or staying late with co-workers at the office. If an evening is spent out in public, it is most likely in order to enjoy food, drink, music, or a movie—not to attend a lodge meeting.

Upside Down

Yet, as bleak as things might seem when considering Freemasonry's future prospects, there are counterforces in play that may enable the Craft to pull back from the precipice.

The same online universe that has introduced millions to the virtual world of social networking has enabled far-flung Masons to meet each other through e-mail lists, blogs, and Yahoo groups of their own.

Starting with the Freemasonry forum on CompuServe in the 1980s, before the Internet became ubiquitous, people who were curious about Masonry were able to connect with real live Masons and have their questions answered. Just as important, Masons from different jurisdictions and countries—some whose grand lodges didn't "recognize" each other—were able to meet online and discuss their differences and commonalities, thereby gaining a global perspective that few ordinary Masons had previously enjoyed.

The growth of the Web enabled both individual lodges and grand lodges to hang out their shingles, and thousands of Masonic Web sites rapidly appeared. This increased Masonic visibility tenfold.

Meanwhile, the growing public interest in certain threads of "alternative spirituality," such as Gnosticism, the Divine Feminine, the mysteries of Egypt, secret societies, and the Knights Templar, has pulled Freemasonry into the mix, feeding romantic notions of Masonic significance.

This, in turn, has caused a new generation of men to come knocking at Masonry's door, curious to see whether it might be worth their time and interest. This presents both an opportunity and a challenge to the aging Masonic leadership.

Time to Retire

Long accustomed to declining numbers and a membership of whom 95 percent qualify to join AARP, most lodges have shaped themselves around their older members' preferences and needs. This has meant early meetings and dinners to accommodate early bedtimes; lodge excursions best suited to retirees, such as cruises; unadventurous dinner menus; and the comfort of the familiar. This has also meant that retired men with plenty of time on their hands have devised a Masonry to occupy that time.

The generation now in their seventies and eighties are those who have held the fort and kept the order going as numbers have declined. In some smaller lodges where only twelve to twenty men may be active members, it is not uncommon to have Past Masters serving two or three times as Master of the lodge, and officers' lines filled out with other Past Masters. In such circumstances, the temptation is strong to take new initiates and immediately make them officers, even before they fully grasp what work this will entail. At the same time, representatives of various concordant and appendant bodies—such as the York Rite, Scottish Rite, Shrine, and Eastern Star—are waiting in the wings, hoping to persuade the new Mason to also join their respective groups and fill the holes in *their* officers' lines.

The recent initiate, who might have been attracted to Masonry without really knowing what to expect, may be thrilled by his sudden popularity, or he may run for the hills and never be seen in lodge again.

Some Masonic leaders, seeing this desperate dynamic too often backfire, have taken a different approach altogether. Rather than attempt to solve the dilemma of a shrinking fraternity by getting the maximum number of warm bodies to join through keeping initiation fees and dues low, and by pumping new candidates through one-day conferrals of all three blue-lodge degrees, they have proposed the exact opposite: an emphasis on quality, not quantity. The advocates of this view champion a new model, called the Traditional Observance Lodge.

Getting Serious

According to the Masonic Restoration Foundation, an advisory organization headed by several prominent Masonic leaders, a Traditional
Observance Lodge is marked by "higher dues, festive boards [i.e.,
formal celebratory dinners], a strict dress code, and higher standards
of ritual" as well as "a solemn approach to holding [meetings] and conferring degrees, the use of the Chamber of Reflection as part of the
initiation ceremony, longer time between degrees, and the requirement for candidates to present a paper before the lodge on the lessons
of their degree prior to advancement."[1]

Many of these ideas have been borrowed from successful European Masonic lodges, which have attracted a better-educated and
well-heeled membership by the counterintuitive tactic of maintaining exclusivity, demanding full participation by all members, and emphasizing intellectual stimulation and initiatory impact. Significantly,
European Freemasonry has seen steady growth in recent decades by
following this approach, even as mainstream Masonry in America has
declined despite relaxing its requirements and standards.

The rationale of the Traditional Observance Lodge is that a higher
grade of committed members will be attracted (and retained) both by
demanding more of them and by delivering more to them. While an
average local blue lodge might serve spaghetti and allow casual dress,
a Traditional Observance (T.O.) lodge might hold regular high-ticket
dinners requiring white ties and evening wear. While your average
blue-lodge meeting might be preceded by members swapping jokes
and gradually settling down, a Traditional Observance meeting might
begin on time with a five-minute silent meditation in which all present participate. The goal, Traditional Observance proponents explain,
is a "quality experience" all around.

This approach is not without its critics. Many Masons who have
been comfortable with Masonry even as it has declined view Traditional Observance lodges as "snobbish" and "elitist." This is under-
standable. If one lodge is serving doughnuts and coffee after a meeting,
and a T.O. lodge is serving pâté and cognac after theirs, the first lodge
is likely to feel one-upped and defensive. On the other hand, the T.O.
proponents would argue, business-as-usual Masonry has failed to at-

tract and excite new members. T.O. lodges, by contrast, *are* growing and initiating more professionals and younger members; the proof is in the pudding.

Nevertheless, it remains highly unlikely that a wholesale shift to the Traditional Observance approach will occur or that the T.O. lodges will be the dominant wave of the future. What the approach *does* represent, however, is the recognition by some Masons that the Craft will not survive if it doesn't provide an entryway and meaningful reception for new Masons who are attracted by the potential for "more light" and initiatory growth. If the inertia in the older lodges is just too great to provide what younger men are looking for, the fraternity should constitute new lodges with space for new (or self-consciously "traditional") approaches and let them flow forth as a parallel stream.

Delivering the Goods

In the course of my search for the truth about Freemasonry, I went through several phases. First, an initial period of idealistic enthusiasm, fed in part by the cheerleading of online Masons who had created a virtual all-good cyber-brotherhood marked by upbeat chatter and camaraderie, unburdened by real-world limitations or responsibilities.

This was followed by a gradual awareness that Freemasonry—whatever its ideals—is very much a real-world institution, populated with men who share the same mix of character strengths and flaws as the general population. As a self-consciously moral and ethical order, Freemasonry has the same problems of hypocrisy and failure to live up to its own values and standards that one finds in churches and other social groups presuming to better their members and serve the greater good.

With the cushion of large numbers and ever-growing assets now diminishing, those in positions of Masonic power are caught in an actuarial bind: the institution is shrinking beneath them no matter what they do. This encourages a climate of defensiveness and wagon circling, which aggravates the Craft's inherent conservatism. The result can be some pretty cranky infighting and power plays. The good news is that such behavior has little interface with or impact upon the world outside the fraternity. The bad news is that it does get played out in some circles within Freemasonry, particularly among the most active.

Eventually, however, my phase of disillusionment was succeeded by a more balanced state and an appreciation for what Freemasonry does have to offer.

For lovers of puzzles and mysteries, its symbols and historical lacunae provide endless opportunities for contemplation and speculation. For those wishing self-improvement, it provides a context that encourages them to live out their ideals. For those seeking brotherhood and sociality, it provides a fellowship of equals and an ongoing series of waist-expanding meals. For those in search of an initiation into manhood and a graduation from perpetual adolescence, Masonry provides a unique service—one developed and tested across three centuries or more. For those Masons who choose to be active, it teaches leadership skills, personal responsibility, group coordination, and individual patience.

What Masonry does *not* provide—and this may be a disappointment to some—is a hidden entrée into the inner circles of political and economic power. Nor does it provide secret sexual rituals, blood sacrifices, contacts with aliens, or a handy way to fix parking tickets.

Alas, I found no hidden Masonic freeways, no tunnels beneath the lodge leading to reptilian shape-shifters, and no Zionist-Illuminati dupes. Watchers of FOX News, yes. Subverters of the republic, no. Christians, Jews, Muslims, and Hindus, yes. Satanists, decidedly not.

When all is said and done, I discovered that, like many human institutions, Freemasonry is neither as perfect as it would like to make itself out to be nor as terrible as its detractors would like to believe. While the criticisms of the anti-Masons are mostly spurious charges based on mistaken notions, hoaxes, faulty interpretations, and urban legends, I did find that the critics occasionally had a point.

For instance, while Masonry is certainly not a cult (its leadership is too decentralized, its personal demands on one's time and money are at the discretion of each member, and a disappointed Mason can simply walk away at any time), some gung-ho Masons act *as if* they've joined a cult. In my own initial enthusiasm over the Craft, I joined several appendant bodies and research groups and signed on to the officers' line in my own lodge and in Scottish Rite. Needless to say, in due course I found myself at Masonic meetings of various kinds, sometimes two or three evenings a week. An external observer might have thought that a cult had swallowed up my life, but it was all of my own doing. Eventually, I pulled back and rebalanced my Masonic commitments, having learned my lesson the hard way.

Similarly, while Masonry is not a religion, as some critics have claimed, it *is* an almost archetypal embodiment of what Rousseau described in *The Social Contract* as a "civil religion"—the minimum religious sentiment that he felt was necessary for social cohesion and good citizenry. Rousseau's list of a civil religion's dogmas—"the existence of a mighty, intelligent and beneficent Divinity, possessed of foresight and providence, the life to come, the happiness of the just, the punishment of the wicked, the sanctity of the social contract and the laws"[2]— could have been lifted directly from the tenets of Freemasonry. Later discussions of civil (or civic) religion have also pointed to ritual expressions of piety and patriotism as common components, and these, too, are omnipresent in American Masonry, where every meeting, dinner, or other occasion is preceded by both a prayer and a pledge of allegiance to the flag.

But perhaps the most valid criticism of Masonry has to do with its handling of oaths (called "obligations" in Masonic jargon). A part of every degree ritual—whether in the blue lodge or York Rite or Scottish Rite—is the candidate's obligation. The actual contents of the obligations are not earth-shattering—they mostly amount to vows to follow Masonic ideals and to keep those vaguely defined secrets confidential, underscored by the invocation of a symbolic penalty—but the specific details are not spelled out beforehand. This places the candidate in the awkward position of swearing, clause by clause, to an agreement that he has had no opportunity to weigh or evaluate. Such a pig-in-the-poke approach would hardly hold up under contract law, and it remains an archaic vestige going back to the days of operative lodges and the protection of trade secrets. Until Masonry reforms this unnecessary bit of peekaboo secrecy through some form of disclosure prior to each degree, it will continue to provide ammunition to its harshest critics.

At the outset of this book I posed the question, Why all the secrecy? I offered various theories along the way, but none of the reasons offered could fully account for the ongoing tradition of Masonic secrecy.

Ultimately, I've come to the reluctant conclusion that secrecy in Freemasonry, like secrecy in government, feeds upon itself and proliferates unnecessarily unless held in check. Like bureaucrats run amok, Masons have figuratively stamped "Top Secret" on everything (and yet nothing) while long since having forgotten why.

Granted, secrecy *can* serve a useful function in helping to preserve the "sacred space" of lodge ritual and in forming a bond of confidentiality and trust between Masonic brethren. Spiritual, creative, or psychological work often requires strict privacy and silence so that one's energies aren't dissipated in idle chatter or gossip. Undoubtedly, secrecy has its place, both in Masonry and in the world at large. However, the judicious application of secrecy is one thing, while a reflexive penchant for secrecy where none is really called for is something else again. As I've noted before, the *real* Masonic secrets cannot be disclosed because they consist of each Mason's subjective experience of Freemasonry itself and his own efforts to fulfill its promise.

In my view, the Masonic fetish for secrecy has obscured the Craft's very real contributions to society and its members. For millions of men, over the course of several centuries, it has provided one of the modern world's few remaining initiations into manhood and maturity, as well as an outlet for sociality and charity. It has provided a template for the common man to undertake a "hero's journey" in search of self-improvement. And perhaps most compelling for many of its members, it has provided a palpable link to a past—partly real, partly mythic—when men built the great cathedrals and temples, and when knightly chivalry was the order of the day. These accomplishments deserve recognition and respect, not secrecy and misunderstanding.

The ideals of human brotherhood and of dealing "squarely" with everyone "on the level" may seem quaint in an era in which hardball tactics, cutthroat competition, and unfettered greed have been enthroned as the norm. But until the final door has been slammed shut on the last remaining Masonic temple, we can derive some satisfaction from knowing that a few decent men are still trying to swim against the tide.

Appendix A

Further Light on Masonry

Recommended Resources for Research on Freemasonry

Books

There are literally thousands of books that have been written on Freemasonry and on Masonic history, symbolism, and philosophy. The following recommendations are books that I have found the most helpful in gaining an overview of the Masonic phenomenon. While most of these books are either in print or available used, a few books (such as those by Knoop and Jones) are out of print and likely to be found only in Masonic libraries.

Freemasons' Guide and Compendium, by Bernard E. Jones (Orpington, U.K.: Eric Dobby Publishing, 1994).

This book, first published in 1950, still stands as possibly the best overview of Freemasonry ever written. The perspective is British, and it doesn't presume to cover American and other variants of Masonry, but for a crash course in Masonic history, there is no better book.

Freemasons' Book of the Royal Arch, by Bernard E. Jones (Orpington, U.K.: Eric Dobby Publishing, 1994).

The author takes the same well-researched and thorough approach as in his *Freemasons' Guide and Compendium.* The concentration here is on the history and symbolism of the Royal Arch degree.

The Origins of Freemasonry: Scotland's Century, 1590–1710, by David Stevenson (Cambridge: Cambridge University Press, 1990).

The First Freemasons: Scotland's Early Lodges and Their Members, by David Stevenson (Edinburgh: Grand Lodge of Scotland, 2001).

These two books by a Scottish professor of history serve as companion volumes covering Scotland's operative lodges and their evolution into speculative lodges. Working with primary documents, Stevenson makes a well-argued case for Scotland's key role in the origins of British Freemasonry.

The Beginnings of Freemasonry in America, by Melvin M. Johnson (New York: George H. Doran Co., 1924).

This volume is not so much a narrative history as a chronology of every documented reference that the author could dig up about 18th-century Freemasonry in America. This is the logical starting place for any investigation of American Masonry leading up to the American Revolution.

The Pocket History of Freemasonry, by Fred L. Pick and G. Norman Knight (New York: Philosophical Library, 1953).

Pick and Knight's little volume is probably the single most reader-friendly and down-to-earth introduction to the history of Freemasonry in England. It covers a lot of ground, considering its size.

Freemasonry and American Culture, 1880–1930, by Lynn Dumenil (Princeton, New Jersey: Princeton University Press, 1984).

This is one of the most insightful and well-written academic books to tackle American Masonry. Dumenil's analysis of the changing focus of Masonic lodges as they moved into the 20th century is especially enlightening.

A Pilgrim's Path: Freemasonry and the Religious Right, by John J. Robinson (New York: M. Evans & Co., 1993).

Robinson is best known for his highly speculative book *Born in Blood*, which attempted to link the origins of Freemasonry to the Knights Templar. This more modest (and credible) volume collects his essays defending Masonry against attacks from religious conservatives.

Secret Ritual and Manhood in Victorian America, by Mark C. Carnes (New Haven, Connecticut: Yale University Press, 1989).

A scholarly look at the role played by Freemasonry and other fraternal orders in men's lives in the 19th century. Carnes is especially good on the shifting status of men and women in relation to family and religion.

Revolutionary Brotherhood: Freemasonry and the Transformation of the American Social Order, 1730–1840, by Steven C. Bullock (Chapel Hill: University of North Carolina Press, 1996).

This dense, scholarly book examines the first century of American Masonry, with particular attention paid to changes in public perceptions of the fraternity. The information it provides is useful in balancing out some of the more romantic notions of the Masonic role in the American Revolution.

The Craft and Its Symbols, by Allen E. Roberts (Richmond, Virginia: Macoy Publishing, 1974).

In many lodges across the United States, this compact book is given to newly initiated Masons. It provides an introductory discussion of the numerous symbols that are referred to within the rituals of the three blue-lodge degrees.

The Theosophical Enlightenment, by Joscelyn Godwin (Albany, New York: SUNY Press, 1994).

While this highly readable history of 19th-century fringe and occult thinkers makes only passing mention of Masonry, it is unparalleled in its portrayal of the cultural context within which English-speaking Masonry evolved.

Freemasonry: A Journey Through Ritual and Symbol, by W. Kirk MacNulty (New York: Thames and Hudson, 1991).

This volume in Thames and Hudson's "Art and Imagination" series brings together numerous color photos of Masonic aprons, artifacts, illustrations, and symbols, all anchored by a thoughtful introductory essay.

The Way of the Craftsman, by W. Kirk MacNulty (London: Central Regalia, 2002).

The author approaches Freemasonry as a system for psychological self-knowledge and growth, drawing upon Jungian psychology and Jewish Kabbalah in his analysis.

The Golden Builders: Alchemists, Rosicrucians, and the First Freemasons, by Tobias Churton (Boston: Weiser Books, 2005).

This is an excellent, well-researched examination of the preoccupations of the 17th century's British intelligentsia with esoteric pursuits, leading into the appearance of speculative Freemasonry.

The Magus of Freemasonry, by Tobias Churton (Rochester, Vermont: Inner Traditions, 2006).

An in-depth portrait of Elias Ashmole, one of the earliest identified English Masons and a founder of the Royal Society.

Freemasonry on Both Sides of the Atlantic, edited by R. William Weisberger, Wallace McLeod, and S. Brent Morris (New York: Columbia University Press, 2002).

A mammoth anthology of scholarly papers covering Masonic history from dozens of angles.

Freemasonry in Context: History, Ritual, Controversy, edited by Arturo de Hoyos and S. Brent Morris (New York: Lexington Books, 2004).

This volume collects twenty of the best papers previously published by the Scottish Rite Research Society.

Early Masonic Pamphlets, edited by Douglas Knoop, G. P. Jones, and Douglas Hamer (Manchester, U.K.: Manchester University Press, 1945).

This is an outstanding annotated collection of reprints of nearly every mention of Freemasons and Masonry in print from 1638 to 1735. It is out of print, but it can be found in major Masonic libraries.

The Genesis of Freemasonry, by Douglas Knoop and G. P. Jones (Manchester, U.K.: Manchester University Press, 1947).

A Short History of Freemasonry to 1730, by Douglas Knoop and G. P. Jones (Manchester, U.K.: Manchester University Press, 1940).

Knoop and Jones represent serious Masonic historical research at its finest. These two volumes present a distillation of the efforts of the "realistic" school of Masonic scholarship as it stood in the mid–20th century.

Lodge of the Double-Headed Eagle: Two Centuries of Scottish Rite Freemasonry in America's Southern Jurisdiction, by William L. Fox (Fayetteville: University of Arkansas Press, 1997).

This is an exhaustive yet very well written history of the Scottish Rite (Southern Jurisdiction), focusing primarily on the leadership of the Supreme Council 33° and the Sovereign Grand Commanders. What might have been an exercise in organizational PR is, in Fox's able hands, a candid look at the all-too-human strengths and weaknesses of this particular Masonic hierarchy.

Is It True What They Say About Freemasonry? by Arturo de Hoyos and S. Brent Morris (New York: M. Evans & Co., 2004).

Now in its third revised edition, this is the definitive answer to the attacks of some of the most prominent anti-Masonic critics.

Duncan's Ritual of Freemasonry, by Malcolm C. Duncan (New York: Crown Publishing, 1976).

This "exposure" of the ritual of the three blue-lodge degrees and four Royal Arch chapter degrees has been continuously in print since the 19th century. It provides a snapshot of the state of American Masonic ritual at the time of its first publication, although it is not without errors and should not be taken as an accurate version of every grand lodge's present ritual.

The Meaning of Masonry, by W. L. Wilmshurst (New York: Gramercy Books, 1980).

Although nearly one hundred years old and based on English Masonic ritual (which differs in some particulars from American ritual), this book remains one of the most popular examples of one Mason's personal reflections on deeper Masonic meanings. Wilmshurst was a Theosophist, and his own beliefs inevitably influence the slant one finds here.

American Freemasons, by Mark A. Tabbert (New York: New York University Press, 2005).

An excellent, lavishly illustrated history of Freemasonry in the United States. Clear prose and color pictures combine to make this one of the most readable histories of its sort.

Freemasons for Dummies, by Christopher Hodapp (Hoboken, New Jersey: Wiley Publishing, 2005).

The ubiquitous "For Dummies" series tackles Freemasonry, and the result is surprisingly good. Written by a knowledgeable Mason, this guide covers Masonry from A to Z in an accessible fashion, although the author gives short shrift to matters esoteric.

Understanding Manhood in America: Freemasonry's Enduring Path to the Mature Masculine, by Robert G. Davis (Lancaster, Pennsylvania: Anchor Communications, 2005).

One of American Masonry's most thoughtful leaders examines the shifting concepts of "manhood" and makes the case for the Craft as a unique rite of passage into maturity.

Freemasonry: Rituals, Symbols and History of the Secret Society, by Mark Stavish (Woodbury, Minnesota: Llewellyn Publications, 2007).

An esoteric Mason makes an intelligent and wide-ranging case for an esoteric Freemasonry.

The Origins of Freemasonry: Fact and Fictions, by Margaret C. Jacob (Philadelphia: University of Pennsylvania Press, 2006).

Jacob is at the forefront of a new scholarly interest in Masonic history. This is a concise, accessible introduction to her research.

Journals and Periodicals

Ars Quatuor Coronatorum: Transactions of Quatuor Coronati Lodge No. 2076 London. Published annually since 1886 by Quatuor Coronati Correspondence Circle, 20 Great Queen Street, London WC2B 5BE, United Kingdom.

The Quatuor Coronati Lodge of London, U.K., is undoubtedly the most outstanding "research lodge" within Freemasonry worldwide. *Ars Quatuor Coronatorum,* the lodge's annual transactions, publishes the papers given at its quarterly meetings, along with incisive critiques and responses by lodge members as well as shorter papers and contributions from its circle of some five thousand–plus corresponding members. *Ars Quatuor Coronatorum*'s 122 volumes (as of 2009) are a treasure trove of serious (and exhaustive) research on Masonic origins, history, and meanings. Subscriptions are available only to Masons and Masonic institutions, but serious scholars should be able to consult *Ars Quatuor Coronatorum* volumes at the larger Masonic libraries.

Heredom: Transactions of the Scottish Rite Research Society. Published annually since 1992 by the Scottish Rite Research Society, 1733 16th Street, NW, Washington, D.C. 20009–3103.

The Scottish Rite Research Society (SRRS) has rapidly become the top Masonic research society in North America, and its annual transactions, *Heredom*, publishes top-quality papers on Masonic history, with a special emphasis on the Scottish Rite. From its inception it has also included papers by non-Masonic academic scholars.

The Plumbline: Newsletter of the Scottish Rite Research Society. Published quarterly since 1992 by the Scottish Rite Research Society, 1733 16th Street, NW, Washington, D.C. 20009–3103.

While primarily a venue for SRRS news, this newsletter also features papers and articles that are too short to warrant publication in *Heredom*. SRRS members receive both *Heredom* and the *Plumbline*, as well as an annual "bonus" book.

Freemasonry Today. Published quarterly. Editorial and administrative offices at Freemasons' Hall, Great Queen Street, London, WC2B 5AZ, United Kingdom.

A well-produced, well-written, slick quarterly magazine, edited by Michael Baigent, and published by the United Grand Lodge of England. Although there is commonly a historical article or two each issue, the primary emphasis is on contemporary Masonry, particularly in Britain. The magazine is also available online (www.freemasonrytoday.com).

The Square. Published quarterly by Lewis Masonic, Riverdene Business Park, Molesey Road, Hersham, Surrey KT12 4RG, United Kingdom.

Edited by Leo Zanelli, the *Square* is an independent Masonic quarterly in Britain. Its style is more informal and chatty than *Freemasonry Today,* but it also runs good material of potential interest to Masons and non-Masons alike. The publisher, Lewis Masonic, is one of the primary Masonic book publishers and distributors in the United Kingdom (www.lewismasonic.com).

Web Sites

Grand Lodge of British Columbia and the Yukon
(freemasonry.bcy.ca/sitemap.html)

This site is much more than just an online PR presence for one of Canada's provincial grand lodges. The wealth of articles here on all aspects of Masonic history and controversy is equal to none. Handsomely designed and well thought out, this site can serve as an excellent introduction to the complexity of contemporary Masonry.

United Grand Lodge of England
(www.ugle.org.uk)

This site reflects the attempt by the United Grand Lodge of England (UGLE) in recent years to foster a more open attitude toward public curiosity about Freemasonry. Much can be found here about Masonry in the UGLE's jurisdiction.

Grand Lodge of California, F&AM
(www.freemason.org)

Each of the fifty-one grand lodges in the United States (including Washington, D.C.) has a Web site, some more interesting than others. The Web site of the Grand Lodge of California is notable not only for its information on Masonry in general, but also for its online access to its well-produced bimonthly magazine, *The California Freemason.*

Scottish Rite of Freemasonry–Southern Jurisdiction
(www.scottishrite.org)

Scottish Rite of Freemasonry–Northern Masonic Jurisdiction
(www.supremecouncil.org)

Between them, these two sites provide information on the northern and southern jurisdictions of the Scottish Rite system of higher degrees in the United States.

YorkRite.org
(yorkrite.org)

This is the official informational site for the various York Rite bodies and their related invitational and honorary groups in the United States. This should provide a glimpse into the multifaceted universe of higher Masonic degrees and orders as provided by the York Rite.

Paul M. Bessel's Masonic Site
(bessel.org/webindex.htm)

Paul Bessel, an active Mason on the East Coast, established this personal Web site as a public resource for information on all aspects of Masonry. Although recent updates have been few and far between, it still contains an outstanding collection of articles, statistics, and research materials.

PhoenixMasonry Masonic Museum
(www.phoenixmasonry.org/masonicmuseum)

This is a fascinating online "museum" of Masonic artifacts, not affiliated with any particular grand lodge. The museum's host, Phoenixmasonry.org, also has electronic editions of many old Masonic books.

Masonicinfo.com
(www.masonicinfo.com)

Ed King, a Mason in New England, maintains this vast Web site with the goal of countering anti-Masonic allegations and misunderstandings with accurate information. The tone is feisty and often sarcastic, and while King does not suffer fools gladly, he does provide an antidote for much of the misinformation out there.

Cornerstone Society
(www.cornerstonesociety.com)

The site of a British Masonic organization dedicated to encouraging discussion of Masonic history, philosophy, and symbolism. It holds two annual conferences, the papers of which are archived here along with other worthwhile Masonic research.

Appendix B

Masonic Lodge Officers and Their Typical Duties

It is common practice in the United States for blue lodges to elect a new line of officers annually. Some lodges maintain a "progressive line" where each officer "moves up a chair" each year, starting with the Marshal or Junior Steward and culminating in a term as Worshipful Master. The officers are responsible for the lodge functioning smoothly, and duties are traditionally divided up among them. Ideally, by the time an officer becomes Worshipful Master, he will have become familiar with all aspects of lodge governance.

The officers and their duties listed here are drawn from typical descriptions for many American jurisdictions, but there may be some variations in officers' titles and duties, depending on the specific grand lodge.

Worshipful Master (WM)—Leads and oversees the lodge during his term. Sets theme or emphasis for the year, if there is one. Appoints committees. Proficient in WM's part in degree rituals, in most jurisdictions.

Senior Warden (SW)—Chief coordinator of lodge activities. Proficient in SW's part in degree rituals. Serves as acting Worshipful Master in the absence of WM.

Junior Warden (JW)—Responsible for lodge dinners. Oversees the Stewards. Proficient in JW's part in degree rituals. Serves as acting Worshipful Master in the absence of WM and SW.

Senior Deacon (SD)—Conducts candidates during degree rituals. Accommodates and introduces visiting Masons at meetings. Most active participant in degree rituals. May have responsibility for lodge newsletter.

Junior Deacon (JD)—Assists SD in ritual. Coordinates with Tyler on controlling access to lodge meetings.

Senior Steward (SS)—Responsible for lodge refreshments. Helps prepare candidates for degrees.

Junior Steward (JS)—Assists SS in refreshments and ritual duties.

Marshal (M)—Greets candidates and helps prepare them for degrees. Accompanies visiting grand lodge officers into lodge.

Chaplain (C)—Offers devotions, prayers, and scriptural readings for lodge functions and rituals. (In some jurisdictions, the Chaplain is typically the immediate past Worshipful Master.)

Tyler (T)—Guards the door of the lodge during degree rituals and stated meetings. May help in setting up and tearing down the lodge room for meetings. (Commonly, the Tyler is a Past Master or older longtime member.) Sometimes spelled "Tiler."

Secretary (S)—Keeps minutes of stated meetings and degree rituals. Maintains lodge records. Handles correspondence and communiqués with grand lodge and other lodges. Collects dues from members; turns over funds and bills to Treasurer.

Treasurer (TR)—Keeps accounts for lodge and disburses funds for various expenses.

Notes

Chapter 1: The Masonic Myth

1. United Grand Lodge of England, "What Is Freemasonry?" http://www.ugle.org.uk/masonry/what-is-freemasonry.htm.

2. William Cooper, *Behold a Pale Horse* (Sedona, AZ: Light Technology, 1991), pp. 77–78.

3. Martin L. Wagner, *Freemasonry Interpreted* (1912; repr., Brooklyn, NY: A&B Books, 1994), p. 251.

4. United Grand Lodge of England, "What Is Freemasonry?"

5. Estimate based on U.S. Census figures for 1960. It appears that at that time there were approximately 78 million white males, of which approximately 50 million were adults. As will be discussed later, Masonry at that time was divided along color lines, with mainstream Masonry being almost exclusively white (and Protestant).

6. Stephen Bullock, *Revolutionary Brotherhood* (Chapel Hill: Univ. of North Carolina Press, 1996), pp. 177–78.

7. John L. Brooke, *The Refiner's Fire: The Making of Mormon Cosmology, 1644–1844* (Cambridge: Cambridge Univ. Press, 1994), p. 168.

8. Bullock, *Revolutionary Brotherhood*, p. 284.

9. R. Keith Muir, "The Morgan Affair and Its Effect on Freemasonry," *Ars Quatuor Coronatorum* 105 (1992): 230.

10. The same preacher who coined the term "Burned-Over District" and popularized the tent revivals in the late 1820s was also a former Mason

turned anti-Mason. This was the Rev. Charles G. Finney, later president of Oberlin College and author of the anti-Masonic book *The Character, Claims and Practical Workings of Freemasonry* (Ohio: Western Tract and Book Society, 1869).

11. Brooke, *Refiner's Fire*, pp. 168–69, 246.

12. Pat Robertson, *The New World Order* (Waco, TX: Word Publishing, 1991), p. 184.

13. See Clement XII's bull *In Eminenti* (1738).

14. Manly Palmer Hall, *The Lost Keys of Freemasonry* (Los Angeles: Philosophical Research Society, 1923; repr., 1976), pp. xxi–xxii.

15. Manly Palmer Hall, *The Secret Teachings of All Ages* (Los Angeles: Philosophical Research Society, 1928), pp. xxxiv–xxxv.

16. See David Icke, *The Biggest Secret* (Scottsdale, AZ: Bridge of Love, 1999). See also http://www.reptilianagenda.com/research/r020500a.shtml.

17. This account follows that in Dennis Stocks, "Leo Taxil and Anti-Masonry," http://www.casebook.org/dissertations/freemasonry/anti2.html. See also Alain Bernheim, A. William Samii, and Eric Serejski, "The Confession of Leo Taxil," *Heredom* 5 (1996): 137–68.

18. Bataille, *Le diable au XIXe siècle*, p. 391, quoted in Lady Queenborough (Edith Starr Miller), *Occult Theocrasy* (Hawthorne, CA: Christian Book Club of America, 1933; repr., 1980), pp. 224–45. Queenborough is generally an unreliable and overly credulous source, but there is no reason to doubt the authenticity of her translation of this passage from Bataille's book.

19. For a full translation of Taxil's confession, see Bernheim, Samii, and Serejski, "Confession of Leo Taxil."

20. Des Griffin, *Fourth Reich of the Rich* (South Pasadena, CA: Emissary Publications, 1976), pp. 69–70.

21. For instance, see Adolf Hitler, *Mein Kampf* (Boston: Houghton Mifflin, 1971), pp. 314–15.

22. Victor Marsden, trans., *The Protocols of the Learned Elders of Zion* (Reedy, WV: Liberty Bell Publications, n.d.), p. 43.

23. For this list of notables I referred to the excellent Web site maintained by the Grand Lodge of British Columbia and Yukon: http://freemasonry.bcy.ca/.

24. For the photo of "Buzz" Aldrin and the flag, see photo page 14 of the

spread between pp. 268 and 269 in William L. Fox, *Lodge of the Double-Headed Eagle* (Fayetteville: Univ. of Arkansas Press, 1997).

25. Jasper Ridley, *The Freemasons* (New York: Arcade, 2001), pp. 118–21.

Chapter 2: Square Roots

1. There appear to have been only two degrees or designations of advancement within operative masonry: apprentice and fellow craft. Masters were, in effect, project managers.

2. There are actually multiple theories about the derivation of the word *free* when appended to *mason*. The one cited here is one of the most popular, but another theory is equally compelling: that the word *free* refers to "free stone"—the variety of stone that masons worked with. For further discussion, see Bernard E. Jones, *Freemasons' Guide and Compendium* (New York: Macoy Publishing, 1950), pp. 145–47; and M. D. J. Scanlan, "Freemasonry and the Mystery of the Acception, 1630–1723—A Fatal Flaw," in *Freemasonry on Both Sides of the Atlantic*, ed. R. William Weisberger, Wallace McLeod, and S. Brent Morris (Boulder, CO: East European Monographs, 2002), pp. 155–60.

3. See, for instance, Christopher Knight and Robert Lomas, *The Book of Hiram* (London: Century, 2003), pp. 331–32.

4. See A. G. Markham, "Some Problems of English Masonic History," *Ars Quatuor Coronatorum* 110 (1997): 13–15.

5. The exception to the rule of alternative historians largely ignoring serious sources of Masonic historical research is Michael Baigent and Richard Leigh, *The Temple and the Lodge* (London: Jonathan Cape, 1989). Though speculative in nature—and authored by two of the three co-authors of *Holy Blood, Holy Grail*—this book avoids some of the more elementary errors of other books in the field, and compared with them its theories and conclusions are relatively modest.

6. Knight and Lomas, *Book of Hiram*, pp. 20–22.

7. Pick and Knight note: "According to the Engraved List of Lodges of 1729, this lodge was constituted in 1691, but it probably had a far earlier origin." Fred L. Pick and G. Norman Knight, *The Pocket History of Freemasonry* (New York: Philosophical Library, 1953), p. 75.

8. Jones, *Freemasons' Guide and Compendium*, p. 171.

9. Jones, *Freemasons' Guide and Compendium*, p. 170.

10. Lists of the seven wonders differ as to which structures are included. The Temple of Solomon is not included in some lists.

11. Pick and Knight, *Pocket History of Freemasonry,* pp. 29, 36.

12. Quote from the transcription of the Regius Poem in Grand Lodge of British Columbia and Yukon, "The Halliwell Manuscript," http://free masonry.bcy.ca/texts/regius.html.

13. Henry Leonard Stillson, ed., *History of the Ancient and Honorable Fraternity of Free and Accepted Masons, and Concordant Orders* (Boston and New York: Fraternity Publishing Co., 1906), pp. 170–71.

14. David Stevenson, *The Origins of Freemasonry: Scotland's Century, 1590–1710* (Cambridge: Cambridge Univ. Press, 1988), pp. 23–24.

15. Harry Carr, "The Transition from Operative to Speculative Masonry" (Prestonian Lecture for 1957), in *The Collected "Prestonian Lectures," 1925–1960,* ed. Henry Carr (London: Quatuor Coronati Lodge no. 2076, 1965), p. 421.

16. Historian Lisa Kahler points out that the terms "operative," "nonoperative," "accepted," and "speculative," in regards to Masonry, have been used by different writers to mean different things, depending on the writer and the circumstances. "Speculative" as a term employed within Masonic circles doesn't seem to have come into usage until the latter half of the 18th century, and some historians have seen fit to use it to describe only post-1730 Masonry. In order not to bog ourselves down in the intricacies of this controversy, I am using the term as a broadly descriptive one to designate Masons or lodges where symbolic or philosophical matters were of primary interest. See Lisa Kahler, "Scottish Definitions and Transitions," *Heredom* 9 (2002): 233–50.

17. I generalize here what is commonly accepted by most Masonic researchers. Scanlan, "Mystery of the Acception," makes a good case for the possibility that both the Acception and other lodges should be seen as part of an overlapping milieu within which operatives and nonoperatives had greater contact than is often supposed.

18. Stevenson, *Origins of Freemasonry,* pp. 44, 49, 196–208.

19. Stevenson, *Origins of Freemasonry,* pp. 198–99.

20. Stevenson, *Origins of Freemasonry,* pp. 49–51, 87–96.

21. For an excellent debunking of the Templar myth, see Robert L. D. Cooper, "The Knights Templar in Scotland: The Creation of a Myth," *Ars Quatuor Coronatorum* 115 (2002): 94–148. This material has been

expanded upon further in Robert L. D. Cooper, *The Rosslyn Hoax?* (London: Lewis Masonic, 2007).

22. Philip Coppens, *The Stone Puzzle of Rosslyn Chapel* (Enkhuizen, Netherlands: Frontier Publishing, 2004), p. 37.

23. Christopher Knight and Robert Lomas, *The Second Messiah* (Gloucester, MA: Four Winds Press, 2001), p. 39.

24. Christopher Knight and Robert Lomas, *The Hiram Key* (Portland, MA: Element Books, 1997), photos no. 7 and 8, following p. 178.

25. Evelyn Lord, *The Knights Templar in Britain* (London: Pearson Education Ltd., 2002), p. 153; Cooper, "Knights Templar in Scotland," p. 129. Lord has it that the St. Clairs testified against the Templars, but I have been unable to confirm this.

26. The first charter was sent to King James VI of Scotland in 1600 and the second to his son Charles I, king of England and Scotland, in 1627–28. The Williams Sinclair on whose behalf they were written were father (1600) and son (1627–28). See David Stevenson, "The Sinclairs of Roslin and the Masters of Works," in Stevenson, *Origins of Freemasonry,* chap. 4.

27. Robert Freke Gould, *The History of Freemasonry,* vol. 3 (Philadelphia: John C. Yorston Publishing, 1902), pp. 303–4.

28. The William Sinclair of 1737 is, needless to say, a descendent of the earlier William Sinclairs who built Rosslyn Chapel (15th century) and sought royal recognition of Masonic patron status (16th century). The genealogical relationships are complicated by there being at least two branches of the family between whom the Rosslyn land and buildings passed.

29. This legend is taken as accepted fact in William Alexander Laurie, *History of Free Masonry and the Grand Lodge of Scotland* (Edinburgh: Seton & Mackenzie, 1859), p. 78. Despite being revised by the Secretary of the Grand Lodge of Scotland from an earlier book by Laurie's father, this work is such a haggis of legend, hearsay, and unreliable sources that it nearly serves as an early precursor of the alternative-history genre. See Cooper, "Knights Templar in Scotland," pp. 112–27.

30. John J. Robinson, *Born in Blood: The Lost Secrets of Freemasonry* (New York: M. Evans & Co., 1989), pp. 165–66.

31. Unfortunately, a search of the novel has not turned up the phrase in question, so the original source of the phrase remains unknown.

32. Albert Mackey, who is not always a reliable source, claims that the skull is not a Masonic symbol, except for its symbolic presence in Masonic Templarism. However, there are numerous examples of symbolic skulls and skull and crossbones to be found on Masonic aprons and tracing boards related to the third degree, especially in Europe. See Albert Mackey, William Hughan, and Edward Hawkins, *An Encyclopaedia of Freemasonry* (New York: Masonic History Co., 1921), p. 694.

33. "Ill. John J. Robinson, 33° Enters Celestial Lodge Above," *Scottish Rite Journal*, November 1993, pp. 34–36.

34. Interestingly enough, the initiatory ritual of the Order of the Temple (the Masonic Templar "degree" in the York Rite) has almost zero reference within it to the rest of the Masonic mythos and does not reference the fate of the historical Knights Templar.

35. As it turns out, the Hermetic and Neoplatonic texts (the *Corpus Hermeticum*) that were translated and assumed to date from ancient Egypto-Hellenic civilization were much later texts actually dating from the second to fourth centuries CE. This was pointed out by Isaac Causabon only in 1614, by which time the Renaissance had already been under way for some 150 years. See Frances A. Yates, *Giordano Bruno and the Hermetic Tradition* (Chicago: Univ. of Chicago Press, 1964), pp. 398–403.

36. Wayne Shumaker, *The Occult Sciences in the Renaissance: A Study in Intellectual Patterns* (Berkeley: Univ. of California Press, 1979), p. 169.

37. The reading of the Old Charges was replaced with a reading of the Constitutions once the premier grand lodge was organized and Anderson had done his work.

38. Certain components of the rituals, particularly the lectures, can be traced to Masonic authors of the late 18th century, such as William Preston and, in the United States, Thomas Smith Webb. The genesis of the rest of the rituals, however, is lost in the mists of tradition.

39. As quoted in Joscelyn Godwin, *The Theosophical Enlightenment* (Albany, NY: SUNY Press, 1994), p. 6.

40. Hans Peters, "Sir Isaac Newton and 'the Oldest Catholic Religion,'" *Ars Quatuor Coronatorum* 100 (1988): 193.

41. *Anderson's Constitutions, 1723 and 1738*, facsimile ed. (London: Quatuor Coronati, 1976), pp. 143–44.

42. See Andrew Prescott, "The Voice Conventional: Druidic Myths and Freemasonry," paper presented at the fourth international confer-

ence of the Canonbury Masonic Research Centre, London, November 2, 2002; also available online at http://www.cornerstonesociety.com/Insight/Articles/voice.pdf.

43. From Moncure Daniels Conway, ed., *Writings of Thomas Paine* (New York: G. P. Putnam's Sons, 1896); also available online at http://freemasonry.bcy.ca/history/paine_t.html. For good measure, Paine also thought that Masonry was descended from the Druids.

44. Pick and Knight, *Pocket History of Freemasonry,* pp. 88–89, 103.

45. The official title of the Antient Grand Lodge was variously "The Most Ancient and Honourable Society of Free and Accepted Masons," "The Grand Lodge of Free and Accepted Masons of the Old Institution," and "The Most Ancient and Honourable Fraternity of Free and Accepted Masons (according to the old Constitutions granted by His Royal Highness Prince Edwin at York, Anno Domini Nine Hundred twenty and six . . .)." See Jones, *Freemasons' Guide and Compendium,* pp. 197–99. The use of the spelling "Antient" became common practice among Masonic scholars at some point, though I have yet to discover exactly when.

46. See Henry Sadler, *Masonic Facts and Fictions* (1887; repr., Wellingborough, Northants, UK: Aquarian Press, 1985).

47. Jones, *Freemasons' Guide and Compendium,* pp. 196–97.

Chapter 3: Continental Ops

1. Baigent and Leigh, *Temple and the Lodge,* p. 91.

2. Margaret Jacob, *Living the Enlightenment* (Oxford: Oxford Univ. Press, 1991), p. 89.

3. R. William Weisberger, "Prague and Viennese Freemasonry, the Enlightenment, and the Operations of the True Harmony Lodge of Vienna," in Weisberger, McLeod, and Morris, *Freemasonry on Both Sides of the Atlantic,* p. 376

4. Knight and Lomas, *Second Messiah,* p. 199.

5. Knight and Lomas, *Hiram Key,* p. 328. The authors have this as the "Lodge of Scoon and Perth," and cite the 1995 yearbook of the Grand Lodge of Scotland as their source.

6. Historian David Stevenson notes that the claim was first set out in an agreement or contract between Lodge of Scone members in 1658, nearly sixty years after the alleged incident. Given that the document

contains numerous other errors or exaggerated claims, Stevenson judges the James I claim to be "implausible." See David Stevenson, *The First Freemasons: Scotland's Early Lodges and Their Members*, 2nd ed. (Edinburgh: Grand Lodge of Scotland, 2001), p. 103.

7. Marsha Keith Schuchard, in her painstakingly researched book *Restoring the Temple of Vision: Cabalistic Freemasonry and Stuart Culture* (Leiden: E. J. Brill, 2002), argues that King James was strongly interested in subjects touching upon both Hermetic and Masonic themes. Her conclusions as to what this might imply—for example, a special Stuart relationship to a more esoteric Masonry—are highly controversial among Masonic scholars.

8. John Cannon and Ralph Griffiths, *The Oxford Illustrated History of the British Monarchy* (Oxford: Oxford Univ. Press, 1988), p. 419.

9. Paul Naudon, *The Secret History of Freemasonry* (Rochester, VT: Inner Traditions, 2005), p. 254.

10. Naudon, *Secret History of Freemasonry*, p. 254.

11. See Lisa Kahler, "Andrew Michael Ramsay and His Masonic Oration," *Heredom* 1 (1992): 32–39.

12. Quoted and translated in Alain Bernheim, letter to the editor, *Heredom* 5 (1996): 12. Ramsay's letter of April 16, 1737, was to the Marquis de Caumont in Avignon.

13. My account here draws upon both Alain Bernheim's research, shared in the source cited in note 12 above, and that of Lisa Kahler, cited in note 11 above.

14. Actually, there are far more than four. However, the four largest grand lodges are those most often referred to in Masonic circles.

15. Pierre Mollier, "News from the 'Russian Archives' About the Early History of the High Degrees: The Scottish Order in Berlin from 1742 to 1752," *Chain of Union*, special issue no. 2 (2003): 59–64.

16. Alain Bernheim, "Did Early 'High' or Écossais Degrees Originate in France?" *Heredom* 5 (1996): 97–98. Pierre Mollier (see note 15) also refers to the Scottish lodges in England.

17. Mollier, "News from the 'Russian Archives,'" p. 64.

18. Gould, *History of Freemasonry*, vol. 3 , p. 346.

19. Gould, *History of Freemasonry*, vol. 3, p. 348.

20. Gould, *History of Freemasonry*, vol. 3, p. 350.

21. Gould, *History of Freemasonry*, vol. 3, pp. 351–52.

22. See Alain Bernheim, "Avatars of the Knight Kadosh in France and in Charleston," *Heredom* 6 (1997): 149–217; and Alain Bernheim, "Johann August Starck: The Templar Legend and the Clerics," *Heredom* 9 (2001): 251–96.

23. Bernheim, "Johann August Starck," p. 253. Bernheim notes the Rite of Strict Observance's dominance as being for the twelve years following 1764. Gould indicates: "For twenty years from its birth [c. 1750] it either lay dormant, or made only infinitesimal progress; during the next twenty years [i.e., 1770–90] it pervaded all continental Europe to the almost exclusion of every other system; within the next ten it had practically ceased to exist" (Gould, *History of Freemasonry*, vol. 3, p. 353).

24. Gould, *History of Freemasonry*, vol. 3, pp. 353–54.

25. Peter Dawkins, *Building Paradise* (Warwickshire, UK: Francis Bacon Research Trust, 2001), p. 142. Yates, *Giordano Bruno*, p. 450.

26. Betty Jo Teeter Dobbs, *The Janus Faces of Genius: The Role of Alchemy in Newton's Thought* (Cambridge: Cambridge Univ. Press, 1991), pp. 151–52.

27. Hans Peters, "Sir Isaac Newton and 'the Oldest Catholic Religion,'" *Ars Quatuor Coronatorum* 100 (1988): 193.

28. Christopher McIntosh, *Eliphas Lévi and the French Occult Revival* (New York: Samuel Weiser, 1974), pp. 27–30.

29. McIntosh, *Eliphas Lévi*, p. 30.

30. A. C. F. Jackson, *Rose Croix: A History of the Ancient and Accepted Rite for England and Wales*, rev. ed. (Addlestone, Surrey, UK: Lewis Masonic, 1987), pp. 25–26.

31. Mike Restivo, "Jean-Baptiste Willermoz and the C.B.C.S.," http://kingsgarden.org/English/Organizations/OM.GB/Willermoz/WillermozBio.html.

32. Lloyd Worley, "The Traditional Martinist Order and the Martinist Order and Synarchy: An Examination of Claims and Relationships," *Philalethes*, October 1990, p. 18.

33. Manly Palmer Hall, *The Secret Teachings of All Ages* (Los Angeles: Philosophical Research Society, 1971), p. cxcviii.

34. McIntosh, *Eliphas Lévi*, p. 30.

35. Hall, *Secret Teachings*, p. cxcviii.

36. See Jasper Ridley, *The Freemasons* (New York: Arcade, 2001), p. 118–21;

Jan Mogens Reimer, "Mozart, The Magic Flute, Freemasonry and Rosi-crucians: An Antithesis," *Ars Quatuor Coronatorum* 116 (2003): 268–72; and H. C. Robbins Landon, *Mozart and the Masons* (New York: Thames and Hudson, 1991).

37. The one possible exception to this might be the unfortunate William Morgan Affair in upstate New York in 1826.

38. Reimer, "Mozart," p. 271.

Chapter 4: Novus Ordo Seclorum

1. J. Hugo Tasch, *The Facts About George Washington as a Freemason* (New York: Macoy Publishing, 1931), p. 2.

2. Melvin M. Johnson, *The Beginning of Freemasonry in America* (New York: George H. Doran Co., 1924), p. 49.

3. Johnson, *Beginning of Freemasonry in America*, pp. 74–91.

4. James Anderson, "New Constitutions of 1738," in *Andersons' Constitutions, 1723 and 1738*, p. 144.

5. Josiah H. Drummond, "The History of Symbolic Masonry in the United States," in Robert F. Gould, *The History of Freemasonry*, vol. 4, rev. ed. (Philadelphia: John C. Yorston and Co., 1896), p. 301.

6. Steven C. Bullock, *Revolutionary Brotherhood* (Chapel Hill: Univ. of North Carolina Press, 1996), pp. 112–14.

7. Bullock, *Revolutionary Brotherhood*, pp. 85–86.

8. Bullock, *Revolutionary Brotherhood*, pp. 148–53.

9. William Moseley Brown, *George Washington Freemason* (Richmond, VA: Garrett and Massie, 1952), p. 170.

10. Tasch, *Facts About George Washington*, p. 8.

11. Bullock, *Revolutionary Brotherhood*, p. 113.

12. Gould, *History of Freemasonry*, vol. 4, p. 347.

13. Allen E. Roberts, *Freemasonry in American History* (Richmond, VA: Macoy Publishing, 1985), pp. 135–36. Roberts asserts that St. Andrew's Lodge did not meet on the night of the Tea Party, as there were not enough members present. This would seem to be just another way to read the same lodge minutes.

14. Baigent and Leigh, *Temple and the Lodge*, pp. 286–87.

15. Brown, *George Washington Freemason*, p. 50.

16. My account here draws upon that of Peter Tompkins, *The Magic of Obelisks*

(New York: Harper and Row, 1981). Tompkins is an erudite researcher and a vastly entertaining writer, but his book's lack of citations and bibliography reduces its value to that of a suggestive narrative. I have tried, as far as possible, to independently verify all facts included here.

17. Graham Hancock and Robert Bauval, *Talisman* (London: Element/ HarperCollins, 2004), p. 446.

18. Cyril N. Batham, "Ramsay's Oration: The Epernay and Grand Lodge Versions," *Heredom* 1 (1992): 53.

19. Batham, "Ramsay's Oration," p. 56.

20. See Richard C. Carrott, *The Egyptian Revival: Its Sources, Monuments, and Meaning, 1808–1858* (Berkeley: Univ. of California Press, 1978); and Peggy McDowell and Richard E. Meyer, *The Revival Styles in American Memorial Art* (Bowling Green, OH: Bowling Green State Univ. Popular Press, 1994).

21. *The Egyptian Obelisk, and the Masonic Emblems Found at Its Base* (Toronto: J. Ross Robertson, 1880); T. A'M. Ward, *The Obelisks* (n.p., 1881). See also Tompkins, *Magic of Obelisks*, pp. 277–307.

22. *Egyptian Obelisk*, p. 50.

23. *Egyptian Obelisk*, p. 52.

24. Information on Weisse drawn from research by John Patrick Deveney, private correspondence, 2005.

25. John A. Weisse, *The Obelisk and Freemasonry* (New York: J. W. Bouton, 1880), p. 47.

26. Alberto Siliotti, *Egypt Lost and Found: Explorers and Travelers on the Nile* (New York: Stewart, Tabori and Chang, 1999), pp. 162–75.

27. See *Ars Quatuor Coronatorum* 98 (1985): 7 [1–12]; cf.: *Ars Quatuor Coronatorum* 102 (1989): 253.

28. S. Brent Morris, "Freemasonry Q&A: Is the 'Eye in the Pyramid' a Masonic Symbol?" *Scottish Rite Journal*, May/June 2009, p. 17.

29. Morris, "Freemasonry Q&A," p. 17.

30. Alan Axelrod, *The International Encyclopedia of Secret Societies and Fraternal Orders* (New York: Facts on File, 1997), p. 108.

31. Mark C. Carnes, *Secret Ritual and Manhood in Victorian America* (New Haven, CT: Yale Univ. Press, 1989), pp. 76–79.

32. See Whitney R. Cross, *The Burned-Over District* (Ithaca, NY: Cornell Univ. Press, 1950, 1982), for an extensive discussion of revivals and revivalists' conscious manipulation of emotions. I find it suggestive that the same evangelist, Charles Finney, who was one of the chief

promulgators of this emotional style was also an anti-Masonic author. See Cross, *Burned-Over District*, pp. 120, 151–69, 354.

33. Allen E. Roberts, *House Undivided: The Story of Freemasonry and the Civil War* (Fulton: Missouri Lodge of Research, 1969), p. 82.

34. Roberts, *House Undivided*, p. 106.

35. Joseph Fort Newton, *River of Years* (New York: J. B. Lippincott, 1946), quoted in Roberts, *House Undivided*, p. 107.

36. Joseph A. Walkes Jr., *Black Square and Compass: 200 Years of Prince Hall Freemasonry* (Richmond, VA: Macoy Publishing, 1979), pp. 11–12.

37. See, for instance, Fox, *Double-Headed Eagle*, pp. 377–79.

38. R. A. Gilbert, "'The Monstrous Regiment': Women and Freemasonry in the Nineteenth Century," *Ars Quatuor Coronatorum* 115 (2002): 164. The following account largely draws upon this source and upon the account given in Harold V. B. Voorhis, *The Eastern Star: The Evolution from a Rite to an Order* (New York: Macoy Publishing, 1954).

39. William B. Melish, *The History of the Imperial Council, Ancient Arabic Order Nobles of the Mystic Shrine for North America, Second Edition, 1872–1921* (Cincinnati: Abingdon Press, 1921), p. 12; Whitney W. Jones, *The Book of Boumi, 1884–1934* (Baltimore: Boumi Temple, 1934), p. 38.

40. Melish, *History of the Imperial Council*, pp. 25–26.

41. Florence's account is quoted at length in Fred Van Deventer, *Parade to Glory* (New York: William Morrow, 1959), pp. 43–53. The original can be found in the *Eighth Annual Proceedings of the Imperial Council, AAONMS* (1882), pp. 50–53.

42. Deveney examines the possibility that Rawson played a more significant role in the Shrine's early years than later Shrine historians were willing to admit. Rawson claimed to have traveled much in the Middle East and northern Africa and was thought to have accompanied Madame Blavatsky on one of her journeys in the region. He also claimed to have been initiated into both the Bektashi Sufi order and the Druze of Lebanon. There remains the remote, but tantalizing, possibility that the Shrine's Orientalist motif was actually inspired by more than a mock ceremonial at a Marseille party. For more on Rawson, see John Patrick Deveney, "Nobles of the Secret Mosque: Albert L. Rawson, Abd al-Kader, George H. Felt and the Mystic Shrine," *Theosophical History* 8, no. 9 (July 2002); and John Patrick Deveney, "The Travels of H. P. Blavatsky and the Chronology of Albert Leighton Rawson," *Theosophical History* 10, no. 4 (October 2004). For my

own further examination of Rawson and the Shrine, see Jay Kinney, "The Mysterious Origins of the Shrine," *Masonic Magazine*, no. 7 (Spring 2007).

43. Lynn Dumenil, *Freemasonry and American Culture, 1880–1930* (Princeton, NJ: Princeton Univ. Press, 1984), p. 115.

44. For an examination of one Mason's anti-Catholic activities, see Jay Kinney, "Tales from a Trunk: Edwin A. Sherman, a Masonic Whirlwind," *Heredom* 12 (2004).

45. Dumenil, *Freemasonry and American Culture*, pp. 120–37; Fox, *Double-Headed Eagle*, p. 195.

46. Joseph A. Walkes Jr., "The Ku Klux Klan and Regular Freemasonry," *Phylaxis*, First Quarter, 1982, p. 3. There is no way of verifying this estimate, and it may well have been inflated for the Klan's recruiting purposes.

47. I don't mean to single out Texas in making this observation. The overlap between Masonry and the KKK occurred in a number of states where the Klan was strong. Members of the Texas Research Lodge are to be commended for having the courage to research this issue and publish papers that shed light on that era. See Donovan Duncan Tidwell, "The Ku Klux Klan and Texas Masonry," *Transactions of the Texas Lodge of Research A.F. & A.M.* 14 (1978–79); and J. Dexter Sammons, "The Ku Klux Klan and Texas Masonry, Part II," *Transactions of the Texas Lodge of Research A.F. & A.M.* 20 (1984–85).

48. Fox, *Double-Headed Eagle*, pp. 193–94; Dumenil, *Freemasonry and American Culture*, p. 260.

49. For instance, the KKK was condemned in 1922–23 by the Grand Lodges of Connecticut, Iowa, Maine, Nebraska, and Pennsylvania, among others. (See the *Proceedings* of those grand lodges for those respective years, for further details.) The Grand Master of Alabama in 1922, on the other hand, maintained a studied neutrality and had "neither commendation nor condemnation for this Order [i.e., the KKK] and thought that [it] would be overstepping the bounds of propriety to give an expression as Grand Master." See *Proceedings of the Grand Lodge AF&AM of Alabama, 1922* (Montgomery, AL: Brown Printing Co., 1923), p. 46.

50. Harold V. B. Voorhis, *Masonic Organizations and Allied Orders and Degrees* (n.p.: Press of Henry Emmerson, 1952), p. 142.

51. Dumenil, *Freemasonry and American Culture*, p. 225.

52. Dumenil, *Freemasonry and American Culture*, p. 149.

53. For more information on this remarkable building, which continues in active use, see http://www.detroitmasonic.com/.

54. The Guthrie Scottish Rite Temple, now assessed at $63,000,000, continues in active use. See http://www.guthriescottishrite.org.

55. This striking photo, probably conceived by *Life*'s photographer, unfortunately plays into misconceptions of Masonic hierarchy and governance. Grand lodges and grand masters owe no allegiance to the Scottish Rite, and the latter exerts no control over grand lodges or grand masters. Moreover, the Scottish Rite (Southern Jurisdiction), whose House of the Temple provided the setting for the photo shoot, includes only approximately half of the total Scottish Rite members in the United States.

56. "Masonic Membership Statistics, 1924–2007," at the Web site of the Masonic Service Association of North America, http://www.msana.com/msastats.asp.

Chapter 5: The Powers That Be

1. William A. Mason, ed., *Photo Souvenir: 26th Triennial Conclave, Boston, 1895* (Boston: A. A. Rothenberg & Co., 1895).

2. Francis J. Scully, *History of the Grand Encampment of Knights Templar of the United States of America* (Greenfield, IN: Wm. Mitchell Printing Co., 1952), p. 141.

3. Mason, *Photo Souvenir*, p. 174. Commanderies are the local organizational units of the Masonic Knights Templar.

4. Mason, *Photo Souvenir*, p. 7. By the Knights Templar's own count, there were "thirty-nine Grand Commanderies, 972 subordinate Commanderies, and about 110,000 members" in the United States in 1895.

5. Scully, *History of the Grand Encampment*, p. 250–51.

6. *History of the Thirty-Ninth Triennial Conclave, Grand Encampment of Knights Templar of the United States of America* (n.p., 1936), pp. 89–90.

7. Strictly speaking, in some countries there are multiple grand lodges, each of which claims the right to charter local lodges (or even lodges in other countries). For instance, there are at least a half dozen grand lodges in France, each with different members and slightly different rules and customs.

8. American grand lodges have included the fifty states plus Washing-

ton, D.C. As this book goes to press, the Grand Lodges of Connecticut and Delaware have been negotiating a merger, which, if it occurs, will bring the number of grand lodges in the United States down to just fifty.

9. The one-year term for grand masters is not universal. For example, the Grand Lodge of Massachusetts elects grand masters to three-year terms, while Pennsylvania's grand masters serve for two-year terms. The Grand Master of the United Grand Lodge of England is, by tradition, a member of the royal family and serves largely in a ceremonial role. The "Pro Grand Master" amounts to a day-to-day grand master and may serve for many years.

10. "Criteria for Webpages," http://www.glofga.org/criteria.html.

11. "Article II: Powers and Restrictions, §15095 Bingo," in *California Masonic Code* (San Francisco: Grand Lodge F & AM of California, 1996), p. 103.

12. Technically, state grand lodges claim jurisdiction over all additional orders and bodies that their members may join, but this jurisdiction is neither administrative nor ideological and is mostly confined to making sure that Masonic principles are upheld.

13. Fox, *Double-Headed Eagle,* p. 15.

14. Frederick G. Speidel, *The York Rite of Freemasonry: A History and Handbook* (n.p.: Mitchell-Fleming Printing, 1989), p. 53.

15. Michael S. Kaulback, "The First Knight Templars in the United States," *Ars Quatuor Coronatorum* 107 (1994): 226.

16. Bernard E. Jones, *Freemasons' Book of the Royal Arch* (London: George G. Harrup & Co., 1957; rev. ed., 1969), p. 100 (rev. ed.).

17. The York Rite's local chapters, councils, and commanderies are governed by state grand chapters, grand councils, and grand commanderies. These, in turn, operate under an umbrella of the General Grand Chapter Royal Arch Masons International, General Grand Council Cryptic Masons International, and Grand Encampment Knights Templar U.S.A. There is no single organizational body overseeing the York Rite as a whole.

18. This was the traditional mode of conferring the degrees. Nowadays, it is increasingly common to confer the degrees en masse at weekend "festivals" that draw participants from York Rite bodies in a common geographical area.

19. Such a schedule might have varied from Scottish Rite Valley to Scottish

Rite Valley, depending on the number of members and available resources.

20. In all fairness, it must be noted that the higher AASR degrees, in jurisdictions other than the United States, often take years to achieve and are, in some countries, by invitation only and in limited numbers.

21. This summary of the AASR administrative hierarchy largely describes that of the Southern Jurisdiction. All 33rd-degree recipients in the Northern Jurisdiction are called SGIGs, while there are forty-eight "active members" who make up the Supreme Council, Northern Jurisdiction. The number of active members in the fifteen states composing that jurisdiction range from two to five per state. See "What Is a Deputy?" *Scottish Rite Journal*, May-June 2005, p. 21.

22. See Keith Arrington, "Ray Shute and the AMD," in *A Daily Advancement in Masonic Knowledge: The Collected Blue Friar Lectures*, ed. Wallace McLeod and S. Brent Morris (Bloomington, IL: Masonic Book Club, 2003), pp. 225–32; and Voorhis, *Masonic Organizations*.

23. A transcript of Martin Luther King's "Drum Major Instinct" sermon can be found at http://www.blackwebportal.com/wire/DA.cfm?ArticleID= 513 and at other archives on the Web. It was originally delivered at Ebenezer Baptist Church, in Atlanta, Georgia, on February 4, 1968.

24. Considering the considerable overlap between African-American churches and Prince Hall Masonry, I think it is likely that MLK was illustrating his point with a Masonic reference that would not have been lost on many congregants.

Chapter 6: Secret Rites and Rituals

1. Hugh B. Urban, "The Adornment of Silence: Secrecy and Symbolic Power in American Freemasonry," *Journal of Religion and Society* 3 (2001), http://moses.creighton.edu/JRS/2001/2001-2.html.

2. In point of fact, there is nothing beyond peer pressure to prevent a Mason from resigning ("demitting") at any time, or letting his membership lapse through nonpayment of dues. The obligations that a candidate recites within the rituals say nothing regarding a specific time span of membership.

3. *Investigation of Applicants: A Manual for Members of Investigating Committees* (San Francisco: Grand Lodge F&AM of California, n.d.), p. 11.

4. See Robert G. Davis, *Understanding Manhood in America: Freemasonry's Enduring Path to the Mature Masculine* (Lancaster, VA: Anchor Communications, 2005).

5. Mircea Eliade, *The Sacred and The Profane: The Nature of Religion* (New York: Harcourt Brace Jovanovich, 1959), pp. 46–47.

6. Contrary to the misunderstandings of anti-Masonic critics, to suggest that a lodge room functions as "sacred space" is *not* to imply that Masonry functions as a religion or presumes to rival its members' chosen religions. It does not.

7. Robert Lomas later published an even more exhaustive account of the three degrees—as experienced by him in his particular British province—in his *Turning the Hiram Key* (Gloucester, MA: Fair Winds Press, 2005).

8. This summary reflects the degree rituals as performed in California. For an account in more detail of the degree rituals as performed in an English lodge, the reader is directed to the first chapter of Knight and Lomas, *Hiram Key*; and to Lomas, *Turning the Hiram Key*.

9. Curiously enough, in some French versions of the ritual, the Master's Word is not lost but is given to the candidate along with a substitute to be used to protect it. In light of such variations, one has to be careful not to read too much significance into the details of any one version of the ritual.

10. There is little point in arguing over whether one temple is holier than another. In the Masonic mythos, the Temple of Solomon represents the holiest.

11. Knight and Lomas, *Hiram Key,* pp. 120–51; Knight and Lomas, *Second Messiah,* p. 217.

12. The earliest evidence of a Hiram-like tale as part of the ritual is the Graham Manuscript (c. 1726), which has the three sons of Noah go to their father's grave and try to disinter him in order to see "if they could find anything about him ffor to lead them to the vertuable secret which this famieous preacher had[,] for I hop[e] all will allow that all things needful for the new world was in the ark with noah" [all sic]. The Hiram story, as such, doesn't appear until a 1730 exposure, Prichard's *Freemasonry Dissected.* However, recent and compelling research by researcher Julia Cleave has pointed toward a French chanson, *Les Quatre Fils Aymon*, which tells of a Masonic murder during the

building of St. Peter's Church in Cologne with numerous parallels to the Hiram tale. Cleave notes that variations on the name of the murdered mason, Aymon, turn up in numerous Old Charges in passages making reference to the Solomonic worker later known as Hiram Abiff. This suggests the possibility that the later myth of Hiram drew upon the traditional story of Aymon. See Julia Cleave, "Of Hiram and Aymon—the Evolution of the Legend of the Third Degree," *Transactions of the Manchester Association for Masonic Research* 98 (2008).

13. It should be noted that this practice of daily prayer in the Sanctum Sanctorum deviates from actual historical Temple practices, which kept the S.S. off limits to all but the high priest, and only accessible to him once a year at which time he was allowed to utter the ineffable name of the Lord. A traditional Masonic explanation for Hiram's privileged use of the S.S. is that the inner chamber, like the Temple itself, was still unfinished.

Chapter 7: Out of the Blue

1. See Roy A. Wells, *Some Royal Arch Terms Examined* (Hersham, Surrey, UK: Ian Allan, 1988), pp. 14–24. Another interpretation has it that the word/phrase means "the flesh falls from the bones"—a reference to the difficulty encountered in the first two attempts to raise Hiram Abiff's body. Yet a third suggests that it is a phonetic contraction of a Hebrew phrase, "stone rejected by the builders," mentioned in Psalm 118:22.

2. *Monitor and Officers' Manual* (Grand Lodge of California, F&AM, 1997), pp. 35–36.

3. Henry Wilson Coil, *Coil's Masonic Encyclopedia* (New York: Macoy Publishing, 1961), p 165.

4. Coil, *Coil's Masonic Encyclopedia*, p. 552. The rituals of most higher degrees have usually been written down and printed, except for their signs and passwords. It would be too much to expect Masonic ritualists to wholly preserve dozens of such degrees through memorization alone.

5. Jones, *Royal Arch*, p. 45.

6. Jones, *Royal Arch*, p. 55. Interestingly enough, a satirical advertisement for a meeting of "Antediluvian Masonry" published in an English newspaper in 1726 refers to "Innovations that have lately been introduced by the Doctor and some other of the Moderns . . ." This

would seem to indicate that there was some sentiment from early on that considered the premier Grand Lodge to be breaking with earlier traditions. The "Doctor" presumably refers to Dr. James Anderson, credited author of the Constitutions of the premier Grand Lodge.

7. J. Ray Shute states that the imitation or copy of the Ark is found only in American Royal Arch ritual, and attributes this detail to Thomas Smith Webb, the famous American Masonic ritualist who was responsible for systematizing what are now commonly known as the York Rite degrees. *Collectanea* 10, no. 2 (1975): 100; cited in Arturo de Hoyos, "The Mystery of the Royal Arch Word," *Heredom* 2 (1993): 23.

8. This summary is based on a popular "exposure" of Royal Arch chapter degrees: E. Ronayne, *Chapter Degrees* (Chicago: Ezra A. Cook, 1988). As with all such exposés, it reflects a possibly faulty transcription from memory of degree rituals as performed in a particular time and place—in this case, in the American Midwest circa 1880. However, I believe that its general contours correctly describe the Royal Arch myth. The Royal Arch, as performed in England, I am told, has some significant differences, among them being the absence of the veils part of the ritual or, in some cases, the use of only three veils. Such differences between versions of the same degree strongly suggest that one should not read too much into the wording or composition of any single version. This is one of the primary errors of anti-Masonic critics who rely on exposures of degree rituals for their faulty interpretations.

9. Jones, *Royal Arch*, pp. 126–30.

10. Jones, *Royal Arch*, p. 127. Jones mentions numerous other publications of the legend, including one in *An Historical Catechism*, c. 1700, "said to have been taken from a Greek manuscript, *Ecclesiastical History*, by Nicephorus Callistus, who is presumed to be a Byzantine writer of the late thirteenth or early fourteenth century."

11. Jones, *Royal Arch*, p. 158.

12. Jones, *Royal Arch*, p.172, notes the removal of Christian elements and references as late as the revisions of 1834–35, in an effort to better universalize the degrees.

13. A tremendous amount of confusion has been sown by anti-Masons who have mistakenly thought that another word given in the ritual, sometimes called the Grand Omnific Royal Arch Word, is the lost "Master's Word" and the name of a supposedly pagan "Masonic God." A close

reading of the Royal Arch lecture will show that the Grand Omnific Royal Arch Word (a synthetic word derived from the word for "God" in three ancient Middle Eastern languages) is merely a cover word employed to supply the vowels for the Tetragrammaton, the latter being the ineffable name of God and the lost "Master's Word." (For confirmation of this, see E. Ronayne, *Chapter Masonry* (1901; repr., Chicago: Ezra A. Cook Publications, 1988), p. 310, par. 2. The confusion is compounded by wording in the version of the Royal Arch ritual found in the widely disseminated exposure *Duncan's Ritual of Freemasonry,* which states that the Grand Omnific Royal Arch Word *is* the Master Mason's Word and that, moreover, it is the Christian Logos. Neither of these statements is to be found in the official degree rituals in print, and it seems likely that these were either mischievous interpolations by Duncan or the results of confusion and faulty memory on the part of whoever transcribed the rituals. It is also possible that such confusion was unknowingly promulgated by Masons who imperfectly passed along the work. An undated and expanded reprint of *Morgan's Freemasonry Exposed and Explained* from the 19th century has a version of the Royal Arch catechism that quotes the opening verses of the Gospel of John and has a muddled and confusing account of the ritual that omits any mention of the Tetragrammaton at all and alleges that the Grand Omnific Royal Arch Word is the sacred name. A footnote explains that there is great variation from chapter to chapter as to which words are given. This may well have been so, especially before the General Grand Chapter of Royal Arch Masons in the United States standardized the ritual in the mid-1800s.

14. Aryeh Kaplan, *Meditation and the Bible* (York Beach, ME: Samuel Weiser, 1978; repr., 1988), p. 58. Kaplan, in turn, cites Talmudic and other sources.

15. See P. G. Maxwell-Stuart, "De Verbo Mirifico: Johannes Reuchlin and the Royal Arch," *Ars Quatuor Coronatorum* 99 (1986): 206–9. Also see Philip Beitchman, *Alchemy of the Word: Cabala of the Renaissance* (Albany, NY: SUNY Press, 1998), p. 76.

16. A MacGuffin, according to Alfred Hitchcock, is a plot device, such as secret plans or documents, that is of great importance to and motivates the characters in a drama, even though it is of negligible importance itself. The classic example is the Maltese falcon in the book and movie of that name.

17. Frederick G. Speidel, *The York Rite of Freemasonry: A History and Handbook* (n.p.: Mitchell-Fleming Printing, 1989), p. 28.

18. Rex Hutchens, *A Bridge to Light*, 2nd ed. (Washington, DC: Supreme Council 33°, AASR-SJ, 1995), p. 318.

19. In recognition of this problem, there has been a recent effort in the AASR-SJ to provide its valleys with a uniform set of revised degree rituals in order to standardize how the rituals are performed. Whether this will entirely succeed remains to be seen. Cast members who have spent years working with their own versions do not always take well to sweeping changes that require memorizing new scripts.

20. For further discussion of *Scotch Rite Masonry Illustrated*, see Arturo de Hoyos and S. Brent Morris, *Is It True What They Say About Freemasonry?* 2nd ed. (Silver Spring, MD: Masonic Information Center, 1997), pp. 31, 39–41. The exposure, first published in 1888, is still in print. See J. Blanchard, *Scotch Rite Masonry Illustrated* (Chicago: Ezra A. Cook Publications, 1962).

21. Albert Pike, *Beauties of Cerneauism* (n.p.: August 25, 1887).

22. Albert Pike in *Transactions of the Supreme Council, 1857* (n.p.: 1857), p. 258.

23. Albert Pike, *Morals and Dogma of the Ancient and Accepted Scottish Rite of Freemasonry* (Charleston, SC: Supreme Council 33°, AASR-SJ, 1951), p. iii.

24. Pike, *Morals and Dogma*, p. iii.

25. Pike, *Morals and Dogma*, p. iv.

26. The passages occur on pages 102 and 321 in *Morals and Dogma* and on pages 36 and 161 in Eliphas Lévi, *The History of Magic*, trans. A. E. Waite (York Beach, ME: Samuel Weiser, 1999).

27. For one interpretation of what Pike might have meant by using the most prominent passage, see John J. Robinson, "Albert Pike and the Morning Star" in *A Pilgrim's Path: Freemasonry and the Religious Right* (New York: M. Evans & Co., 1993), pp. 41–50. Robinson appears to have been unaware that the passage in question was not Pike's own words.

28. The hoax speech is discussed at length in de Hoyos and Morris, *Is It True?* pp. 5–23.

Chapter 8: Veiled in Symbol and Allegory

1. The Rosicrucians I refer to here were not members of an organized Rosicrucian brotherhood or order, as there was none in the 17th century

during the Rosicrucian uproar. Rather, I'm referring to those self-selected intellectuals who became fascinated with the Rosicrucian myth and ideals and entered into a cultural dialogue with each other. See Francis A. Yates, *The Rosicrucian Enlightenment* (Boulder, CO: Shambhala, 1978).

2. Stanislas Klossowski de Rola, *The Golden Game: Alchemical Engravings of the Seventeenth Century* (London: Thames and Hudson, 1988), pp. 214–21.

3. The full passage of this obligation can be found in *Emulation Ritual* (Addlestone, Surrey, UK: Lewis Masonic, 1995), pp. 75–76. The exact wording of the obligation varies according to the individual grand lodge and the ritual version being used. But this general pledge of secrecy is similar in all jurisdictions.

4. De Hoyos and Morris, *Is It True?* p. 4.

5. J. D. Buck, *Mystic Masonry* (Cincinnati: Robert Clarke Co., 1896), p. xxii. It should be underscored that Buck was here stating his personal belief, not an established fact. His entire book is an attempt to equate the "real secrets" of Masonry with the teachings of Theosophy. Other Masons making similar statements have typically been convinced that their pet philosophies furnish the real key to Masonic symbolism. Anti-Masons typically compound their own confusion by trying to weave the conflicting notions of these supposed "experts" into a coherent narrative. Unsurprisingly, the result is incoherence.

6. In the academic study of semiotics, one thing standing for another is referred to as a "sign," not a symbol. However, in this discussion we will stick with the more typical usage of "symbol."

7. One famous symbol, that of a monument depicting a broken pillar and a weeping virgin whose hair is being unfolded and its ringlets counted by Father Time, was introduced into Masonry by Jeremy Cross, a protégé of Thomas Smith Webb, the primary systematizer of the York Rite degrees, circa 1800. The scene incorporates mourning for the slain Hiram Abiff, the unfinished Temple, and the idea that "time, patience, and perseverance accomplish all things." See Malcolm C. Duncan, *Duncan's Ritual of Freemasonry* (New York: David McKay Co., n.d.), p. 125.

8. The custom of having painted or printed tracing boards was preceded by the practice of drawing the symbols, as well as a diagram of the lodge, with chalk or charcoal on the wooden floors of upstairs pub rooms where Masons held meetings in the 1700s. Newly made Masons would be given

the task of mopping away the evidence after such meetings. See T. O. Haunch, *Tracing Boards, Their Development and Their Designers* (London: Quatuor Coronati Correspondence Circle, 2004). In the United States, lithographed charts (or even magic-lantern slides) of Masonic symbols were commonly used as visual aids for degree lectures, a practice that has fallen out of use in many lodges. These days, printed "monitors" containing the explanations of the symbols are often given to new candidates in place of the symbolic parts of the lectures.

9. This traditional description of Masonry can be found in the first-degree catechism of the Emulation ritual used in many lodges under the United Grand Lodge of England. It should be pointed out that at the time it was first composed, *peculiar* meant "singular" or "distinct."

10. Father Thomas Keating, in commenting upon Gregory the Great's advocacy of contemplative prayer and meditation, notes that it can produce "a state of repose, tranquility, and profound interior peace." See Thomas Keating, M. Basil Pennington, and Thomas E. Clarke, *Finding Grace at the Center*, rev. ed. (Still River, MA: St. Bede Publications, 1982), p. 36.

11. John Daniel, *Scarlet and the Beast*, vol. 2 (Tyler, TX: JKI Publishing, 1994), p. 46.

12. Degree lecture by Thomas Dunckerley, quoted in Albert G. Mackey, William J. Hughan, and Edward L. Hawkins, eds., *An Encyclopedia of Freemasonry* (New York: Masonic History Company, 1921), s.v. "Blazing Star," vol. 1, p. 106.

13. Degree lecture by William Preston, quoted in Mackey, Hughan, and Hawkins, *Encyclopedia of Freemasonry*, s.v. "Blazing Star" (vol. 1, p. 106).

14. Quoted in Dobbs, *Janus Faces of Genius*, p. 158.

15. The Blazing Star is mentioned in the catechism of the first degree in the 1730 exposure *Masonry Dissected*, by Samuel Prichard. Its use presumably dates to earlier still. Some Masonic scholars are at pains to distinguish between the symbols of the Blazing Star, the five-pointed star, and the pentagram (also called variously pentacle, pentangle, and pentalpha). See, for instance, Albert Mackey's entries for "Blazing Star" and "Five-Pointed Star" in Mackey, Hughan, and Hawkins, *Encyclopedia of Freemasonry*. Be that as it may, and as Mackey admits, the Blazing Star is often depicted as a five-pointed star, in many cases with the Masonic *G* in its center. I have even seen depictions of lodge-room

floors with a five-pointed Blazing Star in the center of the floor. Viewed from the West, it appears inverted, but viewed from the East, which is where the Worshipful Master sits, it has its usual single upward point. I would not read great significance into this, as it is a practical matter that a five-pointed star is going to appear differently from each of the four cardinal directions.

16. While Rob Morris first authored the rituals, symbolism, and concepts of the OES in 1850, it appears that initiations were given under other organization names up through the mid-1860s. It wasn't until 1867–68 that the order was formally recast as the Order of the Eastern Star. Reproductions of what is now known as the OES "signet" emblem were published as early as 1855 in a monitor for one of these earlier iterations, the American Adoptive Rite. See Voorhis, *Eastern Star.*

17. Eliphas Lévi, *Transcendental Magic: Its Doctrine and Ritual,* trans. A. E. Waite (1896; repr., York Beach, ME: Weiser Books, 2001), p. 237.

18. Ronald Hutton, *The Triumph of the Moon: A History of Modern Pagan Witchcraft* (Oxford: Oxford Univ. Press, 1999), p. 68.

19. The following quote alone—from Rob Morris, describing his choice of women—should make it clear that the founding concept of the OES was about as far from satanism as one could imagine: "From the Holy Writings I culled four biographical sketches to correspond with my first four points, viz., JEPHTHAH'S DAUGHTER (named 'ADAH') RUTH, ESTHER and MARTHA. These were illustrations of four great congeries of womanly virtues, and their selection has proved highly popular. The fifth point introduced me to the early history of the Christian Church, where amidst a 'noble army of martyrs' I found many whose lives and death overflowed the cup of martyrdom with a glory not surpassed by any of those named in Holy Writ. This gave me ELECTA, 'the Elect Lady,' friend of St. John, the Christian woman whose venerable years were crowned with the utmost splendor of the crucifixion." See the Web site of the OES Grand Chapter of Massachusetts, http://www .oestar.org/rob_morris.html.

20. This assessment of Wicca's recent origins follows from the research of Ronald Hutton, Aidan Kelly, and Chas Clifton. See Hutton, *The Triumph of the Moon;* Aidan Kelly, *Crafting the Art of Magic: A History of Modern Witchcraft, 1939–1964,* bk. 1 (St. Paul, MN: Llewellyn Publications, 1991); and Chas Clifton, review of *Gerald Gardner and the Cauldron of*

Inspiration, by Philip Heselton, *Pomegranate* 6, no. 2 (2004). It isn't my intention to dive into the ongoing arguments over whether Wicca is the inheritor of earlier pagan traditions, some of which might have employed the representation of upright pentagrams in rituals for banishing evil. My point here is that Wicca as a systematized nature religion is a relatively recent creation and its use of the pentagram as an identifying "logo" is a product of the 20th century.

21. The listing of modern Rosicrucian groups at http://www.levity.com/alchemy/alvin.html ("The Alchemy Web Site") states that Gardner was a member of the Corona Fellowship of Rosicrucians, described as "co-masonic rosicrucianism." This group is, in turn, called the Fellowship of Cretona, in a posting online at a Web page of requests for correspondence (http://web.mit.edu/dryfoo/www/Masonry/RQ4C/rq4c_97Q4.html). Ronald Hutton has it as the Rosicrucian Fellowship of Crotona, probably the most accurate rendition; see Hutton, *Triumph of the Moon,* p. 213. Janet Farrar and Gavin Bone, in *Progressive Witchcraft* (Franklin Lakes, NJ: Career Press, 2004), p. 26, state that the Fellowship of Crotona included ritual practices coming from Grande Loge Symbolique Ecossaise Mixte de France, a French Co-Masonic order. ("Co-Masonic" refers to a variant version of Masonry that admits both men and women.) Whatever the case, while affiliation with such fringe groups might provide access to the common store of Masonic symbols and motifs, this does not mean that Gardner would have been recognized as a Mason by any regular grand lodge.

22. John Michael Greer has pointed out that Gardner's first draft of the Wiccan Book of Shadows contained numerous quotes from Aleister Crowley and Israel Regardie, both of whom were familiar with such uses in groups such as the Hermetic Order of the Golden Dawn. John Michael Greer, personal communication with author, December 11, 2005.

23. The coat of arms of the United Grand Lodge of England includes a representation of the Ark of the Covenant with cherubim on either side.

24. These quotes from Preston's lectures can be found in P. R. James, "The Second Lecture of Free Masonry by William Preston," *Ars Quatuor Coronatorum* 83 (1970): 211. There are several versions of the lectures, and another similar version of these quotes can be found in Colin Dyer, *William Preston and His Work* (Shepperton, Middlesex, UK: Lewis

Masonic, 1987), pp. 231–32. It should be noted that Preston's lengthy lectures, while influential, were never officially adopted by the premier Grand Lodge of England. Thomas Smith Webb, the American Mason who further polished the three degree rituals and whose work a majority of American lodges still use, took Preston's lectures as raw material and boiled them down to a more abbreviated and manageable size. References to geometry were retained, but abstruse discussions of asymptotic space were deleted.

25. For a discussion of gematria, see David Fideler, *Jesus Christ Sun of God: Ancient Cosmology and Early Christian Symbolism* (Wheaton, IL: Quest Books, 1993).

26. Plato *Republic,* bk. 7, trans. Benjamin Jowett, http://www.classicallibrary .org/plato/dialogues/republic/book7.htm.

27. It is an accepted rule within esoteric traditions that systems or techniques cannot by themselves cause a mystical experience. Such things are due only to the grace of God. That may be true, but certain disciplines do seem to better the chances of their practitioners being open to that grace if it manifests itself.

28. Stevenson, *Origins of Freemasonry,* pp. 90–96.

Chapter 9: The Illuminati Factor

1. Jay Kinney, "What's Left?" *CoEvolution Quarterly*, Winter 1975, pp. 19–30; Jay Kinney, "The Conspiracy Watcher's Field Guide," in *The Fringes of Reason: A Whole Earth Catalog,* ed. Ted Schultz (New York: Harmony Books, 1989), pp. 93–97.

2. Richard Hofstadter, "The Paranoid Style in American Politics and Other Essays," (New York: Alfred A. Knopf, 1965), p. 3.

3. Richard Hofstadter, "Paranoid Style," p. 39.

4. Reprinted in Douglas Knoop, G. P. Jones, and Douglas Hamer, *Early Masonic Pamphlets* (Manchester, UK: Manchester Univ. Press, 1945), p. 35.

5. James Billington, *Fire in the Minds of Men* (New York: Basic Books, 1980), p. 99. "Illuminist ideas influenced revolutionaries not just through left-wing proponents, but also through right-wing opponents. As the fears of the Right became the fascination of the Left, Illuminism gained a paradoxical posthumous influence far greater that it had exercised as a living movement."

6. My account largely follows that in Seymour Martin Lipset and Earl Raab, *The Politics of Unreason* (New York: Harper Torchbooks, 1970).

7. Lipset and Raab, *Politics of Unreason*, p. 36.

8. Boris I. Nicolaevsky, "Secret Societies and the First International," in *The Revolutionary Internationals, 1864–1943*, ed. Milorad M. Drachkovitch (Stanford, CA: Stanford Univ. Press, 1966). However, the meticulous Masonic historian Ellic Howe takes exception to Nicolaevsky's evidence and conclusions and calls them "a contribution to Masonic mythology." See Ellic Howe, "The Rite of Memphis in France and England, 1838–70," *Ars Quatuor Coronatorum* 92 (1979): 1–14.

9. Ellic Howe, "Fringe Masonry in England, 1870–85," *Ars Quatuor Coronatorum* 85 (1972): 242–95.

10. *Freemason*, no. 3, April 1869, quoted in Howe, "Fringe Masonry in England." The parenthetical clarification is Howe's.

11. Making sense of the ins and outs of groups calling themselves the Order (or Rite) of Memphis, as well as of the similar "Egyptian" Rite of Mizraim, is exceedingly difficult. As is often the case with fringe Masonic rites, charters to start new branches were strewn all over the world, abetting a chaos of lineages, not all of which were on speaking terms with each other. The Rite of Memphis and the Rite of Mizraim were reputedly merged into a single order by Garibaldi in 1881 or 1882 (dates vary), but it is unclear whether this merger had anything to do with the apparent merger of the two under John Yarker's auspices. See Howe, "Rite of Memphis."

12. The Grand Orient also claims to hold more faithfully to the 1723 Anderson Constitution's Charges regarding religion, which obliged Masons to hold only to "that Religion in which all Men agree, leaving their particular Opinions to themselves; that is, to be good Men and true, or Men of Honour and Honesty, by whatever Denominations or Persuasions they may be distinguished." The quote is from *The Constitutions of the Free-Masons, 1723*, facsimile ed. (London: QCCC, 1976), p. 50.

13. This account of Reuss and the revived Order of the Illuminati is indebted to Ellic Howe and Helmut Möller, "Theodor Reuss: Irregular Freemasonry in Germany, 1900–23," *Ars Quatuor Coronatorum* 91 (1978): 28–46.

14. Peter-R. Koenig, *Das O.T.O. Phänomen*, chap. 11, http://user.cyberlink.ch/~koenig/illumin.htm.

15. From a 1914 paper, "The Elixir of Life," quoted in Kenneth Grant, *Aleister Crowley and the Hidden God* (New York: Samuel Weiser, 1974), p. 174.

16. Martin P. Starr, "Masonic Origins of the Ordo Templi Orientis," *Plumbline* 11, no. 3 (Fall 2003): 8. See also Martin P. Starr, "Aleister Crowley: Freemason!" *Ars Quatuor Coronatorum* 108 (1995): 150–61.

17. *Oriflamme*, jubilee ed., 1912, quoted in Howe and Möller, "Theodor Reuss," p. 39.

18. R. Swinburne Clymer, *The Rosicrucian Fraternity in America*, vol. 2 (Quakertown, PA: Rosicrucian Foundation, n.d.), pp. 614–15. Clymer includes reproductions of the jubilee issue of the O.T.O. organ, the *Oriflamme*, 1912, in which Kellner, Yoga, and the O.T.O.'s sexual teachings are discussed, albeit briefly.

19. For a thorough discussion of Randolph, see John Patrick Deveney, *Paschal Beverly Randolph: A Nineteenth-Century Black American Spiritualist, Rosicrucian, and Sex Magician* (Albany, NY: SUNY Press, 1997). The Hermetic Brotherhood of Luxor's history and teachings are covered in Joscelyn Godwin, Christian Chanel, and John P. Deveney, *The Hermetic Brotherhood of Luxor: Initiatic and Historical Documents of an Order of Practical Occultism* (York Beach, ME: Samuel Weiser, 1995).

20. Howe and Möller, "Theodor Reuss," p. 39.

21. Koenig, *Das O.T.O. Phänomen*, chap 11.

22. See, for instance, Jack Harris, *Freemasonry* (New Kensington, PA: Whitaker House, 1983), and Ed Decker, ed. *The Dark Side of Freemasonry* (Lafayette, LA: Huntington House, 1994).

23. Adam Parfrey, "Riding the Downardian Nightmare," in *Cult Rapture* (Portland, OR: Feral House, 1995), p. 233.

24. See, for instance, Loretta Napoleoni, *Terror Incorporated* (New York: Seven Stories Press, 2005); Alfred W. McCoy, *The Politics of Heroin* (New York: Lawrence Hill Books, 1991); Jim Hougan, *Spooks* (New York: William Morrow, 1978); and James Ring Adams and Douglas Frantz, *A Full Service Bank* (New York: Pocket Books, 1992).

Chapter 10: Is Masonry Occult?

1. *The Compact Edition of the Oxford English Dictionary* (Oxford: Oxford Univ. Press, 1971), s.v. "Occult," vol. 1, p. 1971.

2. *Compact Oxford English Dictionary*, s.v. "Occult," vol. 1, p. 1971.

3. Peter Hanns Reill and Ellen Judy Wilson, *Encyclopedia of the Enlightenment,* rev. ed. (New York: Facts on File, 2004), pp. 219–21; Yates, *Giordano Bruno,* p. 355. Yates clarifies that while Copernican theories may have been among the causes of Bruno's condemnation, he was condemned primarily on religious grounds.

4. Michael White, *Isaac Newton: The Last Sorcerer* (Reading, MA: Addison-Wesley, 1997), p. 106.

5. Dobbs, *Janus Faces of Genius,* p. 151.

6. White, *Isaac Newton,* p. 127.

7. Reproduced in Knoop, Jones, and Hamer, *Early Masonic Pamphlets,* p. 30.

8. Knoop, Jones, and Hamer, *Early Masonic Pamphlets,* p. 31.

9. See Philip Beitchman, *Alchemy of the Word: Cabala of the Renaissance* (Albany, NY: SUNY Press, 1998), esp. chap. 4, "The Kiss of the Spouse: Cabala in England (1497–1700)."

10. Henry Dana Ward, A.M., ed., *Anti-Masonic Review* 1, no. 6 (May 1829): 184.

11. General Erich Ludendorff, *Destruction of Freemasonry Through Revelation of Their Secrets* (1927; repr., Los Angeles: Noontide Press, 1977), pp. 45–75.

12. C. W. Leadbeater, *Freemasonry and Its Ancient Mystic Rites* (1926; repr., New York: Gramercy Books, 1998), p. 9. The akashic records, according to Theosophical doctrine, are imprints upon a higher "mental plane" of everything that has ever happened, including human thoughts. These are, it is said, accessible to the inner vision of a trained clairvoyant.

13. Manly P. Hall, *The Lost Keys of Freemasonry* (1923; repr., Richmond, VA: Macoy Publishing, 1976), p. 17.

14. Foster Bailey, *The Spirit of Masonry* (Tunbridge Wells, Kent, UK: Lucis Press, 1957), pp. 36–37.

Chapter 11: Back to the Future

1. See the Web site of the Masonic Restoration Foundation: http://www.masonicrestoration.com.

2. Jean-Jacques Rousseau, *The Social Contract; or, Principles of Political Right* (1762), trans. G. D. H. Cole, bk. 4, chap. 8; available online at http://www.constitution.org/jjr/socon.htm.

Credits

Page 3: Stonecutter Homer action figure, photo by Jay Kinney from private collection. The Simpsons™ World of Springfield Interactive Figure by Playmates® Toys.

Pages 28 and 29: Rosslyn Chapel photos by Robert D. L. Cooper © 2009.

Page 106: Print from the collection of the Grand Lodge of British Columbia and Yukon.

Pages 117 and 120: Diagram and "exposure" from *Duncan's Ritual of Freemasonry*.

Pages 169, 170, and 171: Annotated symbol charts of the first, second, and third degrees by Jay Kinney © 2009.

Page 172: Illuminati cover copyright © by Steve Jackson Games. Cover painting by Dave Martin.

Page 212: Masonic promotional literature © Grand Lodge of California, F&AM.